PENNSYLVANIA

GERMAN

DICTIONARY

Pronunciation Guide

SHORT VOWEL SOUNDS

a ---- father, hot, rot, dot ....datt, fatt, vass, hatt, glatt

e ---- get, bed, set, met ....bett, gevva, geld, vesha

i ---- fit, tip, did, miss, wish ....Bivvel, pikk, bisht, biss, ich

o ---- of, oven, love, shove ....Gott, hott, shtobb, kobb

u ---- put, soot, stood...........................hund, mukk, sunn, butza

ae ---- rat, bat, sat, cat ....daett, maemm, naett

LONG VOWEL SOUNDS

ay ---- hay, say, day, lay ....gays, flaysh, kays, ayl, dray

ee ---- feet, heel, seed, meet.................kee, beebli, fees, veetz

eiy ---- height, sight, right.....................feiyah, meiya, sheiyah

oh ---- road, toad, Oh my! ....shohf, broht, roht, bloh

OTHER VOWEL SOUNDS

au ---- laud, laundry, author.................gaul, drauva, graut, haut

aw ---- law, saw, claw, flaw.................haws, glaws, naws, graws

ei ---- their, heir, air, hair ....deitsh, meisli, drei, heit, bei *

oo ---- moon, spoon, soon ....koo, shtool, goot, boova

oi ---- join, boy, toy, enjoy ....Moi, oi, boi, hoi, froiya

*exception: in the Bible *ei* is sometimes pronounced like *i* in time.
example: (heilich, reich, geisht)

Pronunciation Guide

VOWEL GLIDES

(two English sounds put together)

eah	---	($\bar{a}$ + ah).................................	sheah, beah, deah, eah, leah
iah	---	($\bar{e}$ + ah).................................	biah, miah, broviah, diah
oah	---	($\bar{o}$ + ah).................................	boaht, voahm, goahra, oah
uah	---	(oo + ah)................................	fuah, shuah, uah, shnuah

ENDINGS

a	---	Florida, China, above................	lanna, hoffa, nohma, gukka
ah	---	ahh, awl..................................	vassah, bessah, dellah

CONSONANTS

ch	---	(h sound in the back of throat)..	mach, sach, ich, mich, dach
ng	---	song, ring, bang, sing................	shpringa, fanga, langa
tsh	---	(ch sound) child, chin, ...	Deitsh, hutsh, tshumba
z	---	pizza, pretzel, roots..................	katz, zvay, zeit, butza, zung
r	---	beginning of word, normal r	roht, rawt, rumm, rishta, ratt
r	---	anywhere else, rolled r.............	goahra, veahra, fiahra

If Deitsh word begins with r, it can be pronounced like an English r.

Anywhere else r is rolled like a Spanish r.

If you can't roll your r's, pronounce like an English d instead.

A - a

ab   1. off 2. (prefix) 3. strange.

abbashta *v.* to finish off, to brush off, (example: to brush dirt or dust off your shirt).

abbeisa *v.* 1. to bite off 2. to take a bite.

abbel *(m).* apple.

abbezawla *v.* to pay off.

abbezawld *v.* paid off; pp. of abbezawla.

abbild *(neu).* image used for false worship.

abbildah *(f).* images used for false worship; pl. of abbild.

abbinna *v.* tighten loose buggy wheel spokes.

abblayyicha *v.* 1. to fade 2. lose color.

abblohsa *v.* 1. to blow off 2. to express anger.

abblohwa *v.* to apply extra effort or care.

abbrecha *v.* to break off.

abbutza *v.* 1. to clean off 2. to wipe dishes dry after washing them.

abbutz-lumba *(m).* drying off towel.

abdekka *v.* to uncover.

abdrayya *v.* 1. to unscrew 2. to turn or shut off 3. to turn aside 4. to irritate, disgust.

abdrayyish irritating, disgusting.

abdrobsa *v.* to drop off.

abdu *v.* 1. to unload 2. to post pone 3. to shut off (example: alarm, radio).

abedidda *(f).* appetites; pl. of abeditt.

abeditt *(m).* appetite.

abfall *(m).* apostasy.

abfalla *v.* 1. to fall off 2. to fall away, apostatize.

abfiahra *v.* to lead astray.

abfiahrich misleading, false.

abganga *v.* 1. forsaken 2. went off (alarm) 3. having left the faith; pp. of abgay.

abgavla *v.* to unload with a fork.

abgay *v.* 1. to forsake 2. to go off (alarm).

abgebasht *v.* finished off, brushed off; pp. of abbashta.

abgebissa *v.* bitten off; pp. of abbeisa.

abgeblayyicht *v.* faded; pp. of abblayyicha.

abgeblohkt *v.* having applied extra effort or care; pp. of abblohwa.

abgeblohsa *v.* 1. blown off 2. having expressed anger; pp. of abblohsa.

abgebrocha *v.* broken off; pp.

of abbrecha.

abgebunna *v.* having tightened loose buggy wheel spokes; pp. of abbinna.

abgebutzt *v.* 1.cleaned off 2. having wiped dishes dry after washing them; pp. of abbutza.

abgeddah *(f).* idols; pl. of abgott.

abgeddah-deensht *(m).* idol worship.

abgeddah-deenshta *(f).* the worship of idols; pl. of abgeddah-deensht.

abgeddah-machah *(m).* maker of idols.

abgeddahrei *(neu).* idolatry.

abgeddahreiya *(f).* idolatries; pl. of abgeddahrei.

abgeddish idolatrous.

abgedekt *v.* uncovered; pp. of abdekka.

abgedrayt *v.* 1. unscrewed 2. turned or shut off 3. turned aside 4. irritated or disgusted; pp. of abdrayya.

abgedrobst *v.* droped off; pp. of abdrobsa.

abgedu *v.* 1. unloaded 2. postponed 3.shut off 4. upset, ticked off; pp. of abdu.

abgegavveld *v.* unloaded with a fork; pp. of abgavla.

abgeglobt *v.* beat up; pp. of abglobba.

abgegratzt *v.* scratched or screped off; pp. of abgratza.

abgegvaynd *v.* having broken a habit; pp. of abgvayna.

abgekabbit *v.* copied; pp. of abkabbiya.

abgekawft *v.* 1. bought 2. bribed; pp. of abkawfa.

abgekeaht *v.* swept; pp. of abkeahra.

abgekeeld *v.* cooled off; pp. of abkeela.

abgekliaht *v.* cleared off; pp. of abkliahra.

abgekshatt *v.* unharnessed; pp. of abkshadda.

abgepetzt *v.* pinched off; pp. of abpetza.

abgepiktaht *v.* portrayed publicly, published photograph; pp. of abpiktahra.

abgepoaht *v.* paired off; pp. of abpoahra.

abgevva *v.* to emit, give off.

abgevva mitt *v.* to pursue a hobby, profession, or relationship.

abgezayld *v.* counted off; pp. of abzayla.

abgezohmd *v.* unbridled; pp. of abzohma.

abgezohwa *v.* 1. skinned 2. pulled off 3. pulled off (stunt); pp. of abzeeya.

abglawda *v.* unloaded; pp. of ablawda.

abglaykt *v.* laid off; pp. of ablayya.

abglaysa *v.* 1. read aloud to an audience 2. picked off; pp.

of ablaysa.

abglobba *v.* to beat up.

abgloffa *v.* 1. having run off (liquid) 2. deserted, walked away from; pp. of ablawfa.

abgmacht *v.* 1. removed from the surface 2. having cut down a crop; pp. of abmacha.

abgmayt *v.* mowed off; pp. of abmayya.

abgmeikt *v.* marked off; pp. of abmeika.

abgmessa *v.* measured off; pp. of abmessa.

abgnumma *v.* 1. removed 2. having accepted counsel or a confession 3. took off speedily; pp. of abnemma.

abgott *(m).* idol.

abgott-awldah *(m).* altar dedicated to a false god.

abgott-awldahs *(f).* altars dedicated to false gods; pl. of abgott-awldah.

abgott-deenah *(m).* worshiper of idols.

abgott-gleichnis *(neu).* likeness of an idol.

abgott-gleichnissa *(f).* likeness of idols; pl. of abgott-gleichnis.

abgott-kalb *(neu).* idol shaped like a calf.

abgott-kaynich *(m).* the chief among false gods or idols.

abgott-kaynicha *(f).* the chiefs among false gods or idols; pl. of abgott-kaynich.

abgott-kelvah *(f).* idols shaped like calves; pl. of abgott-kalb.

abgott-opfah *(neu).* idolatrous offering or sacrifice.

abgott-opfahra *(f).* idolatrous offerings or sacrifices; pl. of abgott-opfah.

abgott-preeshtah *(m).* priest in the service of false gods or idols.

abgott-zaycha *(m).* special sign given by an idol or false god.

abgratza *v.* to scratch or scrape off.

abgrissa *v.* torn off; pp. of abreisa.

abgrivva *v.* rubbed off; pp. of abreiva.

abgrobt *v.* plucked; pp. of abrobba.

abgrohmd *v.* 1. taken advantage of another in a deal 2. cleared off surface; pp. of abrohma.

abgrold *v.* rolled off; pp. of abrolla.

abgrosht *v.* rusted off; pp. of abroshta.

abgrutsht *v.* slid off; pp. of abrutsha.

abgvayna *v.* to break a habit.

abgveaht *v.* 1. worn off 2. discouraged from, warned about; pp. of abveahra.

abgvesha *v.* washed off; pp. of abvesha.

abgvikkeld *v.* 1. unwraped off

of something 2. uncoiled off of something; pp. of abvikla.

abgvitsht *v.* slipped off or slipped away; pp. of abvitsha.

abgvoaht *v.* served, waited on (as in a store or restaurant); pp. of abvoahra.

abhakka *v.* 1. to chop off 2. to terminate.

abhandla *v.* to trade (not common).

abhayva *v.* 1. to lift off 2. to hold off, postpone 3. to hold off, ward off.

abheahra *v.* to shed hair.

abheicha *v.* to listen to.

abheiyahra *v.* to give in marriage.

abhenka *v.* to unhook.

abkabbiya *v.* to copy.

abkakt *v.* 1. chopped off 2. terminated; pp. of abhakka.

abkandeld *v.* traded; pp. of abhandla.

abkanka *v.* unhooked; pp. of abhenka.

abkawfa *v.* 1. to buy 2. to bribe.

abkeahra *v.* to sweep off.

abkeaht *v.* having shed hair; pp. of abheahra.

abkeela *v.* to cool off.

abkeicht *v.* having listened to; pp. of abheicha.

abkeiyaht *v.* having given in marriage; pp. of abheiyahra.

abkfalla *v.* 1. fallen off 2. fallen away, apostatized; pp. of abfalla.

abkfiaht *v.* led astray; pp. of abfiahra.

abkliahra *v.* to clear off (example: weather).

abkohva *v.* 1. lifted off 2. held off, postponed 3. held off, warded off; pp. of abhayva.

abksaddeld *v.* unsaddled; pp. of absadla.

abksawt *v.* 1. scolded, told off 2. denied, renounced, abstained from; pp. of absawwa.

abksaykt *v.* sawed off; pp. of absayya.

abksetzt *v.* removed from office; pp. of absetza.

abkshadda *v.* to unharness.

abkshaft *v.* worked off a debt; pp. of abshaffa.

abkshayft *v.* shaved off; pp. of abshayfa.

abkshayld *v.* peeled off; pp. of abshayla.

abkshebt *v.* 1. shoveled off 2. skimmed off; pp. of abshebba.

abkshiddeld *v.* shaken off; pp. of abshidla.

abkshlauwa *v.* knocked off; pp. of abshlauwa.

abkshlenkaht *v.* shaken off, waved off; pp. of abshlenkahra.

abkshlohfa *v.* slept off; pp. of absholhfa.

abkshmissa *v.* 1. thrown off 2. reduced the price; pp. of abshmeisa.

abkshmolsa *v.* melted off; pp. of abshmelsa.

abkshnaebt *v.* replied curtly, snapped off; pp. of abshnaebba.

abkshnidda *v.* cut off; pp. of abshneida.

abkshoahra *v.* cut off with sissors; pp. of absheahra.

abkshohva *v.* 1. pushed off 2. procrastinated; pp. of absheeva.

abkshossa *v.* 1. detonated 2. having shown off 3. fired a gun; pp. of absheesa.

abkshpeeld *v.* shriked duty, played hooky; pp. of abshpeela.

abkshprunga *v.* 1. left early 2. ran off; pp. of abshpringa.

abkshritt *v.* measured by stepping off; pp. of abshridda.

abkshrivva *v.* 1. copied by hand 2. written off; pp. of abshreiva.

abkshtauva *v.* died off; pp. of abshtauva.

abkshteaht *v.* started off; pp. of abshteahra.

abkshtikkeld *v.* marked with stakes; pp. of abshtikla.

abkshtohla *v.* snuck away; pp. of abshtayla.

abkshtrohft *v.* rebuked; pp. of abshtrohfa.

abkshvaut *v.* thrashed, beat up; pp. of abshvauda.

abkshvenkt *v.* rinsed off; pp. of abshvenka.

abkshvoahra *v.* sworn off, determined to quit; pp. of abshveahra.

ablawda *v.* to unload.

ablawfa *v.* 1. to run off (liquid) 2. to desert, to walk away from.

ablaysa *v.* 1. to read aloud to an audience 2. to pick off.

ablaysah *(m).* one who reads aloud to an audience.

ablayya *v.* to lay off.

abmacha *v.* 1. to remove from the surface 2. to cut down a crop.

abmayya *v.* to mow off.

abmeika *v.* to mark off.

abmessa *v.* to measure off.

abnemma *v.* 1. to remove 2. to accept counsel or a confession 3. to take off speedily.

aboahma *v.* to show mercy.

aboahmd *v.* having shown mercy; pp. of aboahma.

abpetza *v.* to pinch off.

abpiktahra *v.* to portray publicly, publish a photograph.

abpoahra *v.* to pair off.

abreisa *v.* to tear off.

abreiva *v.* to rub off.

Abrill *(m).* April.

abrobba *v.* to pluck.

abrohma *v.* 1. to get the advantage of another in a deal 2. to clear off a surface.

abrolla *v.* to roll off.

abroshta *v.* to rust off.

abrutsha *v.* to slide off.

absadla *v.* to unsaddle.

absatz *(m).* off set.

absatza *(f).* off set; pl. of absatz.

absawwa *v.* 1. to scold, to tell off 2. to deny for oneself, to renounce, abstain from 3. to deny a request.

absayya *v.* to saw off.

absetza *v.* to remove from office.

abshaffa *v.* 1. to work out impurities 2. to work off a debt.

abshayfa *v.* to shave off.

abshayla *v.* to peel off.

absheahra *v.* to cut off with scissors.

abshebba *v.* 1. to shovel off 2. to skim off.

absheesa *v.* 1. detonate 2. to show off 3. to fire a gun.

absheeva *v.* 1. to push off of 2. to procrastinate.

abshidla *v.* to shake off.

abshlauwa *v.* 1. to knock off 2. to end the bidding on an item.

abshlenkahra *v.* to shake off or wave off.

abshmeisa *v.* 1. to throw off 2. to make a reduction in price.

abshmelsa *v.* to melt off.

abshnaebba *v.* to reply curtly, snap off.

abshneida *v.* to cut off.

absholhfa *v.* to sleep off.

abshpeela *v.* to shirk duty, to play hooky.

abshpringa *v.* 1. to leave early 2. to run off.

abshreiva *v.* 1. to copy by hand 2. to write off.

abshridda *v.* to measure by stepping off.

abshtauva *v.* to die off.

abshtayla *v.* to sneak away.

abshteahra *v.* to start off.

abshtikla *v.* to mark with stakes.

abshtrohfa *v.* to rebuke.

abshvauda *v.* to thrash, beat up.

abshveahra *v.* to swear off from, determine to quit.

abshvenka *v.* to rinse.

abveahra *v.* 1. to wear off 2. to discourage from, to warn.

abvesha *v.* to wash off.

abvikla *v.* 1. to unwrap off of something 2. to uncoil off of something.

abvitsha *v.* to slip off or slip away.

abvoahra *v.* to serve, to wait on (as in a store or restaurant).

abzayla *v.* to count off.

abzeeya *v.* 1. to skin 2. to pull off 3. to pull off (a stunt).

abzohma *v.* to unbridle.

ach expression of disappointment, irritation, or disgust.

acht eight, eighth.

achta *v.* to heed.

acht-gevva *v.* 1. to be careful 2. to take care of.

acht-havva *v.* to notice.

acht-katt *v.* noticed; pp. of acht-havva.

achtzay eighteen.

achtzayt eighteenth.

achtzich eighty.

adda or.

addah *(m).* command.

addahs *(f).* orders; pl. of addah.

adlich pretty much, fairly.

adning *(f).* 1. set of church standards or rules 2. orderliness.

adninga *(f).* sets of church standards or rules; pl. of adning.

aebbeah *(f).* strawberry.

aebbeahra *(f).* strawberries; pl. of aebbeah.

aebt apt, likely.

aedra *(f).* udders; pl. of aeddah.

afoahra *v.* to experience.

afoahring *(f).* experience.

afoahringa *(f).* experiences; pl. of afoahring.

ah he, unstressed form of "eah".

akkah *(m).* acre.

alanga *v.* to attain.

alangt *v.* attained; pp. of alanga.

alawbnis *(f).* permission, allowance.

alawbnissa *(f).* permissions, allowances; pl. of alawbnis.

alawbt *v.* allowed; pp. of alawva.

alawva *v.* to allow.

ald old.

aldvannish lackadaisical, lacking ambition, indifferent.

allah hand miscellaneous.

allaveil presently.

allem 1. all 2. "allem noch" idiomatic construction meaning apparently.

alles everything.

alli 1. every 2. the most 3. all.

alli-ebbah everyone.

alli-gebott every once in a while.

Alli-Haychsht *(m).* the Highest (God).

Alli-Haychsht *(m).* the Holiest (God).

alli-haychsht highest of all.

alli-heilichsht holiest of all.

alli-heilichsht-blatz *(m).* the most holy place.

alli-mohl every time.

alli-sadda all kinds.

alli-shensht 1. nicest 2. loveliest.

alli-vann each one.

alli-veeshta wickedest, most evil.

almechtich almighty (as used in the Bible).

almohsa *(f).* alms, provisions for the poor or needy.

almohsa-shtubb *(f).* alms room, a room used for provisions for the poor or needy.

almohsa-shtubba *(f).* alms rooms; pl. of almohsa-shtubb.

als oftentimes, at one time, at times.

alsamohl sometimes.

alsnoch yet, still.

am 1. + infinitive, express action in progress (English "__ing") 2. at the, contraction of "an em".

amberell *(f)*. umbrella.

ambohs *(m)*. anvil.

ambohsa *(f)*. anvils; pl. of ambohs.

ambrella *(f)*. umbrellas; pl. of amberell.

amd *(neu)*. office, ministry.

amdah *(f)*. offices, ministries; pl. of amd.

amma contraction of "am en".

amohl at once (always preceded by "uf").

amshel *(m)*. robin.

amshela *(f)*. robins; pl. of amshel.

an at once (always preceded by "uf").

andem probably.

andvadda *(f)*. answers; pl. of andvatt.

andvadda *v.* to answer.

andvatt *(f)*. answer.

angsht *(m)*. anxiety.

anna 1. at, there 2. (prefix) at, there.

anna-du *v.* 1. to put there 2. to put down.

anna-falla *v.* to fall down.

anna-ganga *v.* went there; pp. of anna-gay.

anna-gay *v.* to go there.

anna-gedu *v.* 1. put there 2. put down; pp. of anna-du.

anna-glaykt *v.* laid down; pp. of anna-layya; pp. of anna-leiya.

annah other.

anna-heahra *v.* to belong there.

anna-hokka *v.* to sit down.

annahshtah otherwise.

annah-veldlich other worldly.

anna-keaht *v.* belonged there; pp. of anna-heahra.

anna-kfalla *v.* fell down; pp. of anna-falla.

anna-kokt *v.* sat down; pp. of anna-hokka.

anna-kshikt *v.* sent to some place; pp. of anna-shikka.

anna-kshrivva *v.* written down; pp. of anna-shreiva.

anna-kshtanna *v.* stood in a specific place; pp. of anna-shtay.

anna-kshteld *v.* set down; pp. of anna-shtella.

anna-kumma *v.* to arrive.

anna-layya *v.* to lay down.

anna-leiya *v.* to lie down.

anna-shikka *v.* to send to some place.

anna-shreiva *v.* to write down.

anna-shtay *v.* to stand at a specific place.

anna-shtella *v.* to set down.

anrah another one (used with masculine noun).

anres another one (used with neuter noun).

anri another one (used with feminine noun).

anri others.

aposhtel *(m)*. apostle.

aposhtel-deensht *(m)*. office of the apostle.

aposhtel-deenshta *(f)*. offices of the apostles; pl. of aposhtel-deensht.

aposhtla *(f)*. apostles; pl. of aposhtel.

Apostelgeschichte *(f)*. the Bible book of Acts (Acts of the Apostles).

atzi term used for pain with very small children - "ouchy".

auf-nawm *(m)*. reception.

auf-nawma *(f)*. receptions; pl. of auf-nawm.

Augsht *(m)*. August.

aus 1. out of 2. extinguished 3. (prefix) out.

ausa outside of.

ausahlich pertaining to that which is outward and visible.

ausahra outside one, outsider.

ausah-rekk *(f)*. outer robes; pl. of ausah-rokk.

ausahri 1. outer 2. outside ones, non-native.

ausah-rokk *(m)*. outer robe.

ausahsht outermost.

ausbezawla *v*. 1. to disburse, to pay out 2. to profit.

ausbezawld *v*. disbursed, paid out; pp. of ausbezawla.

ausblansa *v*. to transplant.

ausbloowa *v*. to plow out (potatoes).

ausbrecha *v*. to break out (sickness).

ausbrenna *v*. to burn out.

ausbroviahra *v*. 1. to try out 2. to irritate, annoy.

ausbroviaht *v*. 1. tried out, tempted, tested 2. irritated, annoyed; pp. of ausbroviahra.

ausbumba *v*. to pump dry.

ausbutza *v*. to clean out.

ausdauwa *v*. to thaw out.

ausdayla *v*. 1. to deal or portion out 2. to distribute.

ausdenka *v*. to think out, to figure out a solution.

ausdrawk *(m)*. interpretation, explanation.

ausdrawwa *(f)*. interpretations, explanations; pl. of ausdrawk.

ausdrawwa *v*. 1. to carry out an undertaking 2. to define.

ausdrayla *v*. to roll out dough with a rolling pin.

ausdrayya *v*. to turn out.

ausdredda *v*. 1. to tread out 2. to step aside.

ausdreiva *v*. to drive out, expel.

ausdresha *v*. to work through a difficulty, to resolve a matter.

ausdrikka *v*. to squeeze out.

ausdrikla *v*. to dry out.

ausdu *v*. 1. to surpass, out perform, out do 2. to take off clothing.

auseeva *v*. to take revenge.

auseeves *(neu)*. revenge taking.

auseevish revengeful.

ausfafayla-uf *v*. to miss out on.

ausfafayld-uf *v.* having missed out on; pp. of ausfafayla-uf.

ausfakawfa *v.* to sell out.

ausfakawft *v.* sold out; pp. of ausfakawfa.

ausfalla-mitt *v.* to fall out with, to come to be at odds with.

ausfaydla *v.* to unthread.

ausfiahra *v.* to enact, carry out.

ausfinna *v.* to find out.

ausfix upset, out of fix.

ausfoahra *v.* 1. to turn aside, drive around 2. to leave the planned route, make a side trip 3. to depart.

ausfrohwa *v.* 1. to inquire about 2. to question closely, interrogate.

ausgang *(m).* conclusion, termination.

ausganga *v.* 1. gone out (fire, light) 2. adjourned; pp. of ausgay.

ausgay *v.* 1. to go out (fire, light) 2. to adjourn.

ausgeblanst *v.* transplanted; pp. of ausblansa.

ausgeblookt *v.* plowed out (potatoes); pp. of ausbloowa.

ausgebrend *v.* burned out; pp. of ausbrenna.

ausgebrocha *v.* broke out (sickness); pp. of ausbrecha.

ausgebumbt *v.* pumped out, pumped dry; pp. of ausbumba.

ausgebutzt *v.* cleaned out; pp. of ausbutza.

ausgedaut *v.* thawed out; pp. of ausdauwa.

ausgedayld *v.* 1. dealt or portioned out 2. distributed; pp. of ausdayla.

ausgedenkt *v.* thought out, figured out the solution; pp. of ausdenka.

ausgedrawwa *v.* 1. carried out an undertaking 2. defined; pp. of ausdrawwa.

ausgedrayld *v.* having rolled out dough with a rolling pin; pp. of ausdrayla.

ausgedrayt *v.* turned out; pp. of ausdrayya.

ausgedredda *v.* 1. tread out 2. stepped aside; pp. of ausdredda.

ausgedrikkeld *v.* dried out; pp. of ausdrikla.

ausgedrikt *v.* squeezed out; pp. of ausdrikka.

ausgedrivva *v.* 1. driven out, expelled 2. ornery; pp. of ausdreiva.

ausgedrivva unruly.

ausgedrosha *v.* having worked through a difficulty, resolved a matter; pp. of ausdresha.

ausgedrosha fatigued.

ausgedu *v.* 1. surpassed, out performed, outdone 2. taken off clothing; pp. of ausdu.

ausgeebt *v.* taken revenge; pp. of auseeva.

ausgegrawva *v.* excavated, dug out; pp. of ausgrawva.

ausgekawft *v.* bought out; pp. of auskawfa.

ausgekeaht *v.* swept out; pp. of auskeahra.

ausgeprest *v.* pressed out; pp. of auspressa.

ausgetshekt *v.* examined, checked out; pp. of austshekka.

ausglacht *v.* mocked or laughed at; pp. of auslacha.

ausglaybt *v.* 1. having lived out, exemplified 2. out lived; pp. of auslayva.

ausglidda *v.* having suffered patiently; pp. of ausleida.

ausgloffa *v.* 1. having exeeded the expiration date 2. having released milk prematurely (cows); pp. of auslawfa.

ausglost *v.* having let out, adjourned; pp. of auslossa.

ausgluft *v.* aired out, ventilated; pp. of auslufta.

ausgmacht *v.* 1. decided 2. having extinguished a light or fire 3. mattered 4. fared 5.having dug out vegetables (gardening); pp. of ausmacha.

ausgmessa *v.* measured off; pp. of ausmessa.

ausgnayt *v.* embroidered; pp. of ausnayya.

ausgnumma *v.* 1. having taken revenge 2. having removed the entrails, gutted 3. removed (clothes); pp. of ausnemma.

ausgrawva *v.* to excavate, to dig out.

ausgret *v.* excused; pp. of ausredda.

ausgreyyaht *v.* canceled because of rain, rained out; pp. of ausreyyahra.

ausgricht *v.* 1. having set a matter straight 2. accomplished 3. worked out a conflict; pp. of ausrichta.

ausgrissa *v.* torn out; pp. of ausreisa.

ausgrivva *v.* rubbed out; pp. of ausreiva.

ausgrohmd *v.* cleaned out, straightened out; pp. of ausrohma.

ausgroofa *v.* 1. called out 2. engaged or published for marriage; pp. of ausroofa.

ausgroot *v.* having fully rested; pp. of ausroowa.

ausgrosht *v.* rusted out; pp. of ausroshta.

ausgvatzeld *v.* having developed a root system; pp. of ausvatzla.

ausgvaxa *v.* 1. outgrown 2. having reached full growth; pp. of ausvaxa.

ausgvesha *v.* 1. washed out 2. eroded by water; pp. of ausvesha.

ausgvesha pale, colorless.

ausgvikkeld *v.* unwrapped, uncoiled; pp. of ausvikla.

ausgvitsht *v.* having evaded a task, slipped out of a duty;

pp. of ausvitsha.

ausgvoahra *v.* worn out; pp. of ausveahra.

ausgvoaht *v.* waited out; pp. of ausvoahra.

aushakka *v.* to harvest timber.

aushemmahra *v.* to hammer out.

aushohla *v.* to hollow out.

auskakt *v.* having harvested timber; pp. of aushakka.

auskawfa *v.* to buy out.

auskeahra *v.* to sweep out.

auskemmaht *v.* hammered out; pp. of aushemmahra.

auskfalla-mitt *v.* had a falling out with, being at odds with; pp. of ausfalla-mitt.

auskfaydelt *v.* having unthreaded; pp. of ausfaydla.

auskfiaht *v.* carried out, having enacted; pp. of ausfiahra.

auskfoahra *v.* 1. having turned aside, driven around 2. left the planned route, made a side trip; pp. of ausfoahra.

auskfrohkt *v.* 1. inquired about 2. questioned closely, interrogated; pp. of ausfrohwa.

auskfunna *v.* found out; pp. of ausfinna.

auskohld *v.* hollowed out; pp. of aushohla.

auskshaft *v.* 1. paid off a debt by working 2. having resolved a matter 3. worked out; pp. of ausshaffa.

auskshauft *v.* exhaled; pp. of ausshnaufa.

auskshend *v.* mocked; pp. of ausshenda.

auskshiddeld *v.* shaken out; pp. of ausshidla.

auskshlauwa *v.* 1. knocked out 2. beat out flames 3. sprouted; pp. of ausshlauwa.

auskshlossa *v.* locked out; pp. of ausshleesa.

auskshnubbaht *v.* having investigated a matter which is not one's concern; pp. of ausshnubbahra.

auskshpand *v.* unhitched; pp. of ausshpanna.

auskshpott *v.* mocked; pp. of ausshpodda.

auskshprocha *v.* proclaimed; pp. of ausshprecha.

auskshreinaht *v.* having done finish carpentry; pp. of ausshreinahra.

auskshtambt *v.* 1. having stamped out a fire 2. explored; pp. of ausshtamba.

auskshteaht *v.* started out; pp. of ausshteahra.

auskshtocha *v.* removed with a pointy instrument; pp. of ausshtecha.

auskshtohsa *v.* having cast out; pp. of ausshtohsa.

auskshtokka *v.* stuck it out, endured; pp. of ausshtikka.

auskshtrekt *v.* stretched out; pp. of ausshtrekka.

auskshtroit v. spread out, scattered about; pp. of ausshtroiya.

auskshvenkt v. rinsed out; pp. of ausshvenka.

ausksucht v. searched out; pp. of aussucha.

auslacha v. to mock or laugh at.

auslawfa v. 1. to exceed the expiration date 2. of cows - to release milk prematurely.

auslayva v. 1. to live out, exemplify 2. to out live.

ausleida v. to suffer patiently.

auslendah (m). foreigner.

auslendish foreign.

auslossa v. to let out, adjourn.

auslufta v. to air out, to ventilate.

ausmacha v. 1. to decide 2. to extinguish a light or fire 3. to matter 4. to fare 5. in gardening-to dig out vegetables.

ausmessa v. to measure out.

ausnannah adj. 1. spread apart 2. scattered.

ausnayya v. to embroider.

ausnemma v. 1. to take revenge 2. to remove the entrails of, to gut 3. to remove (clothes).

auspressa v. to press out.

ausredda (f). excuses; pl. of ausret.

ausredda v. to excuse.

ausreisa v. to tear out.

ausreiva v. to rub out.

ausret (f). excuse.

ausreyyahra v. to cancel because of rain.

ausrichta v. 1. to set a matter straight 2. to accomplish 3. to work out a conflict.

ausrohma v. to clean out or straighten out.

ausroofa v. 1. to call out 2. to publish a couple for marriage.

ausroowa v. to become fully rested.

ausroshta v. to rust out.

aussatz (m). leprosy.

aussetzich leprous.

ausshaffa v. 1. to pay off a debt by working 2. to resolve a matter 3. to do body building 4.to work out.

ausshenda v. to mock (not common).

ausshidla v. to shake out.

ausshlauwa v. 1. to sprout 2. to beat out flames 3. to knock out.

ausshleesa v. to lock out.

ausshnaufa v. to exhale.

ausshnubbahra v. to investigate a matter which is not one's concern.

ausshnubbahrah busybody in other people's affairs.

ausshpanna v. to unhitch.

ausshpodda v. to mock.

ausshprecha v. to proclaim.

ausshreinahra v. to do finish carpentry.

ausshtamba v. 1. to stamp out a

fire 2. to explore.
ausshteahra *v.* to start out.
ausshtecha *v.* to remove with a pointy instrument.
ausshtikka *v.* to stick to it, to endure.
ausshtohsa *v.* to cast out.
ausshtrekka *v.* to stretch out.
ausshtroiya *v.* to spread out, to scatter abroad.
ausshvenka *v.* to rinse out.
aussucha *v.* to search out.
austshekka *v.* to examine.
ausvatzla *v.* to develop a root system.
ausvaxa *v.* 1. to outgrow 2. to reach full growth.
ausveahra *v.* to wear out.
ausvendich outward, on the outside.
ausvennich memorized, by heart.
ausvesha *v.* 1. to wash out 2. to erode by water.
ausvikla *v.* 1. to unwrap 2. to uncoil.
ausvitsha *v.* to evade a task, slip out of a duty.
ausvoahra *v.* to wait out.
autseidah *(m).* outsider.
autseidahs *(f).* outsiders; pl. of autseidah.
autseit outside.
avayla *v.* 1. to choose 2. to appoint to office.
avayld *v.* chosen, appointed; pp. of avayla.
avayling *(f).* 1. choice 2. appointment to an office.

avaylinga *(f).* 1. choices 2. appointments to office; pl. of avayling.
avvah 1. but 2. particle placed in front of adjectives to add emphasis 3. too (used as an affirmative to contradict a negative statement).
aw also.
awdlah *(m).* eagle.
awdlah-flikkel *(m).* eagle wing.
awdlah-flikla *(f).* eagle-wings; pl. of awdlah-flikkel.
awk *(neu).* eye.
awks-balla *(m).* eyeball.
awks-dekkel *(m).* eyelid.
awks-dekla *(f).* eyelids; pl. of awks-dekkel.
awl all.
awl recht alright.
awl zvay both.
awldah *(m).* altar.
awldah-ksha *(neu).* vessels used in the service of the altar.
awldah-ksharra *(f).* all of the vessels used for service at the altar; pl. of awldah-ksha.
awldahra *(f).* altars; pl. of awldah.
awldah-shtay *(m).* a stone used to build an altar.
awlmechtich almighty.
awwa *(f).* eyes; pl. of awk.
awwa-blikk *(m).* blink of an eye.
awwa-dekkel *(m).* eye lid.
awwa-dekla *(f).* eyelids; pl. of

awwa-dekkel.

awwa-lechah *(f)*. eye sockets; pl. of awwa-loch.

awwa-loch *(neu)*. eye socket.

awwa-shmiah *(f)*. eye salve.

awwa-shmiahra *(f)*. eye salves; pl. of awwa-shmiah.

awwa-vassah *(neu)*. tears.

ax *(f)*. 1. ax 2. axle.

ax-kebb *(f)*. ax heads; pl. of ax-kobb.

ax-kobb *(m)*. ax head.

ay one.

aybrecha *v.* to commit adultery.

aybrechah *(m)*. one who commits adultery.

aybrechich adulterous.

aybruch *(neu)*. adultery.

aybrucha *(f)*. adultries; pl. of aybruch.

aycha made of oak wood.

aycha-baym *(f)*. oak trees; pl. of aycha-bohm.

aycha-bohm *(m)*. oak tree.

aycha-hols *(neu)*. oak wood.

ay-ebbah one person.

Ayfaw *(f)*. Eve, first woman named in the Bible.

ayfeldich having the affections set on one person or object.

ayfeldichkeit *(f)*. singleness of heart.

aygebrocha *v.* having committed adultry; pp. of aybrecha.

ayk *(f)*. harrow.

ayka *(f)*. harrows; pl. of ayk.

ayka *v.* to harrow.

aykel *(m)*. distaste, aversion.

aykla *v.* to be distasteful or undesirable.

ayklich distasteful, disgusting, loathsome.

aykna *v.* 1. to own 2. to owe.

aykna / ayya one's own.

ayknah *(m)*. owner.

ayl *(neu)*. oil.

ayla *(f)*. oils; pl. of ayl.

ayla *v.* to oil, lubricate.

ayl-baym *(f)*. olive trees; pl. of ayl-bohm.

ayl-berg *(m)*. Mount of Olives.

ayl-boddel *(f)*. (olive) oil bottle.

ayl-bodla *(f)*. oil bottles; pl. of ayl-boddel.

ayl-bohm *(m)*. olive tree.

ayl-dichah *(f)*. oil cloths; pl. of ayl-duch.

ayl-duch *(neu)*. oil cloth.

aylend pitiful situation, misery, dysfunctional setting.

aylendich 1. pitiful, miserable 2. dysfunctional.

ayl-frichta *(f)*. olive berries; pl. of ayl-frucht.

ayl-frucht *(neu)*. olive berries.

ayl-goahra *(m)*. olive garden.

ayl-hann *(f)*. hollow horn used as an olive oil container.

aylich oily.

ayl-kenlen *(f)*. small oil cans; pl. of ayl-kenli.

ayl-kenli *(neu)*. small oil can.

ayl-mixah *(m)*. olive oil mixer.

ayl-mixahs *(f)*. olive oil mixers; pl. of ayl-mixah.

aym one.

aymah *(m)*. pail, bucket.

ayn one.

aynd 1. one of several 2. the one 3. one of them.

aynich agreed.

aynichkeit *(f)*. unity.

aynra one.

ayns one of.

aynsisht only.

ayseidich one-sided.

aysel *(m)*. donkey.

aysela *(f)*. donkeys; pl. of aysel.

aysel-hutsh *(m)*. donkey colt.

aysel-hutsha *(f)*. donkey colts; pl. of aysel-hutsh.

aysel-kebb *(f)*. donkey heads; pl. of aysel-kobb.

aysel-kobb *(m)*. donkey head.

aysel-mah *(f)*. donkey mare.

aysel-mahra *(f)*. donkey mares; pl. of aysel-mah.

aysel-shtraych orneriness, stubborn streak.

ayshtand *(m)*. matrimony.

ayva level, flat.

ayva kumma *v.* to get even.

ayvenah more level, more flat.

ayvesht most level, most flat.

ayvich eternal.

ayvichkeida *(f)*. eternities; pl. of ayvichkeit.

ayvichkeit *(f)*. eternity.

ayvichlich eternally, forever.

ayya / aykna one's own.

ayya-fashtand *(m)*. one's own understanding.

ayzechtich not prosperous.

B - b

babba *v.* to stick, to adhere.

babbich sticky.

babiah *(neu)*. paper.

babiahlen *(f)*. small pieces of paper; pl. of babiahli.

babiahli *(neu)*. small piece of paper.

babiahra *(f)*. papers; pl. of babiah.

babla *v.* to babble.

babla poplar (tree).

bablah-baym *(f)*. poplar trees; pl. of bablah-bohm.

bablah-bohm *(m)*. poplar tree.

badda *v.* to aid or benefit.

baddah *(m)*. bother.

baddahra *(f)*. bothers; pl. of baddah.

baddamoll finally, at last.

baddich 1. possessing good quality 2. classy.

badger-haut *(f)*. badger skin.

badger-heidah *(f)*. badger skins; pl. of badger-haut.

badra *v.* to bother.

badreeslen *(f)*. quails; pl. of badreesli.

badreesli *(neu)*. quail.

baetsh *(f)*. batch.

baetshes *(f)*. batches; pl. of baetsh.

bakka *(m)*. cheek.

bakka *v.* to bake.
bakka-gnocha *(m).* cheek bone.
bakkah *(m).* baker.
bakkahrei *(f).* bakery.
bakkahreiya *(f).* bakeries; pl. of bakkahrei.
bakka-shtay *(m).* brick (baked stone).
bakka-shtaynich made of bricks.
bakk-effa *(f).* bake ovens; pl. of bakk-offa.
bakk-offa *(m).* bake oven.
balka *(m).* wooden beam.
ball 1. nearly 2.soon.
balla *(m).* ball.
balsam-shmiah *(f).* balsam salve.
bamgoahra *(m).* orchard (common use).
bamhatzich merciful.
bamhatzichkeida *(f).* mercifulnesses; pl. of bamhatzichkeit.
bamhatzichkeit *(f).* mercifulness.
band *(m).* 1. ring 2. collar 3. fetter.
banda *(f).* collars; pl. of band.
bang worried.
bank *(f).* bench.
basht *(f).* husk.
bashta *(f).* husks; pl. of basht.
bashta *v.* to husk.
batzich bossy, selfish.
bauch *(m).* belly, waist.
bauch-gadda *(f).* surcingles; pl. of bauch-gatt.

bauch-gatt *(m).* surcingle, a band, cinch, strap.
bauchvay *(neu).* stomach ache.
bauma-dekkel *(m).* the pendulum on a clock.
bauma-dekla *(f).* clock pendulums; pl. of bauma-dekkel.
baut nearly, almost.
bauwa *v.* to build.
bavvah *(m).* farmer.
bavvahra *v.* to farm.
bavvahrei *(f).* farm.
bavvahreiya *(f).* farms; pl. of bavvahrei.
bawda *v.* 1. to soak or bathe an injured body part 2. to wade.
bawld bald.
bawl-kebb *(f).* bald heads; pl. of bawl-kobb.
bawl-kebbich baldheaded.
bawl-kobb *(m).* bald head.
bawn *(f).* bean.
bawn *(m).* ban, excommunication, shun.
bawna *(f).* beans; pl. of bawn.
bawna-shtekka *(m).* bean pole.
bawsich bossy.
bawt-shtubb *(f).* bathroom.
bawt-shtubba *(f).* bathroom; pl. of bawt-shtubb.
bay *(neu).* leg.
bayda *v.* to pray.
bay-kedlen *(f).* anklets; pl. of bay-kedli.
bay-kedli *(f).* anklets, jewelry worn on the ankles.

baym *(f)*. trees; pl. of bohm.
baym-nesht *(f)*. tree branches.
bays angry.
baysa *(m)*. broom.
baysa-baym *(f)*. broom trees; pl. of baysa-bohm.
baysa-bohm *(m)*. broom tree.
bayt-box *(f)*. phylactery, frontlet band, scripture containing case worn by Jewish men attached with straps to the arm and forehead (lit.prayer box).
bayt-boxa *(f)*. phylacteries; pl. of bayt-box.
bayt-haus *(neu)*. house of prayer.
bayt-heisah *(f)*. houses of prayer; pl. of bayt-haus.
beah *(f)*. berry.
beah *(m)*. bear.
beahra *(f)*. 1. bears 2. berries; pl. of beah.
beaht *(f)*. 1. beards 2. chins 3. boards; pl. of boaht.
bedanka *v*. to thank.
bedankt *v*. thanked; pp. of bedanka.
bedavvahlich pitiful.
beddah *(f)*. beds; pl. of bett.
bedeida *v*. to signify.
bedeit *v*. signified; pp. of bedeida.
bedekka *v*. to cover, overlay with.
bedekt *v*. covered, overlayed; pp. of bedekka.
bedenklich thought provoking.
bedla *v*. to beg.

bedlah *(m)*. beggar.
bedlen *(f)*. bayby beds, cribs, cradles; pl. of bedli.
bedli *(neu)*. baby bed, crib, cradle.
bedreebnis *(neu)*. affliction, sorrow.
bedreebnisa *(f)*. afflictions, sorrows; pl. of bedreebnis.
bedreebt *v*. grieved; pp. of bedreeva.
bedreeva *v*. to grieve.
bedrohwa betrayed, sad.
beeblen *(f)*. chicks; pl. of beebli.
beebli *(neu)*. chick.
beebli-heislen *(f)*. small chicken coops; pl. of beebli-heisli.
beebli-heisli *(neu)*. small chicken coop.
beeda *v*. 1. to offer 2. to win 3. to bid.
beeya *v*. to bend.
befayla *v*. to command.
befayld *v*. commanded; pp. of befayla.
begawbt gifted.
beglawkt *v*. complained about or bemoaned; pp. of beglawwa.
beglawwa *v*. to complain about, bemoan.
begraybnis *(neu)*. grave or burial place.
begraybnis-blatz *(m)*. cemetery.
begraybnis-bletz *(f)*. cemeteries, burial places; pl. of begraybnis-blatz.
begraybnissa *(f)*. graves or

burial places; pl. of begraybnis.

begreifa *v.* to comprehend.

begreiflich comprehensible.

begriff *(m).* notion, idea, concept.

begriffa *v.* comprehended; pp. of begreifa.

begukka *v.* to examine a matter.

begukt *v.* when a matter is examined; pp. of begukka.

behayfa *v.* to behave.

behayft *v.* behaved; pp. of behayfa.

behilflich helpful.

bei by.

bei-bringa *v.* to bring from somewhere.

beich *(f).* bellies, waists; pl. of bauch.

bei-drawwa *v.* to carry in from somewhere.

bei-falla *v.* to occur to, to come to mind.

bei-gebrocht *v.* brought from somewhere; pp. of bei-bringa.

bei-gedrawwa *v.* carried in from somewhere; pp. of bei-drawwa.

bei-greeya *v.* to get from somewhere, obtain.

bei-grikkt *v.* gotten from somewhere, obtained; pp. of bei-greeya.

bei-hohla *v.* to fetch from somewhere.

bei-kfalla *v.* having come to mind; pp. of bei-falla.

bei-kohld *v.* fetched from somewhere; pp. of bei-hohla.

bei-kshtanna *v.* having encouraged or supported someone; pp. of bei-shtay.

bei-kumma *v.* to come from somewhere.

beilah *(m).* boiler, large container used for canning.

beim by the / it, beside the / it, near the / it (only used with masculine or nueter noun).

bei-nannah together, gathered, assembled.

beis *(m).* bite.

beis zang *(f).* nippers.

beisa *v.* to bite.

bei-shtay *v.* to encourage or support someone.

bei-shtendah supporter.

beisich itchy.

beis-zanga *(f).* nippers; pl. of beis-zang.

bei-vadda *(f).* by words; pl. of bei-vatt.

bei-vatt *(neu).* by word.

beiya *v.* to rock to sleep.

bekand familiar.

bekeahra *v.* to repent.

bekeaht *v.* repented; pp. of bekeahra.

bekend *v.* confessed; pp. of bekenna.

bekendnis *(neu).* confession.

bekendnissa *(f).* confessions; pl. of bekendnis.

bekenna *v.* to confess.

bekimmahnis *(f).* concern.

bekimmahnisa *(f)*. concerns; pl. of bekimmahnis.

bekimmahra *v*. to take concern about.

bekimmaht *v*. concerned; pp. of bekimmahra.

bekk *(f)*. bucks; pl. of bokk.

bekkah *(m)*. oven.

beklen *(f)*. small male deer, sheep, goats, rabbits; pl. of bekli.

bekli *(neu)*. a small male deer, sheep, goat or rabbit.

belaybt *v*. having lived ones faith; pp. of belayva.

belayva *v*. to live one's faith.

beldah *(f)*. belts; pl. of belt.

beleebt beloved.

bell *(f)*. bell.

bella *(f)*. bells; pl. of bell.

belt *(m)*. belt.

bemeet *v*. having put forth effort; pp. of bemeeya.

bemeeya *v*. to put forth effort.

bendel *(m)*. string, shoe lace.

bendla *(f)*. strings, shoe laces; pl. of bendel.

benk *(f)*. benches; pl. of bank.

benklen *(f)*. small benches or footstools; pl. of benkli.

benkli *(neu)*. small bench or footstool.

benohma *v*. to name, to identify.

berg *(m)*. mountain.

berga *(f)*. mountins; pl. of berg.

beroof *(m)*. calling, office of appointment.

beroofa *(f)*. calling, office of appointment; pl. of beroof.

beshneida *v*. to circumcise.

beshneiding *(f)*. circumcision.

beshneidinga *(f)*. circumcisions; pl. of beshneiding.

beshneiding-glawva *(m)*. the belief that circumcision is a requirement for salvation.

beshnidda *v*. circumcised; pp. of beshneida.

besht best.

beshta the best.

beshveahra *v*. to exorcise.

beshveahrah *(m)*. exorcist, one who seeks to expel (an evil spirit) by religious ceremonies.

beshvoahra *v*. exorcised; pp. of beshveahra.

bessah better.

bessahs a better thing.

bett *(neu)*. bed.

bett-kammah *(f)*. bedroom.

bett-kammahra *(f)*. bedrooms; pl. of bett-kammah.

bett-sach *(neu)*. bedding.

bett-shtubb *(f)*. bedroom.

bett-shtubba *(f)*. bedrooms; pl. of bett-shtubb.

bett-zeech *(neu)*. bed sheet.

bett-zeecha *(f)*. bedsheets; pl. of bett-zeech.

bett-zeit *(f)*. bedtime.

betzawla *v*. to pay.

betzawld *v*. paid; pp. of betzawla.

betzawling *(f)*. payment.

bevaykt moved.

biah *(f)*. pear.

biah *(neu)*. beer.
biahra *(f)*. pears; pl. of biah.
biahra-baym *(f)*. pear trees; pl. of biahra-bohm.
biahra-bohm *(m)*. pear tree.
bichah *(f)*. books; pl. of buch.
bichlen *(f)*. small books, pamphlets, booklets; pl. of bichli.
bichli *(neu)*. small book, pamphlet, booklet.
bidda *v*. 1. to ask for, request 2. to bid (peace, greeting etc.).
biddah bitter.
biddah-greidah *(f)*. bitter herbs (wormwood).
biddahlich bitterly.
bikka *v*. 1. to stoop 2. to bow.
bikkel-eisa *(neu)*. appliance used to iron clothes.
bikla *v*. to iron clothes, etc.
bild *(neu)*. image.
bildah *(f)*. images; pl. of bild.
bill *(neu)*. invoice.
bills *(f)*. invoices; pl. of bill.
binn am (verb conj. of sei) "ich binn".
binna *v*. to tie.
birdi *(neu)*. small bird.
birdis *(f)*. small birds; pl. of birdi.
bishof *(m)*. bishop.
bishofs *(f)*. bishops; pl. of bishof.
bisht are (verb conj. of sei) "du bisht".
biskatz *(f)*. skunk.
biskatza *(f)*. skunks; pl. of biskatz.

bisli a little, a tiny bit.
biss until.
bissel a little, a small amount.
Bivla *(f)*. Bibles; pl. of Bivvel.
Bivvel *(f)*. Bible.
bix *(f)*. gun.
bixa *(f)*. guns; pl. of bix.
bladda *v*. to bleat.
blaebbah-maul *(neu)*. blabbermouth.
blaebbah-meilah *(f)*. blabbermouths; pl. of blaebbah-maul.
blaebbahra *v*. to blab.
blaekbeah *(f)*. blackberry.
blaekbeahra *(f)*. blackberries; pl. of blaekbeah.
blaekshmidda *(f)*. blacksmiths; pl. of blaekshmitt.
blaekshmitt *(m)*. blacksmith.
blaetsh-nass soaking wet.
blakk *(m)*. block.
blakka *(m)*. spot.
blakkich spotted.
blaks *(f)*. blocks; pl. of blakk.
blank *(f)*. plank.
blanka *(f)*. planks; pl. of blank.
blansa *(f)*. the category of plants.
blansa *v*. to plant.
blasiah *(m)*. pleasure.
blasiahra *(f)*. pleasures; pl. of blasiah.
blatt *(f)*. 1. leaf 2. set of false teeth.
blatz *(m)*. 1. place 2. space.
blatz-gevva *v*. to yield to.
blatz-nemma *v*. to take place, happen.

blaum *(f)*. plum.
blauma *(f)*. plums; pl. of blaum.
blayyich pale color.
blech *(neu)*. 1. tin 2. tin cup.
blecha *(f)*. tin cups; pl. of blech.
blecha *v*. to suffer consequences.
blechich 1. made of tin 2. tinny, cheaply made 3. having a tinny sound.
blech-sheah *(f)*. tin snips.
blech-sheahra *(f)*. tin snips; pl. of blech-sheah.
bleddah *(f)*. leaves; pl. of blatt.
bleddahrich leafy.
blee-gnebb *(f)*. buds on a plant; pl. of blee-gnobb.
blee-gnobb *(m)*. bud on a plant.
bleeya *v*. to bloom.
bleiva *v*. to remain or stay.
blekk *(f)*. logs; pl. of blokk.
blekka *(f)*. spots; pl. of blakka.
blendi plenty, plenty of.
bleshtah *(neu)*. plaster.
bleshtahra *(f)*. plasters; pl. of bleshtah.
bleshtahra *v*. to plaster.
bleshtahring *(neu)*. the plastered part of a structure.
blesiah *(m)*. pleasure.
blesiahlich pleasantly.
blesiahra *(f)*. pleasures; pl. of blesiah.
bletlen *(f)*. little platters, small serving plates, saucers; pl. of bletli.
bletli *(neu)*. little platter, saucer, small serving plate.
bletsha *v*. 1. to spank 2. to clap.
bletz *(f)*. 1. places 2. spaces; pl. of blatz.

bletzlich immediately.
blikk *(m)*. blink.
blikka *(f)*. blinks of an eye; pl. of blikk.
blikka *v*. 1. to shell peas 2. to blink.
blind blind.
blindheida *(f)*. blindnesses; pl. of blindheit.
blindheit *(f)*. blindness.
blinsla *v*. to blink your eyes.
blitz *(m)*. flash.
blitza *(f)*. flashes; pl. of blitz.
blitza *v*. to flash.
blitz-keffah *(m)*. firefly.
blitz-keffahra *(f)*. fireflies; pl. of blitz-keffah.
bloh blue.
bloh vennich not much, not many.
blohdah *(m)*. blister.
blohdahra *(f)*. blisters; pl. of blohdah.
bloh-fayyel *(f)*. bluebirds; pl. of bloh-fohkel.
bloh-fohkel *(m)*. bluebird.
bloh-hooshta *(m)*. whooping cough.
blohk *(m)*. 1. plague 2. bother.
blohk-frei free from disturbance.
blohsa *v*. to blow.
blohsah *(m)*. blower.
blohs-hann *(f)*. horn or trumpet.
blohs-hanna *(f)*. horns or trumpets; pl. of blohs-hann.
blohwa *(f)*. 1. plaques 2. bothers;

pl. of blohk.
blohwa *v.* to bother or nag.
blohwich bothersome.
blokk *(m).* log.
blokk-haus *(neu).* log cabin.
blokk-heisah *(f).* log cabins; pl. of blokk-haus.
blokk-sheiyah *(f).* log barn.
blokk-sheiyahra *(f).* log barns; pl. of blokk-sheiyah.
blooda *v.* to bleed.
bloodich bloody.
blook *(m).* plow.
blooks-feich *(f).* furrow left by a plow.
blooks-feicha *(f).* furrows left by a plow; pl. of blooks-feich.
blook-sheah *(f).* plow share.
blook-sheahra *(f).* plow shears; pl. of blook-sheah.
blooks-leit *(f).* people who plow.
bloos *(f).* the blues.
bloosich depressed, unhappy.
bloot *(neu).* blood.
bloot-auseevah *(m).* avenger of blood.
bloot-blakka *(m).* blood spot.
bloot-brunna *(m).* well or fountain of blood.
bloot-dashtich blood thirsty.
bloot-fageesah *(m).* shedder of blood.
bloot-fageesich given to bloodshed.
bloot-feld *(neu).* field of blood.
bloot-feldah *(f).* fields of blood; pl. of bloot-feld.
bloot-fluss *(m).* flow of blood.

bloot-opfah *(neu).* offering of blood.
bloot-opfahra *(f).* offerings of blood; pl. of bloot-opfah.
bloot-roht blood red.
bloots-drobba *(m).* drop of blood.
bloots-grankeda *(f).* bleeding sicknesses; pl. of bloots-granket.
bloots-granket *(f).* bleeding sickness.
bloot-shand *(f).* scandal or dishonor involving blood.
bloot-shanda *(f).* scandals involving blood; pl. of bloot-shand.
bloot-shtrayma *(m).* bloodstream.
bloot-shuld an act that incurs blood guilt.
bloot-shuldich blood guilty.
bloot-suklah blood sucker.
bloowa *(f).* plows; pl. of blook.
bloowa *v.* to plow.
blotza *v.* to bump.
blotzah *(m).* bump, rough spot in road.
blotzich bumpy, rough traveling.
blumm *(f).* flower.
blumma *(f).* flowers; pl. of blumm.
blumma-beddah *(f).* flower beds; pl. of blumma-bett.
blumma-bett *(neu).* flower bed.
blumma-goahra *(m).* flower garden.
blumma-krohn *(m).* crown of flowers.

blumma-krohna *(f)*. crowns of flowers; pl. of blumma-krohn.

blumma-land *(neu)*. small plot of land with flowers planted in it.

blumma-lendah *(f)*. small plots of land with flowers; pl. of blumma-land.

blumma-lendlen *(f)*. small flower beds; pl. of blumma-lendli.

blumma-lendli *(neu)*. small flowerbed.

blutt naked, bare.

blutt-kebbich bareheaded.

boah foos *(m)*. barefoot.

boah-fees *(f)*. barefeet; pl. of boah-foos.

boah-feesich barefooted.

boahra *v.* 1. to drill 2. to irk.

boaht *(m)*. 1. beard 2. chin.

boaht *(neu)*. board.

bobb *(f)*. baby (baby doll).

bobba *(f)*. babies (baby dolls); pl. of bobb.

boblen *(f)*. babies; pl. of bobli.

bobli *(neu)*. baby.

bodda *(m)*. ground, floor.

bodda-nesht *(neu)*. blankets arranged on the floor for sleeping on.

bodda-neshtah *(f)*. blankets arranged on the floor for sleeping on; pl. of bodda-nesht.

boddel *(f)*. bottle.

bodla *(f)*. bottles; pl. of boddel.

bodlen *(f)*. tiny bottles; pl. of bodli.

bodli *(neu)*. tiny bottle.

bohl *(f)*. bowl.

bohla *(f)*. bowls; pl. of bohl.

bohlafoll *(f)*. bowls full; pl. of bohlfoll.

bohlfoll *(f)*. bowl full.

bohm *(m)*. tree.

bohm-goahra *(m)*. orchard.

boht *(neu)*. boat.

bohts *(f)*. boats; pl. of boat.

boi *(m)*. pie.

bokk *(m)*. male deer, sheep, goat or rabbit.

bollahra *v.* to rumble (stomach).

boo *(m)*. boy.

boocha *(m)*. beech.

boos *(f)*. repentance.

boova *(f)*. boys; pl. of boo.

boova-leis *(f)*. needles from the stinging nettle plant that stick to clothing.

boovlen *(f)*. little boys; pl. of boovli.

boovli *(neu)*. little boy.

botri *(f)*. pantry.

botrin *(f)*. pantries; pl. of botri.

botshaftah *(m)*. ambassador.

bow *(f)*. bow (for hunting).

bow-hundah *(m)*. bow hunter.

bows *(f)*. bows (for hunting); pl. of bow.

bow-sheesah *(m)*. one who shoots a bow and arrow.

bow-shuss *(m)*. 1. bow shot 2. distance of a bow shot.

box *(f)*. box.

boxa *(f)*. boxes; pl. of box.

box-shtall *(m)*. closed stall for

horses.
box-shtell *(f)*. box stalls; pl. of box-shtall.
braekka *v.* to brag.
braekkah *(m)*. braggart.
brand-opfah *(neu)*. burnt offering.
brand-opfah-awldah *(m)*. altar for burnt offerings.
brand-opfah-awldahra *(f)*. burnt offering alters; pl. of brand-opfah-awldah.
brand-opfahra *(f)*. burnt offerings; pl. of brand-opfah.
brau brown.
braucha *v.* 1. to need 2. to perform magical healing arts (powwow).
brawf well behaved, obedient.
brawlah *(m)*. chicken raised commercially for meat, broiler.
brawlahs *(f)*. broilers (chicken) pl. of brawlah.
brawlah-shtall *(m)*. broiler house.
brawlah-shtell *(f)*. broiler houses; pl. of brawlah-shtall.
brayding *(f)*. width.
brayt wide.
brecha *v.* to break.
breddich *(f)*. sermon.
breddicha *(f)*. sermons; pl. of breddich.
breddicha *v.* to preach.
breddichah *(m)*. preacher.
breddiches *(neu)*. preaching.

bree *(f)*. liquid.
breeda *v.* to breed.
breedah *(f)*. brothers; pl. of broodah.
breedahlich brotherly.
breef *(m)*. letter (postal).
breefa *(f)*. letters (postal); pl. of breef.
breeya *v.* to scald.
breeyich juicy.
breichta *v.* would need.
brenna *v.* to burn.
brenn-aysel *(m)*. stinging nettle.
brenn-aysla *(f)*. stinging nettles; pl. of brenn-aysel.
brennich 1. spicy hot 2. stinging.
brikk *(f)*. bridge.
brikka *(f)*. bridges; pl. of brikk.
brill *(f)*. eyeglasses.
brilla *(f)*. eyeglasses; pl. of brill.
brilla *v.* to cry.
brilles *(neu)*. crying.
bringa *v.* to bring.
brisht *(f)*. breasts; pl. of brusht.
brofayda *(f)*. prophets; pl. of brofayt.
brofayda-fraw *(f)*. prophetess.
brofayda-frawwa *(f)*. prophetesses; pl. of brofayda-fraw.
brofayda-vadda *(f)*. prophecy, words of the prophets.
brofayda-veib *(neu)*. prophetess.
brofayda-veivah *(f)*. prophetesses; pl. of brofayda-veib.
brofayt *(m)*. prophet.

broffetzeiya *v.* to prophesy.
broffetzeiya-vadda words of prophecy.
broffetzeiying *(f).* prophecy.
broffetzeiyinga *(f).* prophecies; pl. of broffetzeiying.
brohda *v.* to fry.
brohdich very warm (ambient temperature).
broht *(neu).* bread.
broht-bakkah *(m).* bread baker.
broht-dayk *(m).* bread dough.
broht-dayka *(f).* bread doughs; pl. of broht-dayk.
broht-fesht *(neu).* feast of bread.
broht-feshta *(f).* feasts of bread; pl. of broht-fesht.
broht-pann *(f).* 1. frying pan 2. bread pan.
broht-panna *(f).* bread pans; pl. of broht-pann.
brokka *(m).* crumb, can refer to solids within a liquid.
brokla *(f).* crumbs, can refer to solids within a liquid; pl. of brokka.
bronze-awldah *(m).* bronze altar.
bronze-awldahra *(f).* bronze alters; pl. of bronze-awldah.
broodah *(m).* brother.
broodah-shaft *(f).* brotherhood.
broodah-shafta *(f).* brotherhoods; pl. of broodah-shaft.

broviahra / boviahra *v.* 1. to try 2. to put to the test.
broviaht / boviaht *v.* tried; pp. of broviahra.
brumma *v.* to buzz or hum.
brummich noisey buzzing or humming.
brunna *(m).* 1. well 2. fountain.
brusht *(f).* breast.
brusht-feedahra *v.* to breast feed.
brusht-kfeedaht *v.* breast fed; pp. of brusht-feedahra.
brusht-playt *(neu).* breastplate.
brusht-playts *(f).* breast plates; pl. of brusht-playt.
brusht-shtikk *(neu).* breast piece.
brutza *v.* to cry, pout, sulk.
brutzich upset, pouting.
buch *(neu).* book.
buch-haldah *(m).* book keeper.
buddah *(m).* butter.
buddah-fass *(neu).* butter churn.
buddah-fessah *(f).* butter churns; pl. of buddah-fass.
buddah-millich *(f).* buttermilk.
bukkel *(m).* back.
bukla *(f).* backs; pl. of bukkel.
bull *(m).* bull.
bulla *(f).* bulls; pl. of bull.
bull-kebbich bull-headed.
bull-rosh *(m).* bull rush.
bull-rosha *(f).* bull rushes; pl. of bull-rosh.
bumb *(f).* pump.
bumba *(f).* pumps; pl. of bumb.

bumba *v.* 1. to bump 2. to pump.
bumbah *(m).* bump.
bumbich bumpy.
bund *(m).* covenant.
bunda *(f).* covenants; pl. of bund.
bundel *(m).* bundle.
bundes-lawt *(m).* ark of the covenant.
bundla *(f).* bundles; pl. of bundel.
bund-shreives *(neu).* written covenant.
bush *(m).* woods, forest.
busha *(f).* woods, forests; pl. of bush.
bushel *(f).* bushel.
bushel-keahb *(f).* bushel baskets; pl. of bushel-koahb.
bushel-koahb *(m).* bushel-basket.

bush-feiyah *(neu).* forest fire.
bush-feiyahra *(f).* forest fires; pl. of bush-feiyah.
bushtawb *(m).* letter of alphabet.
bushtawva *(f).* letters of the alphabet; pl. of bushtawb.
buslen *(f).* kittens; pl. of busli.
busli *(neu).* kitten.
butshah *(m).* butcher.
butshah-haus *(neu).* butcher house.
butshah-heisah *(f).* butcher houses; pl. of butshah-haus.
butshahra *v.* to butcher.
butshahs *(f).* butchers; pl. of butshah.
butza *v.* to clean.
byoosa *v.* to abuse.

C - c

cent *(m).* cent.
Christus *(m).* Christ.
crystal-glaws *(neu).* crystal-glass.

crystal-glessah *(f).* crystal glasses; pl. of crystal-glaws.
curtain *(m).* curtain.

D - d

da the (masculine gender).
dabba *v.* to step into or onto accidentally.
dabbah quickly.
dabbich bumbling, stumbling,

awkward with one's feet.
dabbich clumsy, awkward.
dach *(neu).* roof.
dadda *v.* to wither.
daddel-daub *(f).* turtle dove.

daddel-dauva *(f)*. turtle doves; pl. of daddel-daub.

daedda *(f)*. dads; pl. of daett.

daets *(neu)*. parents (lit.-fathers) used to refer to one's own parents.

daett *(m)*. dad, father.

dalla *(m)*. dent.

damba *v*. to dump.

damf *(m)*. vapor, steam.

damf-gnebb *(f)*. steamed dumplings; pl. of damf-gnobb.

damf-gnobb *(m)*. steamed dumpling.

damm *(m)*. pond.

damma *(f)*. ponds; pl. of damm.

dank *(m)*. thanks.

danka *v*. to thank.

dankboah thankful.

dankboahkeida *(f)*. thankfulness; pl. of dankboahkeit.

dankboahkeit *(f)*. thankfulness.

dankes *(neu)*. giving of thanks.

danki thank you.

danki-shay thank you very much.

dank-leedah *(f)*. songs or hymns expressing thanks; pl. of dank-leet.

dank-leet *(neu)*. song or hymn expressing thanks.

dank-opfah *(neu)*. sacrificial offering of thanksgiving.

dank-opfahra *(f)*. offerings of thankgiving; pl. of dank-opfah.

Dank-Psalm *(m)*. Psalm of thanks.

Dank-Psaltah *(f)*. Psalms of thanks; pl. of Dank-Psalm.

dann *(f)*. thorn.

dann then in that case, then for that reason, then as a consequence.

danna *(f)*. thorns; pl. of dann.

danna-feiyah *(neu)*. thorn fire.

danna-feiyahra *(f)*. thorn fires; pl. of danna-feiyah.

danna-hekka *(f)*. thorn bushes.

danna-putsha *(m)*. clump of thorns.

danna-shtekk *(f)*. thorn bushes; pl. of danna-shtokk.

danna-shtokk *(m)*. thorn bush.

dannich thorny.

dans *(f)*. dance.

dansa *(f)*. dances; pl. of dans.

dansa *v*. to dance.

dasht *(m)*. thirst.

dashtich thirsty.

datt there.

dau *(m)*. dew.

dau thin, emaciated.

daub *(f)*. dove.

daufa *v*. to be allowed.

dauma *(m)*. thumb.

daumlich dizzy.

dausend *(f)*. thousand.

dausends *(f)*. thousands; pl. of dausend.

dauva *(f)*. doves; pl. of daub.

dauwa *v*. to thaw.

davvahlich mournful, pitiful.

davvahlich mournful.

davvahra *v*. to pity.

dawb deaf.
dawdi *(m)*. 1. grandfather, grandpa 2. aged man.
dawdis *(f)*. 1. grandfathers, grandpas 2. aged men; pl. of dawdi.
dawf *(f)*. baptism.
dawfa *(f)*. baptisms; pl. of dawf.
dawfa *v.* to baptize.
dawfah *(m)*. baptizer.
dawk *(m)*. day.
dawk illuminated with daylight.
dawks in the daytime.
dawks-helling *(f)*. day light.
dawlah *(m)*. dollar.
dawwa *(f)*. days; pl. of dawk.
dawwa-veis 1. a day at a time 2. whole days at a time.
dayk *(m)*. dough.
dayka *(f)*. doughs; pl. of dayk.
dayk-drayk *(f)*. dough troughs; pl. of dayk-drohk.
dayk-drohk *(m)*. dough trough.
dayklen *(f)*. small doughs; pl. of daykli.
daykli *(neu)*. small dough.
dayklich daily.
dayk-shisla *(f)*. dough bowls; pl. of dayk-shissil.
dayk-shissil *(f)*. dough bowl.
dayl *(neu)*. portion.
dayl some, certain ones.
dayla *v.* 1. to share 2. to deal or portion out.
dayla *v.* to portion.
daylah *(f)*. portions; pl. of dayl.
dayl-zeit sometimes.
daymeedich humble, meek.
daymeedicha *v.* to humble oneself.
daymeedichkeit *(f)*. attitude of humility.
daymoot *(f)*. humility.
dayt would.
deah *(f)*. door.
deah *(m)*. 1. this (only used with masculine nouns) 2. this one.
deah-heedah *(m)*. doorkeeper.
deahlen *(f)*. small gates or doors; pl. of deahli.
deahli *(neu)*. small gate or door.
deahm *(f)*. intestines.
deahmenszinda *(f)*. appendicitis.
deah-poshta *(m)*. doorpost.
deahra *(f)*. doors; pl. of deah.
deahra this.
deahra-fraym *(neu)*. door frame.
deahra-frayms *(f)*. door frames; pl. of deahra-fraym.
deahra-gnebb *(f)*. door knobs; pl. of deahra-gnobb.
deahra-gnobb *(m)*. door knob.
deahra-shvell *(f)*. threshold.
deahra-shvella *(f)*. thresholds; pl. of deahra-shvell.
deahravayk 1. this way 2. in this manner.
dechah *(f)*. roofs; pl. of dach.
dechtah *(f)*. daughters; pl. of dochtah.
dee *(f)*. this (only used with feminine nouns) , these.
deeb *(m)*. thief.
deef deep.
deefa *(neu)*. the deep.

deefing *(f)*. depth.
deena *v.* 1. to worship 2. to serve.
deena those.
deenah *(m)*. 1. servant of God 2. ordained minister in a church.
deensht *(m)*. ministry.
deensht-glaydah *(f)*. clothing worn for service or ministry; pl. of deensht-glayt.
deensht-glayt *(neu)*. specific clothing worn for service or ministry.
deensht-gnecht *(m)*. servant or slave of God.
deensht-gnechta *(f)*. servants or slaves of God; pl. of deensht-gnecht.
deensht-haus *(neu)*. house of worship.
deensht-heisah *(f)*. houses of worship; pl. of deensht-haus.
deensht-leit *(f)*. servants or ministers.
deensht-mawda *(f)*. servant maids; pl. of deensht-mawt.
deensht-mawt *(f)*. servant maid.
dei your.
deich *(neu)*. depression, hollow, small valley.
deich through.
deicha *(f)*. depressions, hollows, small valleys; pl. of deich.
deich-blohsa *v.* to squander.
deich-brechah *(m)*. one who breaks through.

deich-falla *v.* to fall through.
deich-geblohsa *v.* squandered; pp. of deich-blohsa.
deich-gedrivva rambunctious.
deich-glaysa *v.* 1. read through 2. sorted through; pp. of deich-laysa.
deich-gmacht *v.* 1. seperated 2. suffered, endured; pp. of deich-macha.
deich-gveeld *v.* rummaged through; pp. of deich-veela.
deich-gvitsht *v.* slipped through, escaped; pp. of deich-vitsha.
deich-kfalla *v.* fell through; pp. of deich-falla.
deich-lawf *(f)*. diarrhea "Eah hott di deich-lawf.".
deich-laysa *v.* 1. to read through 2. to sort through.
deich-macha *v.* 1. to separate 2. to suffer, endure.
deich-nannah mixed together.
deich-veela *v.* to rummage through.
deich-vitsha *v.* to slip through, escape.
deift *v.* would be allowed.
deiksel *(f)*. wagon tongue.
deiksla *(f)*. wagon tongues; pl. of deiksel.
deim your (dative case).
dein yours.
deina your.
deinra your.
deitlich clearly, explicitly.
deitshah *(m)*. a speaker of the Pennsylvania-German

language (PA-German or "Deitsh").

Deivel *(m)*. devil.

deivela *(f)*. demons, devils; pl. of deivel.

deivilish devilish.

deiyah expensive.

dekk *(f)*. 1. blanket 2. deck.

dekka *(f)*. blankets; pl. of dekk.

dekka *v.* 1. to cover 2. to put roof on.

dekkel *(m)*. lid, cover.

dekla *(f)*. lids, covers; pl. of dekkel.

deklen *(f)*. small lids; pl. of dekli.

dekli *(neu)*. small lid.

dellah *(m)*. plate.

dellahlen *(f)*. small plates; pl. of dellahli.

dellahli *(neu)*. small plate.

dellahra *(f)*. plates; pl. of dellah.

demm this (dative case).

demmahra *v.* make a banging noise.

demnohch according to, depending on.

denka *v.* to think.

denkes opinion, viewpoint.

denki thank you (common use).

denki-shay thank you very much (common use).

dess this (only used with neuter nouns).

dessamohl this time.

dexel *(m)*. adze.

dexla *(f)*. adzes; pl. of dexel.

di the (gender used for feminine and plural nouns).

diah *(neu)*. animal.

diah you (nominative plural) (dative singular).

diahra *(f)*. animals; pl. of diah.

dibei present or included with.

dich you (accusative singular).

dichah *(f)*. cloths; pl. of duch.

dichli *(neu)*. small piece of fabric.

dich-selvaht yourself.

dideich 1. because of it 2. through it 3. thereby.

difammidawk this forenoon, this day before noon.

difoah 1. previously 2. in favor of.

difreind in relation by blood or marriage.

difunn 1. from 2. from here.

digans *adj.* the whole.

digayya against, opposed.

digeyya against, opposed.

dihaym at home.

dihelft the half.

dikk thick.

dikk-kebbich stubborn.

diksak *(m)*. chubby person.

diksekkich chubby.

dill *(neu)*. anise, dill.

dimeiya this morning.

dimiddawk this noon, this day at noon.

dimla *(f)*. thunders; pl. of dimmel.

dimla *v.* to thunder.

dimmel *(m)*. thunder.

Dimmels-kinnah children of thunder.

dinda *(f)*. ink.

ding *(neu)*. thing.

dinga *v.* to hire.
dingah *(f).* things; pl. of ding.
dinka *v.* to seem.
dinn thin.
dinochmidawk this afternoon.
dinohch 1. afterward 2. depending on, according to - "Miah henn pizza katt dinohch.".
dinohvet tonight.
Dinshdawk Tuesday.
dish *(m).* table.
disha *(f).* tables; pl. of dish.
dishtel *(m).* thistle.
dishtembah *(f).* distemper.
dishtla *(f).* thistles; pl. of dishtel.
dishtlich full of thistles.
ditzu 1. to it 2. to whom 3. included.
ditzudu *v.* to add to.
diveaht worthwile.
diveyya about it.
divorce-shreives *(neu).* divorce writing.
divorce-shreivinga *(f).* divorce writings; pl. of divorce-shreives.
do here.
doah *(neu).* 1. gate 2. large barn door.
doah-heedah gate keeper.
doah-poshta *(m).* post holding large door or gate.
doahra *(f).* 1. gates 2. large barn doors; pl. of doah.
doah-rikkel *(f).* door rail.
doah-rikla *(f).* door rails; pl. of doah-rikkel.

dobbeld double.
doch after all, still, wherefore.
dochtah *(f).* daughter.
dochtah-mann *(m).* son-in-law.
dochtah-mennah *(f).* sons-in-law; pl. of dochtah-mann.
doddah *(m).* yolk of an egg.
dodra *(f).* egg yolks; pl. of doddah.
dohdes-beddah *(f).* death beds; pl. of dohdes-bett.
dohdes-bett *(neu).* death bed.
dohdes-blohk *(m).* death blow.
dohdes-blohwa *(f).* death blows; pl. of dohdes-blohk.
dohdes-engel *(m).* death angel.
dohdes-engla *(f).* death angels; pl. of dohdes-engel.
dohdes-grankeda *(f).* terminal illness (common use); pl. of dohdes-granket.
dohdes-granket *(f).* terminal illness (common use).
dohdes-grankheida *(f).* terminal illness (as used in the Bible); pl. of dohdes-grankheit.
dohdes-grankheit *(f).* terminal illness (as used in the Bible).
doht dead.
doht-geboahra stillborn, dead at birth, born dead.
doht-gmacht *v.* killed, murdered, made dead; pp. of doht-macha.
doht-grank deathly ill.
doht-macha *v.* to kill, murder.
doht-shlakk death blow.

doht-shlayyah *(m)*. murderer.

doktah *(m)*. doctor.

doktahra *v*. 1. to doctor, to get medical help 2. to add to, to enhance the flavor by adding something to it.

doktahs *(f)*. doctors; pl. of doktah.

donkey-hutsh *(m)*. donkey colt.

donkey-hutsha *(f)*. donkey colts; pl. of donkey-hutsh.

donkey-mah *(f)*. female donkey.

donkey-mahra *(f)*. female donkeys; pl. of donkey-mah.

doovakk *(m)*. tobacco.

dracha-diah *(neu)*. dragon.

dracha-diahra *(f)*. dragons; pl. of dracha-diah.

draub *(f)*. grape.

draus out there.

drauva *(f)*. grapes; pl. of draub.

drauva-feld *(neu)*. vineyard, (lit.- grape field).

drauva-feldah *(f)*. vinyards; pl. of drauva-feld.

drauva-goahra *(m)*. vineyard, small vineyard, (lit.- grape garden).

drauva-rank *(f)*. grapevine, tendril, shoot.

drauva-ranka *(f)*. grapevines, tendrils, shoots; pl. of drauva-rank.

drauva-rankla *(f)*. grapevines; pl. of drauva-rankel.

drauva-shtekk *(f)*. grapevines (lit.- grape plants) (common use); pl. of drauva-shtokk.

drauva-shtokk *(m)*. grapevine (lit.- grape plant) (common use).

drauwa *v*. 1. to trust 2. to dare.

drawk-pohls carrying poles.

drawwa *v*. to carry.

drawwich pregnant.

dray *(f)*. a turn or bend.

dray-bank *(f)*. lathe.

dray-benk *(f)*. lathes; pl. of dray-bank.

dray-hels *(f)*. rolling pins; pl. of dray-hols.

drayk *(f)*. troughs; pl. of drohk.

drayl-hols *(neu)*. rolling pin.

draynah *(m)*. sieve, strainer.

drayshta *v*. to comfort.

drayshtah *(m)*. one who comforts.

drayshtlich comforting.

drayya *(f)*. turns or bends; pl. of dray.

drayya *v*. to turn.

drayyich having many turns (of roads).

drebb *(f)*. stair tread.

drebba *(f)*. stair treads; pl. of drebb.

drechtah *(m)*. funnel.

dredda *v*. to tread.

dreeb cloudy, overcast.

dreebsawl *(f)*. sorrow.

dreffa *v*. to make contact with, to meet or hit.

drei three.

drei-eikkich triangle shaped, three cornered.

drei-ekk *(neu)*. 1. triangle, three

(m) = da　　　(f) = di　　　(neu) = es　　　33

cornered 2. triangular field or wood lot.

drei-faddel three-quarters.

drei-fimfdel three-fifths.

dreisich thirty.

dreitzay thirteen.

dreiva *v.* 1. to drive, chase 2. to propel physically 3. to motivate.

drei-zinkichi three pronged, having three tines.

drekk *(m).* dirt.

drekkich dirty.

drekk-loch *(neu).* 1. mud puddle 2. muddy patch of ground.

drenka *v.* to give water to livestock, to lead livestock to water.

dresha *v.* to thresh.

dresha-floah *(m).* threshing floor.

dresha-floahra *(f).* threshing floors; pl. of dresha-floah.

dresha-gavla *(f).* threshing forks; pl. for dresha-gavvel.

dresha-gavvel *(f).* fork used for threshing.

dresha-ksha *(neu).* threshing utensils.

dresha-rawt *(neu).* threshing wheel.

dresha-reddah *(f).* threshing wheels; pl. of dresha-rawt.

dresha-shaufel *(f).* winnowing fork.

dresha-shaufla *(f).* winnowing forks; pl. of dresha-shaufel.

dresha-shlayf *(f).* a tool used for threshing.

dridda third.

driddel *(neu).* a third part.

drikka *v.* to press or squeeze.

drikla *v.* to dry.

drink *(m).* a drink.

drinka *v.* to drink.

drinkes *(neu).* beverage, a drink.

drink-koblen *(f).* drinking cups; pl. of drink-kobli.

drink-kobli *(neu).* drinking cup.

drink-ksha *(neu).* drinking vessel.

drink-ksharra *(f).* drinking vessels; pl. of drink-ksha.

drink-opfah *(neu).* drink offering.

drink-opfahra *(f).* drink offerings; pl. of drink-opfah.

drinks *(f).* drinks; pl. of drink.

drinn in there.

dritt third.

drivva over there.

drivvah across.

drivvah-naus exceedingly.

drobba *(m).* drop.

drobsa *v.* to drop.

droh 1. doing it 2. near it 3. fastened to it 4. (separable prefix) about, at, concerning, of.

drohda *(f).* wires; pl. of droht.

drohk *(m).* trough.

drohm *(m).* dream.

drohma *(f).* dreams; pl. of drohm.

drohma *v.* to dream.

drohmah *(m).* dreamer.

drohsht *(m)*. comfort, assurance.
drohshta *v.* to comfort.
droht *(m)*. wire.
droiya *v.* to threaten.
drovva up there.
drubb *(f)*. group, crowd, flock.
drubba *(f)*. groups, crowds, flocks; pl. of drubb.
druff upon, on there.
druff-dabba *v.* to find or discover by chance.
druff-gedabt *v.* found or discovered by chance; pp. of druff-dabba.
drukka *v.* to print, produce type with a machine.
drukka dry.
drukkanah dryer, more dry.
drukkesht driest of all.
drumm 1. closely around it 2. concerning it 3. therefore.
drunna down there.
drunnah underneath.
druvla *(f)*. troubles; pl. of druvvel.
druvla *v.* to trouble.
druvvel *(m)*. trouble.
druvvel-machah *(m)*. troublemaker.
du 1. you (nominative, singular) 2. to do 3. to put.
duahk *(m)*. tobacco.
dubba *(m)*. dot.
duch *(neu)*. cloth.
duch-belt *(neu)*. cloth belt.
duch-belts *(f)*. cloth belts; pl. of duch-belt.
duch-loom *(f)*. loom to make cloth.

duch-veshah *(m)*. one who washes cloth.
dufta *v.* to fog over glass.
dulda *v.* 1. to tolerate 2. to bear with patience.
duldich patiently.
dumhayda nonsense, foolishness.
dumhaydichkeida *(f)*. foolishnesses; pl. of dumhaydichkeit.
dumhaydichkeit *(f)*. foolishness.
dumla *v.* to hurry.
dumm 1. not intelligent 2. funny, silly.
dumm-kebb *(f)*. ignorant people; pl. of dumm-kobb.
dumm-kobb *(m)*. ignorant person.
dunka *v.* to dip, to dunk.
dunkel dark.
dunkelhayda *(f)*. darknesses; pl. of dunkelheit.
dunkelheit *(f)*. darkness.
dunk-oi *(neu)*. egg cooked over easy, soft yolk.
dunk-oiyah *(f)*. eggs cooked over-easy, soft yolks; pl. of dunk-oi.
dunnahra *v.* to make a thundering noise.
Dunnahshdawk Thursday.
dunshtich humid.
dushbah *(m)*. dusk, twilight (evening).
dutzend dozen.

E - e

eah *(f)*. honor.
eah he.
eahblich contagious.
eahbshaft *(f)*. inheritance.
eahbshafta *(f)*. inheritances; pl. of eahbshaft.
eahbshaft-fadaylah *(m)*. one who apportions an inheritance.
eahda *(f)*. earths; pl. of eaht.
eahdich earthen.
eahgeitz *(m)*. selfish desire for honor.
eahgeitzich covetous of honor.
eahlich honest.
eahm *(f)*. arms; pl. of oahm.
eahmel *(m)*. sleeve.
eahmlich 1. pitiful 2. weak 3. very sick 4. sickly.
eahnd *(f)*. harvest.
eahnda *(f)*. harvests; pl. of eahnd.
eahnda *v*. to reap.
eahnsht *(m)*. zeal.
eahnshtlich 1. earnest 2. diligent.
eahnshtlichkeit *(f)*. 1. earnestness 2. diligence.
eahps *(f)*. pea.
eahpsa *(f)*. peas; pl. of eahps.
eahra *v*. to honor.
eahsht first, only now, only yet.
eahshtah formerly.
eahsht-doah *(neu)*. first gate.

eahsht-frucht *(f)*. first fruit.
eahsht-frucht-dawk *(m)*. first fruit day.
eahsht-frucht-opfah *(neu)*. sacrificial offering of the first fruit.
eahsht-frucht-opfahra *(f)*. special offerings of the first fruits; pl. of eahsht-frucht-opfah.
eahsht-geboahra firstborn.
eahshti-frichta *(f)*. first fruits; pl. of eahsht-frucht.
eaht *(f)*. earth.
eaht-bayben *(f)*. earthquake.
eaht-baybens *(f)*. earthquakes; pl. of eaht-bayben.
eahtlich earthly.
eahva *v*. to inherit.
eahvah *(m)*. heir.
eahveda *(f)*. 1. work 2. occupations, jobs; pl. of eahvet.
eahvet *(f)*. 1. work 2. occupation, job.
eb 1. if, whether 2. before.
ebbah someone.
ebbel *(f)*. apples; pl. of abbel.
ebbes something.
ebdihand beforehand.
edlichi quite a few.
eedah either; used with "adda" (or) , to offer a choice between two alternatives.

eem *(f)*. bee.
eem him (dative case).
eema *(f)*. bees; pl. of eem.
eems *(m)*. meal (not common).
een him.
eena them (dative case).
eesi easy.
eest east.
eevel-ab undecided.
eevila *(f)*. evils; pl. of eevil.
eevil-shaffah *(m)*. worker of
     evil.
effa *(f)*. ovens, stoves; pl. of
     offa.
effangaylish 1. evangelistic 2.
     Scriptural.
effangaylium *(neu)*. gospel.
effangelisht *(m)*. evangelist.
effangelishta *(f)*. evangelists;
     pl. of effangelisht.
eftahs frequently.
ei   1. (prefix) in 2. allied with
     3. idiomatic,
     interjection - example: "Ei,
     ich vays naett!" ("Why, I
     don't know!").
eibendla *v.* to sew on a binding.
eibilda *v.* to imagine.
eich you all (accusative plural).
eich-selvaht yourselves.
eidah *(neu)*. udder.
eidahra *(f)*. udders; pl. of eidah.
eidenka *v.* to keep in
     remembrance.
eidi *(f)*. idea.
eidis *(f)*. ideas; pl. of eidi.
eidrinka *v.* to drink in.
eidruk *(m)*. impression,
     sensation.

eidrukka *(f)*. impressions,
     sensations; pl. of eidruk.
eifah *(m)*. 1. enthusiasm 2. frenzy.
eifahra *v.* to rage.
eifahrich 1. enthusiastically 2.
     frenzied.
eifaydla *v.* to thread a needle.
eifensa *v.* to fence in - "Ich zayl
     dess feld eifensa fa di kee
     nei du.".
eifilla *v.* to fill in.
eigang *(m)*. entrance.
eiganga *(f)*. entrances; pl. of
     eigang.
eiganga *v.* 1 associated with 2.
     shrunk 3. went in; pp. of
     eigay.
eigang-shtubb *(f)*. entrance
     room, entry.
eigang-shtubba *(f)*. entrance
     rooms, entryways; pl. of
     eigang-shtubb.
eigay *v.* 1. to associate with 2. to
     shrink 3. to go in.
eigebendeld *v.* having sewn on a
     binding; pp. of eibendla.
eigebild *v.* imagined; pp. of
     eibilda.
eigedenkt *v.* mindful of; pp. of
     eidenka.
eigedrunka *v.* drank in; pp. of
     eidrinka.
eigendlich actually.
eigendshaft *(f)*. disposition,
     nature.
eigevva *v.* to surrender, concede
     to, to give in to, comply.
eiglawda *v.* invited; pp. of
     eilawda.

eiglaykt *v.* having given alms; pp. of eilayya.

eigmavvaht *v.* walled in; pp. of eimavvahra.

eignumma *v.* 1. taken in 2. included 3. conquered 4. attended; pp. of einemma.

eigraynd *v.* 1. reined in 2. restrained; pp. of eirayna.

eigringd *v.* ringed in; pp. of eiringa.

eigvand *v.* walled in; pp. of eivanda.

eigvatzeld *v.* having become rooted; pp. of eivatzla.

eigvikkeld *v.* wrapped in; pp. of eivikla.

eikfaydeld *v.* threaded; pp. of eikfaydla.

eikfenst *v.* fenced in; pp. of eifensa.

eikfild *v.* filled in; pp. of eifilla.

eiksammeld *v.* 1. gathered in 2. harvested; pp. of eisamla.

eiksayt *v.* having sowed seeds; pp. of eisayya.

eikseit *v.* 1. having agreed with 2. having sided with; pp. of eiseida.

eiksenna *v.* having had insight; pp. of eisayna.

eiksetzt *v.* 1. ordained 2. established in an office 3. having decreed a ruling as law; pp. of eisetza.

eikshlohfa *v.* having fallen asleep; pp. of eishlohfa.

eikshlossa *v.* locked in; pp. of eishleesa.

eikshlukt *v.* having taken in by swallowing; pp. of eishlukka.

eikshnauft *v.* breathed in; pp. of eishnaufa.

eikshpand *v.* having hitched an animal to a carriage or implement; pp. of eishpanna.

eikshpatt *v.* confined; pp. of eishpadda.

eiksht in a unique or excessive manner.

eikshtekt *v.* jailed; pp. of eishtekka.

eikshtimd *v.* agreed or matched with; pp. of eishtimma.

eilawda *v.* to invite.

eilayya *v.* to give alms, to give to the poor or needy.

eimavvahra *v.* to foundation in.

einemma *v.* 1. to take in 2. to include 3. to conquer 4. to attend.

einemmah *(m).* receiver.

eirayna *v.* 1. to rein in 2. to restrain.

eiringa *v.* to ring in.

eisa *(neu).* 1. the substance of iron 2. made of iron.

eisamla *v.* 1. to gather in 2. to harvest.

Eisamling-Fesht *(neu).* Harvest Feast.

Eisamling-Feshta *(f).* Harvest Feasts; pl. of Eisamling-Fesht.

eisa-offa *(m).* forge, iron furnace.

eisa-shmelsah *(m)*. one who works with iron, iron smelter.

eisa-shmelsich hot enough to melt iron.

eisa-shmidda *(f)*. iron smiths; pl. of eisa-shmitt.

eisa-shmitt *(m)*. iron smith.

eisayna *v.* to have insight.

eisayya *v.* to sow seeds.

eiseida *v.* 1. to agree with 2. to side up with.

eisetza *v.* 1. to ordain 2. to establish in an office 3. to decree a ruling as law.

eishaufa *v.* 1. to inform, to give inside information 2. to instruct firmly.

eishleesa *v.* to lock in.

eishlohfa *v.* to fall asleep.

eishlukka *v.* to take in by swallowing.

eishnaufa *v.* to breathe in.

eishpadda *v.* to confine.

eishpanna *v.* to hitch an animal to a carriage or implement.

eishtekka *v.* to incarcerate, imprison.

eishtekka *v.* to put in jail.

eishtimma *v.* to agree or match with.

eisich made of iron.

eisicht *(f)*. insight.

eisichta *(f)*. insights; pl. of eisicht.

eivanda *v.* to wall in.

eivatzla *v.* to become rooted.

eivikla *v.* to wrap in.

eiyah 1. your (plural) 2. to a greater degree 3. sooner, rather.

eiyahlich causing offense.

eiyahm your (plural) (dative case).

eiyahnis *(neu)*. irritation, something which causes offense.

eiyahnisa *(f)*. irritations, things that cause offense; pl. of eiyahnis.

eiyahra *v.* to speak offensively or argumentatively.

eiyetz somewhere (shortened form).

eiyetzvo somewhere.

ekk *(neu)*. corner.

ekkah *(f)*. corners; pl. of ekk.

ekkich having corners.

ekk-poshta *(m)*. corner post.

ekk-shtay *(m)*. corner stone.

eld *(f)*. age.

eldah older.

eldishtah *(m)*. elder in a church.

eldishti *(f)*. elders in a church; pl. of eldishtah.

eldlich aged.

eldra *(f)*. parents.

eldsht oldest.

elf eleven.

elft eleventh.

em 1. oneself (personal pronoun, accusative case) 2.the (dative case).

en 1. a, an 2. unstressed form of "een" (him).

end *(neu)*. end.

end one of several.

enda *v.* to end.

endah *(f)*. ends; pl. of end.

endlich finally.

eng narrow (not common).

engel *(m)*. angel.

engla *(f)*. angels; pl. of engel.

engshta *(f)*. anxieties; pl. of angsht.

engshtlich anxious.

enkah *(m)*. anchor.

enkah-hohka *(m)*. anchor hook.

enkahs *(f)*. anchors; pl. of enkah.

enkel *(m)*. ankle.

enkels *(f)*. ankles; pl. of enkel.

ennich any.

ennichah 1. anyhow 2. any (masculine form).

ennich-ebbah anyone.

ennich-ebbes anything.

es / 's 1. it 2. the (neuter form) 3. she, her (when referring to unmarried girls) 4. that, who, which (relative pronoun) 5. there (pronoun used to start a sentence or clause) example: "Es is feel eahvet fa du.".

esh *(f)*. ashes.

esh-haufa *(m)*. pile of ashes.

esh-heifa *(f)*. piles of ashes; pl. of esh-haufa.

esh-pann *(f)*. ash pan.

esh-panna *(f)*. ash pans; pl. of esh-pann.

essa *(neu)*. meal (common use).

essa *v*. to eat.

essah *(m)*. eater.

ess-fesht-dawk *(m)*. day of feast.

ess-fesht-dawwa *(f)*. days of feast; pl. of ess-fesht-dawk.

essich *(neu)*. vinegar.

ess-sach *(neu)*. food.

ess-sach-opfah *(neu)*. food offering.

ess-sach-opfahra *(f)*. food offerings; pl. of ess-sach-opfah.

etmohls sometimes.

even 1. indeed, actually 2. nevertheless.

evil *(neu)*. evil.

evil-shaffah *(m)*. worker of evil.

evva 1. an expression used to explain or justify some previously given idea 2. an expression used to contradict.

evvah *(m)*. boar.

evvah 1. ever, always; usually followed by "siddah" (since).

evvahra *(f)*. boars; pl. of evvah.

evvahsht uppermost.

evvahsht-hand *(f)*. ruling authority.

evvahshti-shpeichahra *(f)*. attics, (the part of houses directly beneath the roof); pl. of evvahsht-shpeichah.

evvahst shpeichah *(m)*. attic, the part of a house directly beneath the roof.

ex *(f)*. axes; pl. of ax.

extri extra.

F - f

fa 1. for 2. before 3. type, kind, sort.

fa'acht *v.* 1. despised, scorned 2. considered unimportant; pp. of fa'achta.

fa'achta *v.* 1. to despise, scorn 2. to consider unimportant.

fa'achtung *(f).* contempt.

fa'achtunga *(f).* contempts; pl. of fa'achtung.

fa'andvadda *v.* 1. to answer 2. to express.

fa'andvadlich accountable.

fa'andvatt *v.* 1. answered 2. expressed opinion; pp. of fa'andvadda.

fa'aynicha *v.* to express agreement.

fa'aynicht *v.* expressed agreement; pp. of fa'aynicha.

fabaddahra *v.* to disturb.

fabaddaht *v.* disturbed; pp. of fabaddahra.

fabeeda *v.* to forbid.

fabeeya *v.* to bend out of shape.

fabei past.

fabessahra *v.* to improve, to make better.

fabessaht *v.* improved, made better; pp. of fabessahra.

fabiddahra *v.* to grow bitter, disillusioned.

fabiddaht *v.* embittered; pp. of fabiddahra.

fabindnis *(neu).* bondage.

fabindnisa *(f).* bondages; pl. of fabindnis.

fabinna *v.* to bind.

fablend *v.* blinded by a bright light; pp. of fablenna.

fablenna *v.* to blind with a bright light.

fablohsa *v.* 1. to squander 2. to blow away 3. to burst.

fabobbeld *v.* babied; pp. of fabobla.

fabobla *v.* to baby.

fabodda *v.* forbidden; pp. of fabeeda.

fabodda *v.* forbidden; pp. of fabidda.

fabohwa *v.* bent out of shape; pp. of fabeeya.

fabost *v.* having burst; pp. of fabosta.

fabosta *v.* to burst.

fabraekt disposed to bragging.

fabrecha *v.* to break into pieces, shatter.

fabrend *v.* burned up; pp. of fabrenna.

fabrenna *v.* to burn up.

fabrocha *v.* broken; pp. of fabrecha.

fabrochani-heffa broken pots.

fabumbt *v.* banged up, bruised; pp. of fabummba.

fabummba *v.* to bump, bruise.

fabunna *v.* bound; pp. of

fabinna.

fabutza *v.* to leave quickly, skedaddle "Eah hott sich fabutzt.".

fabutzt *v.* 1. scrawny, undersized 2. to have left quickly; pp. of fabutza.

fadadda *v.* to wither completely.

fadambt *v.* dumped by accident.

fadamd *v.* condemned; pp. of fadamma.

fadamins *(f).* condemnation.

fadamma *v.* to condemn.

fadamnisa *(f).* condemnations; pl. of fadamins.

fadasht *v.* died of thirst; pp. of fadashta.

fadashta *v.* to die of thirst.

fadatt *v.* completely withered; pp. of dadda.

fadatt *v.* withered completely; pp. of fadadda.

fadauva *v.* 1. to damage 2. to rot.

fadayla *v.* to separate.

fadayld *v.* separated; pp. of fadayla.

faddah *(m).* father.

faddah-land *(neu).* fatherland.

faddah-lendah *(f).* fatherlands; pl. of faddah-land.

faddel quarter.

faddi 1. forward 2. done.

faddi forward.

faddi-bringa *v.* to accomplish.

faddich finished, done.

faddi-gebrocht *v.* accomplished; pp. of faddi-

bringa.

fadeahbnisa *(f).* corruptions, ruins; pl. of fadeahbnis.

fadeahblich destructive, harmful.

fadeahbnis *(neu).* corruption, ruin.

fadeahva *v.* 1. to damage 2. to rot.

fadeahvah *(m).* one who harms or destroys.

fadeahving *(f).* destruction.

fadechtich lowly esteemed.

fadeena *v.* to earn.

fadeend *v.* earned; pp. of fadeena.

fadeensht *(m).* 1. livelihood 2. wages 3. meritorious works.

fadeitsha *v.* to explain clearly.

fadeitsht *v.* clearly explained; pp. of fadeitsha.

fademmahra *v.* to dent, batter.

fademmaht *v.* dented, battered; pp. of fademmahra.

fadenka *v.* to think evil of.

fadenkt *v.* having thought evil of; pp. of fadenka.

fadilkt *v.* destroyed, annihilated; pp. of fadilya.

fadilya *v.* to destroy, annihilate.

fadinga *v.* to hire out oneself or another.

fadinnahra *v.* 1. to thin out 2. to dilute.

fadinnaht *v.* 1. thinned out 2. diluted; pp. of fadinnahra.

fadobbeld *v.* crumpled, bent out of shape; pp. of fadobla.

fadobla *v.* to crumple, to bend out of shape.

fadotza *v.* to spoil or ruin.

fadotzt *v.* spoiled or ruined; pp. of fadotza.

fadraut *v.* entrusted; pp. of fadrauwa.

fadrauwa *(m).* confidence.

fadrauwa *v.* to entrust.

fadrauwung *(f).* confidence, trust.

fadrawunga *(f).* confidences, trusts; pl. of fadrauwung.

fadrawwa *v.* to forbear, show tolerance.

fadraysht *v.* comforted; pp. of fadrayshta.

fadrayshta *v.* to comfort.

fadrayt *v.* 1. having turned - usually in a negative sense 2. having twisted the truth; pp. of fadrayya.

fadrayya *v.* 1. to turn (usually negative in meaning, as to turn dials out of adjustment) 2. to twist the truth.

fadredda *v.* to trample underfoot.

fadreeslich discouraging, troublesome.

fadreiva *v.* 1. to while away or waste time 2. to drive apart, scatter.

fadrekka *v.* to soil or dirty.

fadrekt *v.* soiled or dirty; pp. of fadrekka.

fadrikka *v.* 1. to squeeze or embrace, sometimes with excessive force 2. to squeeze flat 3. to embrace warmly.

fadrikkeld *v.* dried up; pp. of fadrikla.

fadrikla *v.* to dry up.

fadrikt *v.* 1. squeezed or embraced, sometimes with excessive force 2. squeezed flat 3. warmly embraced; pp. of fadrikka.

fadrivva *v.* 1.having whiled away or wasted time 2. driven apart, scattered; pp. of fadreiva.

fadrossa disappointed.

fadunga *v.* having hired out oneself or another; pp. of fadinga.

fadunkeld *v.* darkened; pp. of fadunkla.

fadunkla *v.* to darken.

fa'eiyahra *v.* to irk or irritate, to annoy.

fa'eiyaht *v.* irked, irritated, annoyed; pp. of fa'eiyahra.

fa'eld *v.* aged, gotten older; pp. of fa'elda.

fa'elda *v.* to age, to become older.

fa'ennahra *v.* to change something.

fa'ennahring *(f).* alteration.

fa'ennahringa *(f).* alterations; pl. of fa'ennahring.

fa'ennaht *v.* changed; pp. of fa'ennahra.

fafaula *v.* to spoil or rot.

fafauld *v.* spoiled or rotted; pp. of fafaula.

fafayla *v.* to miss.

fafayld *v.* missed; pp. of fafayla.

fafiahra *v.* to deceive.

fafiahrah *(m).* one who deceives.

fafiahrahrei *(f).* 1. deception 2. the act of deception.

fafiahrich deceptive.

fafiahrichkeit *(f).* deceptiveness.

fafiaht *v.* decieved; pp. of fafiahra.

fafingahra *v.* to finger, touch with the fingers.

fafingaht *v.* fingered, touched with the fingers; pp. of fafingahra.

fafleeya *v.* to fly to pieces, to fly apart.

faflikka *v.* to cover with patches.

faflikt *v.* covered with patches; pp. of faflikka.

faflohwa *v.* having flown to pieces, flown apart; pp. of fafleeya.

faflucha *v.* 1. to place a curse on 2. to swear at.

faflucht *v.* 1. cursed 2. sworn at; pp. of faflucht.

fafochta *v.* given to squabbling.

fafolka *v.* to persecute.

fafolkt *v.* persecuted; pp. of fafolka pp. of fafolya.

fafolya *v.* to persecute.

fafressa *v.* 1. eaten away 2. voracious.

fafriahra *v.* to freeze.

fafroahra *v.* froze; pp. of fafriahra.

fagaffa *v.* 1. to make a mistake 2. to reveal a secret unintentionally.

fagaft *v.* 1. having made a mistake 2. having revealed a secret unintentionally; pp. of fagaffa.

fagakst one given to much chatter.

faganga *v.* disappeared or evaporated; pp. of fagay.

fagay *v.* to disappear or evaporate.

fagaysheld *v.* lashed or whipped; pp. of fagayshla.

fagayshla *v.* to lash or whip.

fageesa *v.* to pour out, spill.

fagelshtahlich startling.

fagelshtahra *v.* to surprise or shock.

fagelshtaht *v.* surprised or shocked; pp. of fagelshtahra.

fagenglich transient, passing.

fagessa *v.* to forget.

fagesslich forgetful.

fagevva *v.* to forgive.

fagift *v.* poisoned; pp. of fagifta.

fagifta *v.* to poison.

faglawkt *v.* 1. accused or scolded 2. having complained about; pp. of faglawwa.

faglawwa *v.* 1. to accuse or scold 2. to complain about.

fagleicha *v.* to liken to.

fagleichnis *(f).* 1. likeness 2. parable.

fagleichnissa *(f).* 1. likenesses 2. parables; pl. of

fagleichnis.
faglennahra *v.* to belittle.
faglennaht *v.* belittled; pp. of faglennahra.
faglicha *v.* likened to; pp. of fagleicha.
faglobba *v.* to beat up.
faglobt *v.* having been beat up; pp. of faglobba.
fagneekt *v.* having made oneselve comfortable with a situation; pp. of fagneeya.
fagneeya *(m).* comfort, pleasure.
fagneeya *v.* to make oneself comfortable with a situation.
fagnibba *v.* to tie in knots.
fagnibt *v.* tied in knots; pp. of fagnibba.
fagnohtsha *v.* to handle or squeeze unnecessarilly.
fagnohtsht *v.* handled or squeezed unnecessarily; pp. of fagnohtsha.
fagnohtsht *v.* finicky.
fagossa *v.* poured out, spilled; pp. of fageesa.
fagratza *v.* to scratch up, mar.
fagratzt *v.* schatched up, marred; pp. of fagratza.
fagrawbnissa *(f).* graves; pl. of fagrawbnis.
fagrawva *v.* 1. to bury 2. to dig around in the ground.
fagrefticha *v.* 1. to strengthen 2. to emphasize by using expletives.
fagrefticht *v.* 1. strengthened 2. emphasized by using expletives; pp. of

fagrefticha.
fagreisha *v.* to bawl out, to yell at.
fagribbeld *v.* crippled; pp. of fagribla.
fagribbelda *(f).* crippled ones.
fagribla *v.* to cripple.
fagrimla *v.* to break into crumbs, to crumble.
fagrimmeld *v.* broke into crumbs, crumbled; pp. of fagrimla.
fagrisha *v.* bawled out, yelled at; pp. of fagreisha.
fagrohtza *v.* to become moldy.
fagrohtzt *v.* having become moldy; pp. of fagrohtza.
fagrumla *v.* 1. to scold 2. to complain about.
fagrummeld *v.* having complained about; pp. of fagrumla.
fagunna *v.* 1. to envy 2. to desire misfortune for another.
fagunnish/fagunshtlich 1. envious 2. malicious.
fagunsht *(m).* 1. envy 2. ill will.
fahadda *v.* to harden the heart.
fahakka *v.* to mar or damage with striking blows, to gouge.
fahakt *v.* marred or damaged by striking blows, gouged; pp. of fahakka.
fahalda *v.* to prevent.
fahandeld *v.* 1. discussed 2. traded; pp. of fahandla.
fahandla *v.* 1. to discuss 2. to

trade.

fahast 1. hateful 2. to be hated.

fahatt *v.* having hardened the heart; pp. of fahadda.

faheahra *v.* to give a formal hearing or trial.

faheaht *v.* having been given a formal hearing or trial; pp. of faheahra.

fahexa *v.* 1. to perform magic or sorcery 2. to cast a spell or curse.

fahext *v.* 1. performed magic or sorcery 2. having cast a spell or curse; pp. of fahexa.

fahinnahra *v.* to hinder.

fahinnaht *v.* hindered; pp. of fahinnahra.

fahuddeld *v.* 1. confused 2. cluttered, in disarray; pp. of fahudla.

fahudla *v.* 1. to confuse 2. to cause disarray, clutter.

fahungahra *v.* to starve.

fahungaht *v.* starved; pp. of fahungahra.

fahunsa *v.* 1. to tease 2. to disorient.

fahunst *v.* 1. teased 2. disoriented; pp. of fahunsa.

fa'immah forever.

fa'ivvah over, past, concluded.

fakaekka *v.* to respond very expressively.

fakaekt *v.* having responded very expressively; pp. of fakaekka.

fakaffeld *v.* dribbled or spilled; pp. of fakafla.

fakafla *v.* to dribble or spill.

fakatza *v.* 1. to shorten 2. to give less than owed.

fakatzt *v.* 1. shortened 2. having given less than owed; pp. of fakatza.

fakawfa *v.* to sell.

fakawfa-blatz *(m).* market place.

fakawfah *(m).* seller.

fakawft *v.* sold; pp. of fakawfa.

fakeffahra *v.* 1. to act overly concerned 2. to act overly surprised.

fakeffaht *v.* 1. having acted overly concerned 2. having acted overly surprised; pp. of fakeffahra.

fakiddahra *v.* to giggle.

fakiddaht *v.* giggled; pp. of fakiddahra.

fakindicha *v.* to proclaim, make known.

fakindicht *v.* proclaimed, made known; pp. of fakindicha.

fakleahra *v.* 1. to glorify 2. to clarify.

fakleaht *v.* 1. glorified 2. clarified; pp. of fakleahra.

fakosseld *v.* having eaten or worked sloppily; pp. of fakossla.

fakossla *v.* to eat or work sloppily.

falabba *v.* to fail to perform because of neglect.

falabt *v.* failed to perform because of neglect; pp. of falabba.

falacha *v.* 1. to mock 2. to esteem lightly, not take seriously.

falacht *v.* 1. mocked 2. lightly esteemed, not taken seriously; pp. of falacha.

falanga *v.* to desire.

falanga *(m).* desire or want.

falanginga *(f).* desires; pl. of falanga.

falangt *v.* desired; pp. of falanga.

falaykeld *v.* denied; pp. of falaykla.

falaykla *v.* to deny.

falaykt *v.* misplaced, forgot where it was put; pp. of falayya.

falaysa *v.* 1. to sort 2. given to spending much time to reading.

falayt not eager, feeling reluctance.

falayya *v.* to misplace, forget where it was put.

fald *(f).* pleat.

falda *(f).* pleats; pl. of fald.

faleahra *v.* to spill.

faleaht *v.* spilled; pp. of faleahra.

falechaht full of holes, worn.

faleimda *v.* to slander.

falengahra *v.* to lengthen.

falengaht *v.* lengthened; pp. of falengahra.

faleshtahra *v.* to blaspheme.

faleshtaht *v.* blasphemed; pp. of faleshtahra.

faletza *v.* to wrong, to use wrongly, mistreat.

faletzt *v.* wronged, mistreated; pp. of faletza.

faliahra *v.* to lose.

fall *(f).* trap.

falla *(f).* traps; pl. of fall.

falla *v.* to fall.

falla-glost *v.* droped, having let fall; pp. of falla-lossa.

falla-lossa *v.* to drop or let fall.

faloahra *v.* lost; pp. of faliahra.

falohwa given to lying.

falossa *v.* 1. to leave or go away from someone 2. to depart 3. "falossa uf" (to rely on).

falsh false.

falshhayda *(f).* falsehoods; pl. of falshhayt.

falshhayt *(f).* falsehood.

falshheida *(f).* falsehoods; pl. of falshheit.

falusht *(m).* lust.

falushta *(f).* lusts; pl. of falusht.

famacha *v.* to express excessive astonishment or admiration.

famacht *v.* expressed excessive astonishment or admiration; pp. of famacha.

famawla *v.* to grind up completely.

famawla ground up.

famayya *(f).* 1. ability, power 2. possessions, goods.

fameahra *v.* to increase.

fameaht *v.* increased; pp. of fameahra.

fameika *v.* 1. to notice 2. to make marks on.

fameikt *v.* 1. noticed 2. marked

up; pp. of fameika.

family-drubb *(f)*. group of families.

family-drubba *(f)*. groups of families; pl. of family-drubb.

family-shtamm *(m)*. family roots.

family-shtemm *(f)*. families roots; pl. of family-shtamm.

fammidawk *(m)*. forenoon.

fammidawks in the forenoon.

famohna *v.* to admonish.

famohnd *v.* admonished; pp. of famohna.

famohning *(f)*. admonition.

famohninga *(f)*. admonitions; pl. of famohning.

fanemma *v.* to perceive.

fanga *v.* to catch.

fangah *(m)*. one who catches or captures.

fang-net *(neu)*. net used for catching or capturing.

fang-nets *(f)*. nets used for catching or capturing; pl. of fang-net.

fang-shtrikk *(m)*. snare.

fang-shtrikka *(f)*. snares; pl. of fang-shtrikk.

fanichta *v.* to consider unimportant.

faniddahra *v.* the act of lowering ones standards.

faniddaht *v.* having lowered one's standards; pp. of faniddahra.

fanna in front, at the front.

fanna-bei head on, from the front.

fanna-draus up ahead.

fanna-drinn in the front part.

fanna-droh 1. in front of 2. fastened to the front.

fanna-druff on the front.

fanna-heah 1. in the lead 2. ahead of, before hand.

fanna-naus in advance.

fanna-nei entering at the front.

fanna-rumm 1. around the front 2. openly exposed, not hidden.

fanna-vekk openly, completely.

fannich 1. in front of 2 .funny.

fanumma *v.* perceived; pp. of fanemma.

faraykt *v.* moved; pp. of farayya.

farayya *v.* to move.

fareisa *v.* to tear.

farenkt *v.* sprained, twisted.

fareyyaht rained on.

farissa *v.* torn; pp. of fareisa.

farobba *v.* 1. to tear, pull apart into pieces 2. to disassemble.

farobt *v.* 1. torn apart 2. disassembled; pp. of farobba.

farohda *v.* to betray.

farosht *v.* rusted; pp. of faroshta.

faroshta *v.* to become rusty.

faroshta *v.* to rust.

farukt *v.* crazy.

farummaniahra *v.* 1. to maneuver 2. to apply effort.

farummaniaht *v.* maneuvered; pp. of farummaniahra.

farunseld *v.* wrinkled; pp. of

farunsla.

farunsla *v.* to wrinkle.

fasalsa salted too much.

fasamla *v.* to gather, to assemble.

fasamling-blatz *(m).* meeting place.

fasamling-bletz *(f).* meeting places; pl. of fasamling-blatz.

fasamling-haus *(neu).* meeting house.

fasamling-heisah *(f).* meeting houses; pl. of fasamling-haus.

fasamling-tent *(m).* tent used for assemblies.

fasamling-tents *(f).* tent used for meeting or assembling; pl. of fasamling-tent.

fasammeld *v.* gathered, assembled; pp. of fasamla.

fasaufa *v.* to drown.

fasauma *v.* to waste time, opportunity, etc.

fasaumd *v.* having wasted time, opportunity, etc; pp. of fasauma.

fasaut *v.* damaged, rendered inoperable; pp. of fasauwa.

fasauwa *v.* to damage, to render inoperable.

fasavvahra *v.* to sour.

fasavvaht *v.* soured; pp. of fasavvahra.

fasayna *v.* to reconcile, to make peace with.

fasaynd *v.* reconciled, made peace with; pp. of fasayna.

faseikt *v.* taken care of; pp. of

faseiya.

faseima *v.* to waste time, opportunity, etc.

faseiya *v.* to take care of.

fasell therefore, for that reason.

fasenka *v.* to singe, burn.

fasenkt *v.* singed, burned; pp. of fasenka.

fashaycha *v.* to scare, to intimidate.

fashaycht *v.* scared, intimidated; pp. of fashaycha.

fashelda *v.* to scold, berate.

fashiddeld *v.* shaken up; pp. of fashidla.

fashidla *v.* to shake up.

fashimfa *v.* 1. to scold 2. to speak evil of.

fashimft *v.* 1. scolded 2. having spoken evil of; pp. of fashimfa.

fashlabba *v.* to spill (only used with liquids).

fashlabt *v.* spilled (only used with liquids); pp. of fashlabba.

fashlauwa *v.* to beat up.

fashlavvahra *v.* to slobber.

fashlavvaht *v.* slobbered; pp. of fashlavvahra.

fashlayfa *v.* to misplace, by someone else.

fashlayft *v.* misplaced by someone else; pp. of fashlayfa.

fashleesa *v.* to completely lock up.

fashlohfa *v.* to oversleep.

fashlossa *v.* completely locked up; pp. of fashleesa.

fashlubba *v.* 1. to hide 2. to soak in (as paint into wood).

fashlubt *v.* 1. hidden 2. soaked in (as in paint into wood); pp. of fashlubba.

fashmaesha *v.* to smash.

fashmaesht *v.* smashed; pp. of fashmaesha.

fashmelsa *v.* to melt.

fashmiahra *v.* to smear.

fashmiaht *v.* smeared; pp. of fashmiahra.

fashmoddahra *v.* to suffocate.

fashmoddaht *v.* suffocated; pp. of fashmoddahra.

fashmolsa *v.* melted; pp. of fashmelsa.

fashnabba *v.* to reveal a secret unintentionally.

fashnabt *v.* having revealed a secret unintentionally; pp. of fashnabba.

fashneida *v.* to cut up.

fashnidda *v.* cut up; pp. of fashneida.

fashohma *v.* to shame, mock.

fashohmd *v.* shamed, mocked; pp. of fashohma.

fashohna *v.* to overlook or dismiss another's fault or mistake.

fashohnd *v.* having overlooked or dismissed another's fault or mistake; pp. of fashohna.

fasholda *v.* scolded, berated; pp. of fashelda.

fashpalda *v.* to split apart.

fashpautza *v.* to spit on.

fashpautzt *v.* having been spit on; pp. of fashpautza.

fashpeeld playful.

fashpodda *v.* to mock.

fashpott *v.* mocked; pp. of fashpodda.

fashprecha *v.* to promise.

fashpreching *(f).* promise.

fashprechinga *(f).* promises; pl. of fashpreching.

fashprechnis *(f).* promise.

fashprechnissa *(f).* promises; pl. of fashprechnis.

fashpritza *v.* 1. to burst, explode as a firecracker 2. to spray or splash with liquid.

fashpritzt *v.* 1. burst, exploded as in a firecracker 2. sprayed or splashed with liquid; pp. of fashpritza.

fashprocha *v.* promised; pp. of fashprecha.

fashprunga *v.* 1. over run by or covered with animal tracks 2. sprung (door, window).

fashpukka *v.* to startle, to frighten.

fashpukkich easily startled, frightened.

fashpukt *v.* startled, frightened.

fashrekka *v.* to startle, to scare.

fashrivva *v.* covered with writing.

fashrokka *v.* startled, scared; pp. of fashrekka.

fasht *v.* to fast.

fasht / shiah almost, nearly.

fashtamba *v.* to stomp on, to

trample.

fashtambt *v.* stomped on, trampled; pp. of fashtamba.

fashtand *(m).* 1. moderation, decency 2. understanding.

fashtanna *v.* understood; pp. of fashtay.

fashtatza *v.* 1. to confuse 2. to cause to stumble.

fashtatzt *v.* 1. confused, bewildered 2. caused to stumble; pp. of fashtatza.

fashtauna *v.* to astonish.

fashtaund *v.* astonished; pp. of fashtauna.

fashtaundlich suprisingly.

fashtay *v.* to understand.

fasht-dawk *(m).* day of fasting.

fasht-dawwa *(f).* days of fasting; pl. of fasht-dawk.

fashteika *v.* to strengthen.

fashteiking *(f).* oath.

fashteikinga *(f).* oaths; pl. of fashteiking.

fashteikt *v.* strengthened; pp. fashteika.

fashtekkel-blatz *(m).* hiding place.

fashtekkel-bletz *(f).* hiding places; pl. of fashtekkel-blatz.

fashtekkeld *v.* hidden; pp. of fashtekla.

fashtekla *v.* to hide.

fashteld *v.* having altered one's appearance in order to deceive; pp. of fashtella.

fashtella *v.* alter one's appearance in order to

deceive.

fashtelling *(f).* false appearance.

fashtellinga *(f).* false appearances; pl. of fashtelling.

fashtendich reasonable.

fashtendlichkeit *(f).* reasonableness.

fashtendnis *(f).* comprehension, understanding.

fashtikka *v.* 1. to suffocate 2. to smother.

fashtikt *v.* 1. suffocated 2. smothered; pp. of fashtikka.

fashtocha *v.* covered with stings.

fashtokka *v.* to harden one's heart, to be stubborn.

fashtokt *v.* stubborn.

fashtrekka *v.* to stretch out or shape.

fashtrekt *v.* stretched out of shape; pp. of fashtrekka.

fashtroit *v.* scattered; pp. of fashtroiya.

fashtroiya *v.* to scatter.

fashuah for sure, assuredly.

fashuldicha *v.* 1. to accuse 2. to transgress against.

fashuldicht *v.* 1. accused 2. transgressed against; pp. of fashuldicha.

fashunna *v.* to scrape or bruise.

fashveahra *v.* to forswear.

fashveaht *v.* forsworn; pp. of fashveahra.

fashvecha *v.* to weaken, dilute.

fashvecht *v.* weakened, diluted; pp. of fashvecha.

fashvetza *v.* 1. to discuss 2. to persuade by talking.

fashvetzt *v.* 1. discussed 2. persuaded by talking; pp. of fashvetza.

fashvitza *v.* to get sweaty.

fashvitzt *v.* having become sweaty; pp. of fashvitza.

fasindicha *v.* to transgress or sin.

fasindicht *v.* transgressed or sinned; pp. of fasindicha.

fasoffa *v.* drowned; pp. of fasaufa.

fass *(neu).* barrel.

fassa *v.* to fill a container.

fassich / feddahsich forward direction.

fasucha *v.* 1. to tempt (as used in the Bible) 2. to attempt 3. to taste.

fasuchah *(m).* tempter.

fasucht *v.* 1. tempted (as used in the Bible) 2. tasted; pp. of fasucha.

fasuchung *(f).* temptation.

fasuddeld *v.* 1. soiled or dirtied 2. having become unclean by sinning; pp. of fasudla.

fasudla *v.* 1. to soil or dirty 2. to become unclean by sinning.

fatt away (as in away from home).

fatt-shridda *(f).* advances; pl. of fatt-shritt.

fatt-shritt *(m).* advance.

fatzay fourteen.

fatzayt fourteenth.

fatzich forty.

faub *(m).* color.

faul 1. lazy 2. rotten.

faulensah *(m).* lazy person.

faunreinicha *v.* to corrupt, defile.

faunreinicht *v.* corrupted, defiled; pp. of faunreinicha.

fausht *(f).* fist.

faushta *(f).* fists; pl. of fausht.

fauva *(f).* colors; pl. of faub.

favach why.

favand *v.* forewarned; pp. of favanna.

favanna *v.* to forewarn.

favass why.

favaxa *v.* to grow over, to become impenetrable.

favaysvass who knows what all.

favaysvi very, really, a great amount.

faveesht *v.* devastated; pp. of faveeshta.

faveeshta *v.* 1. to devastate 2. to fall into ruin.

faveeshtung *(f).* devastation, ruin.

faveeshtunga *(f).* devestations, ruins; pl. of faveeshtung.

faveila *v.* to pass the time, to occupy one's time.

favelka *v.* to wilt.

favelkt *v.* wilted; pp. of favelkt.

favikkeld *v.* 1. wrapped up 2. tangled up; pp. of favikla.

favikla *v.* 1. to wrap up 2. to tangle up.

favillicha *v.* to accept a proposal or assignment.

favillicht *v.* having accepted a

proposal or assignment; pp. of favillicha.

favisha *v.* to locate or encounter.

favisht *v.* having located or encountered; pp. of favisha.

favunnahra *v.* to astonish.

favunnaht *v.* having astonished; pp. of favunnahra.

fawbel *(f).* fable.

fawbla *(f).* fables; pl. of fawbel.

fawbla-shtoahri *(f).* fabel, story.

fawbla-shtoahris *(f).* fables, stories; pl. of fawbla-shtoahri.

fawda *(m).* thread.

fawna *(f).* corn tassels.

faxa *v.* to fax.

fayammahra *v.* to bemoan.

fayammaht *v.* bemoaned; pp. of fayammahra.

fayawkt *v.* disturbed or chased away; pp. of fayawwa.

fayawwa *v.* to disturb or chase, to chase away.

faydla *v.* to thread.

fayl 1. defect, fault 2.doubtless "unni fayl".

fayla 1. error 2. sickness.

faylah *(m).* 1. fault 2. sin.

faylah-suchah *(m).* fault finder (lit.- fault seeker).

fazand *v.* enraged; pp. of fazanna.

fazanna *v.* to enrage.

fazatt frustrating, unfair.

fazayla *v.* to tell or narrate.

fazayld *v.* told or narrated; pp. of fazayla.

fazeahra *v.* to consume, as by fire.

fazeahrich consuming.

fazeaht *v.* consumed (as by fire); pp. of fazeahra.

fazoddeld *v.* dropped, spilled, spread on the ground (not used with liquids); pp. of fazodla.

fazodla *v.* to drop, spill, spread on the ground (not used with liquids).

feah fair.

feahsht *(m).* verse.

feahshta *(f).* verses; pl. of feahsht.

feahva *v.* to color usually by dying.

febla *v.* to make light of, to not take seriously.

fecht *(f).* fight.

fechta *(f).* fights; pl. of fecht.

fechta *v.* to fight.

fechta-feld *(neu).* battle field.

fechta-feldah *(f).* battle fields; pl. of fechta-feld.

fechtah *(m).* fighter.

fechtich contentious.

feddah *(f).* fathers; pl. of faddah.

feddah *(m).* feather.

feddahra / fedra *(f).* pl. of feddah ("fedra" - common pronunciation).

feddahsht forward most.

feddahsich / fassich forward direction.

fee *(neu).* livestock (animal).

feedra *v.* to feed.

fee-heedah *(m).* animal herder.

feel 1. many 2. much.
feela *v.* to feel.
fees *(f).* feet; pl. of foos.
feesich footed.
fees-sohla *(f).* soles of the feet; pl. of foos-sohl.
feevah *(m).* fever.
feevahrich feverish.
fei 1. very small or fine 2. fancy.
feich *(f).* furrow.
feicha *(f).* furrows; pl. of feich.
feicha *v.* to fear.
feichboah fearful.
feichbutzich fearful, "fraidy cat".
feicht damp, moist.
feichtlohs fearless.
fei-gmawla finely ground.
feil *(f).* file.
feila *(f).* files; pl. of feil.
feila *v.* to file.
feind *(m).* enemy.
feinda *(f).* enemies; pl. of feind.
feinda-hend *(f).* enemy hands.
fei-shtenglich delicately structured.
feiya *(f).* figs.
feiya-baym *(f).* fig trees; pl. of feiya-bohm.
feiya-blashtah *(m).* burn blister.
feiya-bohm *(m).* fig tree.
feiyah *(neu).* fire.
feiyah-dawk *(m).* holiday.
feiyah-dawk-fesht *(neu).* religious holiday, feast.
feiyah-dawk-feshta *(f).* religious holidays, feasts; pl. of feiyah-dawk-fesht.
feiyah-dawwa *(f).* holidays; pl. of feiyah-dawk.
feiyah-effa *(f).* fire ovens; pl. of feiyah-offa.
feiyah-flamm *(neu).* flame of fire.
feiyah-flamma *(f).* flames of fire; pl. of feiyah-flamm.
feiyah-funk *(f).* spark.
feiyah-funka *(f).* sparks; pl. of feiyah-funk.
feiyah-grate *(f).* the grate in a furnace.
feiyah-grates *(f).* grates in a furnace; pl. of feiyah-grate.
feiyah-hols *(neu).* firewood.
feiyahlen *(f).* small fires; pl. of feiyahli.
feiyahli *(neu).* small fire.
feiyah-offa *(m).* fire oven.
feiyah-opfah *(neu).* sacrificial fire.
feiyah-opfahra *(f).* sacrificial fires; pl. of feiyah-opfah.
feiyah-pann *(m).* fire pan.
feiyah-panna *(f).* fire pans; pl. of feiyah-pann.
feiyah-pits *(f).* fire pits; pl. of feiyah-pitt.
feiyah-pitt *(m).* fire pit.
feiyahra *(f).* fires; pl. of feiyah.
feiyahra to fire (lose job).
feiyahrich fiery.
feiyah-shtekka *(m).* torch (lit.- fire stick).
feiya-kucha *(m).* cake made of figs.
fekkel *(f).* birds (as used in the

Bible); pl.of fokkel.
fekkel-fangah *(m)*. bird
　catcher.
feld *(neu)*. field.
feldah *(f)*. fields; pl. of feld.
feld-hauptmann *(m)*. field
　overseer, captain.
feld-hauptmennah *(f)*. field
　overseer, captain; pl. of
　feld-hauptmann.
fellich 1. relatively,
　comparatively 2. slightly
　more than.
fellicha-deensht *(m)*. bishop
　office.
felsa *(m)*. boulder, rock.
felsa-badger *(m)*. rock badger.
felsa-badgers *(f)*. rock badger;
　pl. of felsa-badger.
felsa-vanda *(neu)*. rock walls.
felya *(m)*. inner rim to which
　outer ends of spokes are
　attached on a buggy wheel.
fens *(f)*. fence.
fensa *(f)*. fences; pl. of fens.
fensa-meislen *(f)*. chipmunks;
　pl. of fensa-meisli.
fensa-meisli *(neu)*. chipmunk.
fenshtah *(neu)*. window.
fenshtah-dichah *(f)*. window
　curtains; pl. of fenshtah-
　duch.
fenshtah-duch *(neu)*. window
　curtain.
fenshtahra *(f)*. windows; pl. of
　fenshtah.
fenyoo *(f)*. auction.
fenyoos *(f)*. auctions; pl. of
　fenyoo.

fesht *(neu)*. religious holiday,
　feast, festival.
fesht fastened, connected to.
feshta *(f)*. religious holidays,
　feasts, festivals; pl. of fesht.
feshtah-blatz *(m)*. solidly
　grounded (lit.- fastened in
　place).
fesht-fasmling *(f)*. festival
　gathering.
fesht-zeida *(f)*. festival times;
　pl. of fesht-zeit.
fesht-zeit *(f)*. festival time.
fessah *(f)*. barrels; pl. of fass.
fett *(neu)*. lard, fat.
fett *adj*. fat.
fett-kucha *(m)*. doughnut.
fett-opfahra *(f)*. pl. of fett-
　opfah.
feyyel *(f)*. birds (as used in
　everyday speech); pl.of fohl.
fiah four.
fiah-ekkich having four
　corners.
fiah-feesich four-footed.
fiahra *v*. to lead.
fiaht forth.
fikkahra *v*. 1. to calculate 2. to
　plan on.
filla *v*. to fill.
fimf five.
fimft fifth.
fingah *(m)*. finger.
fingah-heet *(f)*. thimbles; pl. of
　fingah-hoot.
fingah-hoot *(m)*. thimble (lit.-
　finger hat).
fingah-nakkel *(m)*. fingernail.
fingah-nekkel *(f)*. fingernails;

pl. of fingah-nakkel.

fingahra *v.* to finger something, to touch with the fingers.

fingah-ring *(m).* finger ring.

fingah-rings *(f).* finger rings; pl. of fingah-ring.

finna *v.* to find.

firchta *v.* to fear.

fisha *v.* to fish.

fishah *(m).* one who fishes.

fishah-mann *(m).* fisherman.

fishah-mennah *(f).* fishermen; pl. of fishah-mann.

fish-awdlah *(m).* osprey.

Fish-Doah *(neu).* Fish Gate.

fish-fangah *(m).* fish catcher.

fishgatt *(f).* fishing pole or rod.

fish-hohka *(m).* fish hook.

fish-lein *(f).* fish line.

fish-leina *(f).* fishing lines; pl. of fish-lein.

fish-voi *(neu).* a large bird that eats fish.

fish-voiya *(f).* large birds that eat fish; pl. of fish-voi.

fitz *(f).* 1. twig 2. whip.

fitza *(f).* 1. twigs 2. whips; pl. of fitz.

flabbah *(m).* flap.

flabbahs *(f).* flaps; pl. of flabbah.

fladra *v.* to flap vigorously.

flaetsh *(m).* slap or whack on the behind.

flaetshah *(f).* slaps or whacks on the behind; pl. of flaetsh.

flamm *(neu).* flame.

flamma *(f).* flames; pl. of flamm.

flamma *v.* to flare up, flame,

blaze.

flammich flaming.

flauma *(m).* piece of lint.

flay *(f).* flea.

flaysh *(neu).* flesh, meat.

flaysh-fekkel *(f).* buzzards, birds of prey; pl. of flaysh-fokkel.

flaysh-fokkel *(m).* buzzard.

flaysh-gavla *(f).* meat forks; pl. of flaysh-gavvel.

flaysh-gavvel *(f).* meat fork.

flayshlich fleshly, carnal, sensual.

flaysh-market *(m).* meat market.

flaysh-markets *(f).* meat markets; pl. of flaysh-market.

flayvah *(m).* flavor.

flayvahs *(f).* flavors; pl. of flayvah.

flechta *v.* to weave.

fleddah-maus *(f).* bat (animal).

fleddah-meis *(f).* bats (animal); pl. of fleddah-meis.

fleeya *v.* 1. to fly 2. to flee.

fleicht maybe.

fleishleit *(neu).* flashlight.

fleishleits *(f).* flashlights; pl. of fleishleit.

fleisich diligent.

fleisichkeit *(f).* diligence.

flekka *(m).* 1. spot, stain 2. flake of dirt 3. particle of matter.

flelsa-vand *(f).* rock wall.

flexa *(f).* sinews, tendons.

flikka *v.* to mend.

flikkel *(m)*. wing.
flikla *(f)*. wings; pl. of flikkel.
flint-shtay *(m)*. flint.
floah *(m)*. floor.
floahra *(f)*. floors; pl. of floah.
floahra *v.* to surprise, to floor.
flokka *(m)*. flake.
flots *(f)*. floods; pl. of flott.
flott *(f)*. flood.
fluch *(m)*. curse.
flucha *(f)*. curses; pl. of fluch.
flucha *v.* to swear, curse.
fluch-vadda *(f)*. curse words, swear words; pl. of fluch-vatt.
fluch-vatt *(neu)*. swearword.
foah fore-, a prefix meaning "before", "taking the lead".
foahbau *(m)*. fore bay, a lean to attached to the front of a barn to store things.
foahbild *(neu)*. example.
foahbilda *v.* to set an example or pattern.
foahbildah *(f)*. examples; pl. of foahbild.
foahdenkes *(neu)*. thinking ahead.
foaheldra *(f)*. forefathers; pl. of foahfaddah.
foahfaddah *(m)*. forefather.
foahfeddah *(f)*. forefathers; pl. of foahfaddah.
foahgang *(m)*. 1. preeminence 2. example.
foahganga *v.* having led, having been in charge; pp. of foahgay.
foahgay *v.* to lead, be in charge.

foahgayyah *(m)*. leader, foreman.
foahgegukt *v.* having looked forward to; pp. of foahgukka.
foahgezayld *v.* planned ahead; pp. of foahzayla.
foahgnumma *v.* undertook; pp. of foah-nemma.
foahgricht *v.* predetermined; pp. of foahrichta.
foahgrisht *v.* prepared ahead; pp. of foahrishta.
foahgroofa *v.* chosen ahead of time; pp. of foahroofa.
foahgukka *v.* to look forward to.
foahgvist *v.* having known ahead of time; pp. of foahvissa.
foahhalda *v.* to accuse of something.
foah-haut *(f)*. foreskin.
foah-heah *v.* earlier, before a specified time.
foah-heit *(f)*. foreskins; pl. of foah-haut.
foahkalda *v.* accused of something; pp. of foah-halda.
foahksawt *v.* predicted; pp. of foahsawwa.
foahksenna *v.* foresaw; pp. of foahsayna.
foahksetzt *v.* having been set in a position of eminence; pp. of foahsetza.
foahkshpeeld *v.* having played lead, such as a musical instrument; pp. of foahshpeela.

foahkshteld *v.* having set forth; pp. of foahshtella.

foahksunga *v.* having sang lead; pp. of foahsinga.

foahkumma *v.* to take place, to occur.

foahnaymsht *v.* preeminent, most important.

foahnemma *v.* to undertake.

foahra *v.* 1. to drive 2. to ride 3. to haul.

foahrich just now, before now.

foahrichta *v.* to predetermine.

foahrishta *v.* to prepare ahead.

foahroofa *v.* to choose ahead of time.

foahs *(m).* force.

foahsawwa *v.* to predict, prophesy.

foahsawwah *(m).* soothsayer.

foahsayna *v.* to foresee.

foahsetza *v.* 1. to set in a position of eminence 2. to set forth.

foahshein *(m).* appearance, exposure.

foahshpeela *v.* to play lead, such as musical instrument.

foahshtella *v.* to set forth.

foahsicht *(f).* foresight (lit.-seeing ahead).

foahsichtich foreseeing, wise, prudent.

foahsinga *v.* to sing lead, to take the lead in singing.

foahsingah *(m).* lead singer.

foahvissa *v.* to know ahead of time.

foahvitzich bossy, presumptuous.

foahzayla *v.* to plan ahead.

foahzeida *(f).* foretimes, earlier times; pl. of foahzeit.

foahzeit *(f).* earlier time.

foddahra / fodra *v.* 1. to require 2. to demand.

fohl *(m).* bird (as used in everyday speech).

fokkel *(m).* bird (as used in the Bible).

folfilla *v.* to fulfill.

folheit *(f).* fullness.

folk *(neu).* people, nation.

folkfild *v.* fulfilled; pp. of folfilla.

folkumma *v.* perfect.

folkummaheit *(f).* fullness, perfection.

folkummashaft *(f).* perfection.

foll full.

folshtendich fully.

folya *v.* to follow.

foodah *(neu).* feed.

foodah-drayk *(f).* mangers; pl. of foodah-drohk.

foodah-drohk *(m).* manger.

foodah-gang *(m).* ally in barn where livestock is fed.

foos *(m).* foot.

foos-bank *(f).* foot rest.

foos-benk *(f).* foot rests; pl. of foos-bank.

foos-dredda *(f).* footsteps.

foos-hohld *(m).* foot hold.

foos-hohlds *(f).* foot holds; pl. of foos-hohld.

foos-shteel *(f).* ottomans, foot stools; pl. of foos-shtool.

foos-shteelen *(f)*. foot stools; pl. of foos-shteeli.

foos-shteeli *(neu)*. little footstool.

foos-shtool *(m)*. footstool, ottoman.

foos-sohl *(m)*. sole of the foot.

fox *(m)*. fox.

fransel *(m)*. 1. fringe 2. ragged piece of thread 3. stray piece of thread or fabric.

fransla *(f)*. fringes; pl. of fransel.

franslich tattered.

fratzich fancy.

fraw *(f)*. 1. wife 2. woman.

fraw-brofayda *(f)*. female prophets, women prophets; pl. of fraw-brofayt.

fraw-brofayt *(f)*. female prophet, woman prophet.

frawwa *(f)*. 1. wives 2. women; pl. of fraw.

fraylich joyful.

fraylichkeit *(f)*. joyfulness.

fraym *(neu)*. frame.

frayms *(f)*. frames; pl. of fraym.

frays *(m)*. phrase.

frayses *(f)*. phrases; pl. of frays.

frayt *(f)*. joy.

frech 1. bold 2. immodest 3. fancy.

free early.

free-reyyah *(m)*. early rain.

free-yoah *(neu)*. spring, the season.

free-yoahrich spring like.

frei free.

Freidawk Friday.

frei-drayyah *(m)*. deliverer.

frei-glost *v.* having let loose or set free; pp. of frei-lossa.

freiheit *(f)*. freedom.

frei-kshteld *v.* having set free; pp. of frei-shtella.

frei-lossa *v.* to let loose, to set free.

freind *(m)*. 1. friend 2. relative.

freindlich friendly.

freindlichkeit *(f)*. friendliness.

freindshaft *(f)*. relatives.

freindshaft-regishtah *(m)*. genealogy register.

freindshaft-regishtahra *(f)*. genealogy registries; pl. of freindshaft-regishtah.

freindshaft-shtamm *(m)*. genealogy, persons roots.

freindshaft-shtemm *(f)*. genealogies, person's roots; pl. of freindshaft-shtamm.

frei-setzah *(m)*. one who sets free.

frei-setz-yoah *(neu)*. the year when all are set free, year of Jubilee.

frei-shtella *v.* to set free.

frei-shtellah *(m)*. one who releases.

frei-shtelling *(f)*. deliverance.

frei-villich willingly, voluntarily.

frei-villich-opfah *(neu)*. free will offering.

frei-villich-opfahra *(f)*. free will offerings; pl. of frei-villich-opfah.

fremd 1. unfamiliar 2. strange,

unusual.

fresh *(f)*. frogs; pl. of frosh.

fressa *v*. 1. to eat (animals only) 2. to overeat 3. to eat too fast or impolitely 4. devour.

fressah *(m)*. glutton.

fressahrei *(f)*. gluttony.

freyyaheit *(f)*. joy.

friahra *v*. to freeze.

frichta *(f)*. fruits; pl. of frucht.

fridda *(m)*. peace.

fridda-machah *(m)*. peace maker.

fridda-opfah *(neu)*. peace offering.

fridda-opfahra *(f)*. peace offerings; pl. of fridda-opfah.

fridlich peacefully, peaceful.

frish fresh.

froh glad.

frohk *(m)*. question.

frohwa *(f)*. questions; pl. of frohk.

frohwa *v*. to ask.

froiya *v*. to rejoice.

fromm pious.

frosh *(m)*. frog.

frosht *(m)*. frost.

froshtich frosty.

frucht *(f)*. fruit.

fruchtboah fruitful.

frucht-feld *(neu)*. field with a crop in it.

frucht-feldah *(f)*. fields of crops; pl. of frucht-feld.

frucht-kashta *(m)*. grain bin.

fuah *(f)*. 1. team of horses or oxen 2. a horse and carriage in hitch.

fuah-dreivah *(m)*. driver of a team of horses.

fuah-mennah *(f)*. pl. of fuah-mann.

fuahra *(f)*. teams; pl. of fuah.

fuddah *(m)*. the foundation wall in a building which extends below the frost line, footer.

fuddahs *(f)*. foundation walls in a building which extend below the frostline, footers; pl. of fuddah.

fuftzay fifteen.

fuftzayt fifteenth.

fuftzich fifty.

fuftzichsht fiftieth.

fumm of the (used with masculine or neuter noun, dative case).

fumma of a (used with masculine or neuter noun, dative case).

funka *(m)*. spark.

funn 1. of 2. from.

funn-nannah separate from each other.

furcht *(f)*. fear.

fussah *(m)*. lint.

fussahra *(f)*. lints; pl. of fussah.

fussahra *v*. 1. to fill the air with dust or lint 2. to snow.

fussahrich 1. lint covered 2. lightweight.

G - g

gabiddel *(neu)*. chapter.

gabidla *(f)*. chapters; pl. of gabiddel.

gacht *v.* heeded; pp. of achta.

gaksa *v.* to cackle.

gall *(f)*. gallon.

galla *(f)*. gallons; pl. of gall.

gandvat *v.* answered; pp. of andvadda.

ganga *v.* went; pp. of gay.

gans *(f)*. goose.

gans entire, whole.

gans-deich throughout, completely through.

gaul *(m)*. horse.

gaunsh *(f)*. swing.

gaunsha *(f)*. swings; pl. of gaunsh.

gaunsha *v.* to swing.

gautza *v.* to bark.

gavla *(f)*. forks; pl. of gavvel.

gavvel *(f)*. fork.

gay *v.* to go.

gaygend *(neu)*. 1. community 2. area.

gaygenda *(f)*. 1. communities 2. areas; pl. of gaygend.

gaykeld *v.* has been distasteful or undesireable; pp. of aykla.

gaykend *v.* owned; pp. of aykna.

gaykt *v.* harrowed; pp. of ayka.

gayl yellow.

gayld *v.* oiled, lubricated; pp. of ayla.

gays *(m)*. goat.

gaysa-haut *(f)*. goatskin.

gaysa-heit *(f)*. goat skins; pl. of gaysa-haut.

gayshel *(f)*. whip, scourge.

gayshla *(f)*. whips, scourges; pl. of gayshel.

gayshla *v.* to scourge or whip.

gayshtling *(f)*. whipping, scourging.

gayshtlinga *(f)*. whippings, scourgings; pl. of gayshtling.

gayslen *(f)*. baby goats, kids; pl. of gaysli.

gaysli *(neu)*. baby goat, kid.

gayya 1. steep 2. against, opposed to 3. toward.

gayyich 1. against, opposed to 2. toward.

geahbt *v.* inherited; pp. of eahva.

geahn 1. gladly 2. with desire.

geahnd *v.* reaped; pp. of eahnda.

geahsht *(f)*. barley.

geahsht-broht *(neu)*. barley bread.

geaht *v.* honored; pp. of eahra.

gebabbeld *v.* babbled; pp. of babla.

gebabt *v.* stuck, adhered; pp. of babba.

gebaddaht *v.* bothered; pp. of badra.

gebakka *v.* baked; pp. of bakka.

gebasht *v.* husked; pp. of bashta.

gebatt *v.* aided or benefited; pp. of badda.

gebaut *v.* built; pp. of bauwa.

gebavvaht *v.* farmed; pp. of bavvahra.

gebawda *v.* 1. soaked or bathed an injured body part 2. waded; pp. of bawda.

gebayda *v.* prayed; pp. of bayda.

gebaydah *(f).* prayers; pl. of gebayt.

gebayt *(neu).* prayer.

gebeddeld *v.* begged; pp. of bedla.

gebei *(neu).* building.

gebeiyah *(f).* buildings; pl. of gebei.

gebeiyt *v.* rocked to sleep; pp. of beiya.

gebikkeld *v.* ironed (clothes); pp. of bikla.

gebikt *v.* 1. stooped 2. bowed; pp. of bikka.

gebiss *(neu).* mouthpiece of a bridle, bit.

gebissa *v.* bitten; pp. of beisa.

gebissah *(f).* mouthpieces of bridles, bits; pl. of gebiss.

geblaebbaht *v.* blabbed; pp. of blaebbahra.

geblanst *v.* planted; pp. of blansa.

geblatt *v.* bleated; pp. of bladda.

geblecht *v.* having suffered consequences; pp. of blecha.

gebleet *v.* bloomed; pp. of bleeya.

gebleshtaht *v.* plastered; pp. of bleshtahra.

gebletsht *v.* 1. spanked 2. clapped; pp. of bletsha.

geblikt *v.* 1. shelled (peas) 2. blinked; pp. of blikka.

geblinseld *v.* having blinked your eyes; pp. of blinsla.

geblitzt *v.* flashed; pp. of blitza.

geblivva *v.* remained or stayed; pp. of bleiva.

geblohkt *v.* bothered; pp. of blohwa.

geblohsa *v.* blown; pp. of blohsa.

geblooda *v.* bled; pp. of blooda.

geblookt *v.* plowed; pp. of bloowa.

geblotzt *v.* bumped; pp. of blotza.

geboahra *v.* born.

geboahra *v.* drilled; pp. of boahra.

geboaht *v.* irked; pp. of boahra.

gebodda *(f).* commands; pl. of gebott.

gebodda *v.* 1. offered 2. won 3. having bid; pp. of beeda.

gebohwa *v.* bent; pp. of beeya.

gebollaht *v.* rumbled (stomach); pp. of bollahra.

gebott *(neu).* command.

gebraekk *(neu).* the act of bragging.

gebraekt *v.* bragged; pp. of braekka.

gebrauch *(m).* 1. custom 2. habit.

gebraucha *(f).* 1. customs 2. habits; pl. of gebrauch.

gebraucht *v.* 1. needed 2.

performed magical healing arts (powwowed); pp. of braucha.

gebreddich *(neu)*. preaching, teaching.

gebreddicht *v.* preached; pp. of breddicha.

gebreed *v.* 1. scalded; pp. of breeya 2. bred; pp. of breeda.

gebreicht *v.* would have needed; pp. of breichta.

gebrend *v.* burned; pp. of brenna.

gebrild *v.* cried; pp. of brilla.

gebrill *(neu)*. constant crying.

gebrocha *v.* broke; pp. of brecha.

gebrocht *v.* brought; pp. of bringa.

gebroffetzeit *v.* prophesied; pp. of broffetzeiya.

gebrohda *v.* fried; pp. of brohda.

gebrumd *v.* buzzed or hummed; pp. of brumma.

gebrutzt *v.* cried, pouted sulked; pp. of brutza.

gebumpt *v.* 1. bumped 2. pumped; pp. of bumba.

gebunna *v.* tied; pp. of binna.

gebutshaht *v.* butchered; pp. of butshahra.

gebutzt *v.* cleaned; pp. of butza.

gebyoost *v.* abused; pp. of byoosa.

gedabt *v.* stepped into or onto accidentally; pp. of dabba.

gedambt *v.* dumped; pp. of damba.

gedanka *(f)*. thoughts.

gedankt *v.* thanked; pp. of danka.

gedanst *v.* danced; pp. of dansa.

gedatt *v.* withered; pp. of dadda.

gedaut *v.* thawed; pp. of dauwa.

gedavvaht *v.* pitied; pp. of davvahra.

gedawf *(neu)*. the practice of baptizing.

gedawft *v.* baptized; pp. of dawfa.

gedayld *v.* portioned; pp. of dayla.

gedaymeedicht *v.* humbled; pp. of daymeedicha.

geddahra *v.* to gather.

gedeend *v.* 1. worshipped 2. served; pp. of deena.

gedekt *v.* covered; pp. of dekka.

gedemmaht *v.* having made a banging noise; pp. of demmahra.

gedenkt *v.* thought; pp. of denka.

gedimmeld *v.* thundered; pp. of dimla.

gedinkt *v.* seemed; pp. of dinka.

gedoktaht *v.* doctored; pp. of dokahra.

gedraut *v.* 1. trusted 2. dared; pp. of drauwa.

gedrawwa *v.* carried; pp. of drawwa.

gedraysht *v.* comforted; pp. of drayshta.

gedrayt *v.* turned; pp. of drayya.

gedrenkt *v.* having given water to livestock; pp. of drenka.

gedrikkeld *v.* dried; pp. of

drikla.

gedrikt　*v.* squeezed or pressed; pp. of drikka.

gedrivva　*v.* 1. driven 2. propelled physically 3. motivated; pp. of dreiva.

gedrodda　*v.* treaded; pp. of dredda.

gedroffa　*v.* 1. hit 2. met; pp. of dreffa.

gedrohmd　*v.* dreamed; pp. of drohma.

gedrohsht　*v.* comforted; pp. of drohshta.

gedroit　*v.* threatened; pp. of droiya.

gedropst　*v.* dropped; pp. of drobsa.

gedrosha　*v.* threshed; pp. of dresha.

gedrukt *v.* printed, type produced by a machine; pp. of drukka.

gedrunka　*v.* drank; pp. of drinka.

gedruvveld　*v.* troubled; pp. of druvla.

gedu　*v.* 1. done 2. put (in the past sense); pp. of du.

geduft　*v.* fogged or steamed up glass; pp. of dufta.

geduld　*v.* 1. tolerated 2. bore with patience; pp. of dulda.

geduld　patience.

geduldheit　*(f).* patience (as a noun).

geduldich　patient, forbearing.

gedummeld　*v.* hurried; pp. of dumla.

gedunga　*v.* hired; pp. of dinga.

gedunkt　*v.* dipped, dunked; pp. of dunka.

gedunnaht　*v.* having made a thundering niose; pp. of dunnahra.

geedichkeit　*(f).* kindness, benevolence.

geeskann　*(f).* watering can.

geeskanna　*(f).* watering cans; pl. of geeskann.

gefecht　*(neu).* habitual fighting.

gegakst　*v.* cackled; pp. of gaksa.

gegaunsht　*v.* swung (on a swing); pp. of gaunsha.

gegautzt　*v.* barked; pp. of gautza.

gegaysheld　*v.* scourged or whipped; pp. of gayshla.

gegeddaht　*v.* gathered; pp. of geddahra.

gegiet　*v.* guided, steered; pp. of geida.

gegikst　*v.* pricked; pp.of giksa.

geglawbt　*v.* 1. believed 2. having an opinion 3. having faith; pp. of glawva.

geglawkt　*v.* complained; pp. of glawwa.

geglayt　*v.* clothed; pp. of glayda.

geglicha　*v.* liked; pp. of gleicha.

geglobt　*v.* 1. having beat 2. knocked on a door; pp. of globba.

geglusht　*v.* desired; pp. of glushta.

gegmohnd　*v.* 1. seemed 2. reminded; pp. of gmohna.

gegneet　*v.* kneeled; pp. of gneeya.

gegneikst *v.* complained; pp. of gneiksa.

gegnibt *v.* knotted; pp. of gnibba.

gegnuddaht *v.* grumbled or muttered; pp. of gnudra.

gegraddeld *v.* crawled, climbed; pp. of gradla.

gegraebt *v.* grabbed; pp. of graebba.

gegratzt *v.* scratched; pp. of gratza.

gegraust *v.* repulsed or made sick to stomach; pp. of grausa.

gegrawva *v.* dug; pp. of grawva.

gegrayt *v.* crowed (like a rooster); pp. of grayya.

gegreest *v.* greeted; pp. of greesa.

gegreitzicht *v.* crucified; pp. of greitzicha.

gegrekst *v.* creaked; pp. of greksa.

gegribbeld *v.* crippled; pp. of gribla.

gegrisha *v.* yelled, screamed, shouted, cried out; pp. of greisha.

gegrummeld *v.* grumbled; pp. of grumla.

gegrund *v.* 1. established, grounded 2. founded; pp. of grunda.

gegukt *v.* looked; pp. of gukka.

gegvayld *v.* tormented; pp. of gvayla.

gegvaynd *v.* gotten used to; pp. of gvayna.

gegveahvt *v.* squirmed; pp. of gveahva.

gegvild *v.* quilted; pp. of gvilda.

geida *v.* to guide, to steer.

geifaht *v.* raged; pp. of eifahra.

geil *(f).* horses; pl. of gaul.

geils-mann *(m).* horseman.

geils-mennah *(f).* horsemen; pl. of geils-mann.

Geisht *(m).* the Holy Spirit.

geisht *(m).* spirit.

geishtah *(f).* spirits; pl. of geisht.

geishtlich spiritual.

geishtlichkeit *(f).* spirituality.

geitz *(m).* covetousness.

geitzich covetous.

geiyaht *v.* spoken offensively or argumentatively; pp. of eiyahra.

gekaund *v.* counted (English word using Deitsh rules); pp. of kaunda.

gekawft *v.* bought; pp. of kawfa.

gekawld *v.* called on the phone; pp; of kawla.

gekeaht *v.* swept; pp. of keahra.

gekebt *v.* beheaded; pp. of kebba.

gekeeld *v.* cooled; pp. of keela.

gekemd *v.* combed; pp. of kemma.

gekend *v.* recognized or having known someone or something; pp. of kenna.

gekikt *v.* kicked; pp. of kikka.

gekist *v.* kissed; pp. of kissa.

gekitzeld *v.* tickled; pp. of kitzla.

gekliaht *v.* cleared; pp. of

kliahra.
gekocht *v.* cooked; pp. of kocha.
gekollaht *v.* colored; pp. of
kollahra.
gekosht *v.* having cost; pp. of
koshta.
gekotzt *v.* vomited; pp. of kotza.
gekrohnd *v.* crowned; pp. of
krohna.
geld *(neu).* money.
geld-box *(f).* money box,
donation box.
geld-boxa *(f).* money boxes,
donation boxes; pl. of geld-
box.
geld-sakk *(m).* money bag.
geld-sekk *(f).* money bags; pl.
geld-sakk.
geld-vexlah *(m).* money
changer.
geleshtah habitual
blaspheming.
gend *v.* ended; pp. of enda.
gens *(f).* geese; pl. of gans.
gensa-heidich goosebumpy.
genunk *v.* enough.
gepeddeld *v.* peddled; pp. of
pedla.
gepeepst *v.* peeped; pp of
peepsa.
gepeild *v.* piled; pp. of peila.
gepetzt *v.* pinched; pp. of petza.
gepiffa *v.* whistled; pp. of peifa.
gepikt *v.* picked, chosen; pp. of
pikka.
gepishpaht *v.* whispered; pp. of
pishpahra.
gepoft *v.* puffed; pp. of poffa.
geprissa *v.* praised; pp. of

preisa.
gepsucht *v.* visited; pp. of
psucha.
gepusht *v.* pushed; pp. of pusha.
gerecht righteous.
gerechtichkeit *(f).*
righteousness.
gericht *(neu).* judgement.
gerichta *(f).* judgements; pl. of
gericht.
gericht-haus *(neu).* court
house.
gericht-heisah *di.* court
houses; pl. of gericht-haus.
gerichtichkeit *(f).* judgement.
gerichts-dawk *(m).* judgement
day.
gerichts-dawwa *(f).* judgement
days; pl. of gerichts-dawk.
geshtah yesterday.
geshtayl *(neu).* habitual
stealing.
gessa *v.* ate; pp. of essa.
getaend *v.* tanned; pp. of taena.
getaybt *v.* taped; pp. of tayba.
getayst *v.* tasted; pp. of taysta.
geteetsht *v.* taught; pp. of teesha.
geteidend *v.* tightened; pp. of
teidna.
getempt *v.* tempted (informal);
pp. of tempta.
getlich godly.
getlichkeit *(f).* godliness.
getotsht *v.* touched; pp. of totsha.
getraesht *v.* trashed; pp. of
traesha.
getraynd *v.* trained; pp. of
trayna.
getrayt *v.* traded; pp. of trayda.

getrikt *v.* tricked; pp. of trikka.

getshawt *v.* chewed; pp. of tshawwa.

getshaynsht *v.* changed; pp. of tshaynsha.

getsheahtsht *v.* charged; pp. of tsheahtsha.

getsheet *v.* cheated; pp. of tsheeda.

getshumbt *v.* jumped; pp. of tshumba.

gettah *(f).* gods.

gettin *(f).* goddess.

getza-opfah *(neu).* offering made to an idol.

gevislich surely, undoubtedly.

geviss for sure.

gevva *v.* 1. to give 2. to happen.

gevvah *(m).* giver.

gevvich "I give".

geyya 1. steep 2. against, opposed to 3. toward.

geyyich 1. against, opposed to 2. toward.

gezahh *(neu).* arguing, debating.

gezankt *v.* scolded; pp. of zanka.

gezatt *v.* teased, argued; pp. of zarra / zadda.

gezauft *v.* bickered; pp. of zaufa.

gezayld *v.* counted; pp. of zayla.

gezaymd *v.* tamed; pp. of zohma.

gezebt *v.* braided; pp. of zebba.

gezeigt *v.* witnessed or testified; pp. of zeiya.

geziddaht *v.* shivered or trembled; pp. of ziddahra.

gezimmaht *v.* to have worked as a carpenter.

gezohwa *v.* 1. pulled 2. moved to another residence; pp. of zeeya.

gezveicht *v.* grafted.

gezveifeld *v.* doubted.

gezvunga *v.* compelled.

gichtahra *(f).* seizures, convulsions.

gift *(neu).* poison.

giftich poisonous.

giksa *v.* to prick.

giksah *(m).* pricker.

giksah-shtekk *(f).* prickly plants; pl. of giksah-shtokk.

giksah-shtokk *(m).* prickly plant.

giksich prickly.

glacht *v.* laughed; pp. of lacha.

gland *v.* 1. learned 2. taught; pp. of lanna.

glangt *v.* reached; pp. of langa.

glantz *(m).* brightness.

glatt smooth.

glaut *v.* sounded or appeared to someone; pp. of lauda.

glawda *v.* loaded; pp. of lawda.

glawk *(f).* 1. complaint 2. accusation.

glaws *(neu).* 1. glass (the material) 2. water glass.

glawsich 1. made of glass 2. glassy.

glawva *(m).* 1. faith 2. belief 3. religion.

glawva *v.* 1. to believe 2. to be of the opinion 3. to have faith.

glawvich 1. believing, having faith 2. "I believe".

glawwa *(f)*. 1. complaints 2. accusations; pl. of glawk.

glawwa *v.* to complain.

glay *(m)*. clover.

glay small, tiny.

glaybt *v.* lived; pp. of layva.

glayda *v.* to clothe.

glaydah *(f)*. clothing, clothes, garments; pl. of glayt.

glaydah-sakk *(m)*. garment bag.

glaydah-sekk *(f)*. garment bags; pl. of glaydah-sakk.

glaykt *v.* laid; pp. of layya.

glaynd *v.* 1. borrowed 2. lent; pp. of layna.

glaysa *v.* read; pp. of laysa.

glayt *(neu)*. garment.

gleaht *v.* 1. poured 2. taught; pp. of leahra.

gleebt *v.* loved; pp. of leeva.

gleedah *(f)*. members; pl. of gleet.

gleekt *v.* lied, told untruth; pp. of leeya.

gleet *(neu)*. member.

glei soon.

gleicha *v.* to like.

gleicha 1. same, identical 2. equal.

gleichaveis likewise.

gleichnis *(neu)*. 1. parable 2. likeness.

gleichnissa *(f)*. 1. parables 2. likenesses; pl. of gleichnis.

glennah smaller.

glensht smallest.

gleshtaht *v.* blasphemed; pp. of leshtahra.

glessah *(f)*. water glasses; pl. of glaws.

gleyya *v.* laid, having assumed a prone position; pp. of leiya.

gleyyaheida *(f)*. opportunities; pl. of gleyyaheit.

gleyyaheit *(f)*. 1. opportunity 2. privilege.

glidda *v.* suffered; pp. of leida.

glikk *(m)*. good fortune, luck.

gliklich fortunate.

glitzahrich glittering.

gloahheit *(f)*. 1. glory 2. clearness.

globb shtekka *(m)*. club.

globba *v.* 1. to beat 2. to knock on a door.

gloffa *v.* walked; pp. of lawfa.

glohbt *v.* praised; pp. of lohva.

glost *v.* to have let; pp. of lossa.

glukk *(f)*. setting hen.

glukka *(f)*. setting hens; pl. of glukk.

glumba *(m)*. clump (such as clump of dirt).

glumsich clumsy.

glusht *v.* 1. lusted 2. desired; pp. of lushta.

glushta *(m)*. desire.

glushta *v.* to desire.

glushtich desirous.

gmacht *v.* 1. made 2. sounded 3. used in idioms "uf gmacht" (opened) "zu gmacht" (closed) "um gmacht" (cut down); pp. of macha.

gmauld *v.* argued; pp. of maula.

gmawla *v.* ground (such as meat or coffee); pp. of mawla.

gmay *(f)*. 1. congregation 2.

church, group of believers 3.
worship service.

gmay-haus *(neu)*. church
house, house of worship,
place of worship.

gmay-heisah *(f)*. church
houses, houses of worship;
pl. of gmay-haus.

gmayna *(f)*. congregations,
churches; pl. of gmay.

gmaynd *v*. 1. meant 2. having
an opinion 3. being
conceited "sich gmaynd";
pp. of mayna.

gmayt *v*. mowed; pp. of mayya.

gmeikt *v*. marked; pp. of meika.

gmeind *v*. 1. remembered 2.
minded, cared; pp. of
meinda.

gmeinshaft *(f)*. fellowship.

gmessa *v*. measured; pp. of
messa.

gmohna *v*. 1. to seem 2. to
remind.

gmolka *v*. milked; pp. of melka.

gnadda *(f)*. knots in wood; pl. of
gnatt.

gnaddich knotty (used in wood).

gnakeld *v*. nailed; pp. of nakla.

gnatt *(m)*. knot in wood.

gnawda-shtool *(m)*. mercy seat
(theological).

gnawdi grace (grace of God).

gnawt *(f)*. grace (God's grace).

gnaymd *v*. named; pp. of
nayma.

gnayt *v*. sewn; pp. of nayya.

gnebb *v*. buttons; pl. of gnobb.

gnecht *(m)*. servant, slave, hired

hand.

gnechta *(f)*. servants, slaves,
hired hands; pl. of gnecht.

gnechta-geisht *(m)*. spirit or
attitude of servant hood.

gnechtshaft *(f)*. servant hood.

gnee *(neu)*. knee.

gneeya *v*. to kneel.

gneiksa *v*. to complain.

gneiksich *adj*. complainer,
nagger, verbaly grumpy,
cranky, fussy.

gnibb *(m)*. knot.

gnibba *(f)*. knots; pl. of gnibb.

gnibba *v*. to knot.

gnobb *(m)*. button.

gnocha *(m)*. bone.

gnoddel *(m)*. lump (such as in
batter).

gnodla *(f)*. lumps (such as in
batter) ; pl. of gnoddel.

gnodlich lumpy (such as in
batter).

gnovlich knobby.

gnudra *v*. to mutter.

gnumma *v*. taken, took; pp. of
nemma.

goah completely, entirely.

goahra *(m)*. garden.

goahra-haldah *(m)*. gardener.

goaht *(f)*. quart.

goldich golden.

gold-shtikk *(neu)*. peice of
gold.

gold-shtikkah *(f)*. gold peices.

goot good.

goot-gukkich good looking.

goot-maynich kind, well
meaning.

goot-maynichkeida *(f).* kindnesses; pl. of goot-maynichkeit.

goot-maynichkeit *(f).* kindness.

goot-shmakkich having a good smell.

gopfaht *v.* sacrificed; pp. of opfahra.

Gott *(m).* God.

Gottes God's.

Gottes-deensht *(m).* 1. worship service 2. the act of serving God.

Gottes-furcht *(f).* fear of God.

Gott-firchtich *(f).* God fearing.

Gottheit *(f).* Godhead.

gottlohs ungodly.

grabb *(f).* crow.

grabba *(f).* crows; pl. of grabb.

grabbelt *v.* rattled; pp. of rabla.

graddel *(m).* crotch.

gradla *v.* to crawl, to climb.

graebba *v.* to grab.

graft *(f).* strength.

grank sick.

grankada *(f).* sicknesses (common use); pl. of granket.

granket *(f).* sickness (common use).

grankheida *(f).* sicknesses (used in the Bible); pl. of grankheit.

grankheit *(f).* sickness (used in the Bible).

gratza *v.* to scratch.

gratzah *(m).* scratch.

gratzahs *(f).* scratches; pl. of gratzah.

grausa *v.* to repulse or sick to stomach.

grausam revolting, repulsive.

grausht *v.* having made a rushing sound; pp. of rausha.

grausich gruesome, disgusting.

grauslich revolting, repulsive.

graut *(neu).* cabbage.

grawb *(neu).* grave (common use).

grawb-blatz *(m).* burial place.

grawb-hohf *(m).* graveyard, cemetary.

grawb-hohfa *(f).* graveyards, cemetaries; pl. of grawb-hohf.

grawbt *v.* robbed; pp. of rawva.

graws *(neu).* grass.

grawsa *(f).* grasses; pl. of graws.

grawst *v.* 1. moved energetically 2. raved 3. ranted or raged; pp. of rawsa.

grawt 1. straight 2. immediately 3. directly 4. exactly.

grawt-nau right now, right away, straight away.

grawtzu by shortcut.

grawva *(m).* 1. ditch 2. gully 3. crevice.

grawva *v.* to dig.

graysah bigger, larger.

graysht biggest, largest.

grayvah *(f).* graves; pl. of grawb.

grayya *v.* to crow (as a rooster).

grebs *(f).* crab, crayfish.

grebs *(neu).* cancer.

grebsa *(f)*. crabs, crayfish; pl. of grebs.

grecht *v*. raked; pp. of recha.

gree green.

greedich greedy.

greek *(m)*. war.

greeka *(f)*. wars; pl. of greek.

greeks-deenah *(m)*. military employee.

greeks-gaul *(m)*. war horse.

greeks-geil *(f)*. war horses; pl. of greeks-gaul.

greeks-gnecht *(m)*. soldier.

greeks-gnechta *(f)*. soldiers; pl. of greeks-gnecht.

greeks-hauptman *(m)*. military captain.

greeks-hauptmennah *(f)*. military captians; pl. of greeks-hauptmennah.

greeks-heet *(f)*. helmets; pl. of greeks-hoot.

greeks-hoot *(m)*. military helmet.

greeks-ksha *(neu)*. armor.

greeks-ksharra *(f)*. pieces of armor; pl. of greeks-ksha.

greeks-leit *(f)*. army people.

greeks-mann *(m)*. soldier.

greeks-mennah *(f)*. soldiers; pl. of greeks-mann.

greeks-shtekka *(m)*. war club.

greeks-tavvah *(m)*. an instrument of war.

greeks-vammes *(m)*. military clothing (lit.- war coat).

greeks-vemmes *(f)*. military clothing (lit. war coats); pl. of greeks-vammes.

greesa *v*. to greet.

greeya *v*. to get.

greeyish *adj*. Greek.

grefta *(f)*. strengths; pl. of graft.

grefta strength.

greftich 1. strong 2. hearty.

greftichlich 1. strongly 2. heartily.

greidah *(f)*. herbs.

greidah-ayl *(neu)*. ointment, herbal oil for medicinal purposes.

greilich shameful, bad.

greinicht *v*. cleansed, purefied; pp. of reinicha.

greisha *v*. to yell, to scream, to shout, to cry out.

greislich vile.

greitz *(neu)*. cross (torture stake).

greitza *(f)*. crosses (torture stakes); pl. of greitz.

greitzicha *v*. to crucify.

greksa *v*. to creak.

grend *v*. poked or shoved; pp. of renna.

greyyaht *v*. rained; pp. of reyyah.

griaht *v*. stirred; pp. of riahra.

gribbel *(m)*. cripple.

gribla *(f)*. cripples; pl. of gribbel.

gribla *v*. to cripple.

gricht *v*. judged; pp. of richta.

gridda *v*. ridden, rode; pp. of reida.

grikk *(f)*. 1. brook 2. crutch.

grikka *(f)*. 1. brooks 2. crutches; pl. of grikk.

grikt *v*. got; pp. of greeya.

grimla *(f).* crumbs; pl. of grimmel.

grimlich crumbly.

grimmel *(f).* crumb.

grind *(neu).* scab.

grind *v.* leaked; pp. of rinna.

grish *(m).* a shout, a loud call.

grisha *(f).* shouts, loud calls; pl. of grish.

grisht *v.* prepared; pp. of rishta.

Grishta-leit *(f).* people having Christian beliefs; pl. of Grishta-mensh.

Grishta-mensh *(m).* person having Christian beliefs.

grishtlich christian.

grissa *v.* torn; pp. of reisa.

grivva *v.* rubbed; pp. of reiva.

grobt *v.* plucked, picked (as in picked fruit from a tree) ; pp. of robba.

grodda *(f).* toads; pl. of grott.

groh gray.

grohda *v.* 1. advised 2. counseled 3. voted; pp. of rohda.

grohna *(m).* faucet, spigot.

grohs big, large, huge.

grohs-dawdi *(m).* great-grandfather.

grohs-dawdis *(f).* great-grandfathers; pl. of grohs-dawdi.

grohs-feelich conceited, arrogant, feeling "big" about yourself.

grohs-hansich acting conceited, arrogant, acting like you are "big and

tough".

grohs-mammi *(f).* great-grandmother.

grohs-mammis *(f).* great-grandmothers; pl. of grohs-mammi.

grohtz *(neu).* mold, mildew.

grohtzich moldy, musty.

grold *v.* rolled; pp. of rolla.

groofa *v.* called; pp. of roofa.

groofa called out, chosen.

groos *(m).* greeting.

groosht *v.* roosted; pp. of rooshta.

groot *v.* rested; pp. of roowa.

grosha *(m).* small coin of little value.

grott *(f).* toad.

grumbeah *(f).* potato.

grumbeahra *(f).* potatos; pl. of grumbeah.

grumla *v.* to grumble.

grumlah *(m).* grumbler.

grumm crooked, not straight.

grund *(m).* 1. ground 2. the reason or basis for an action or belief.

grunda *v.* 1. to establish, ground 2. to found.

grund-lechah *(f).* holes in the earth, dens; pl. of grund-loch.

grund-loch *(neu).* hole in the earth, den.

grundsau *(f).* groundhog, woodchuck.

grundsei *(f).* groundhogs, woodchucks; pl. of grundsau.

grusht *(f)*. crust.
grutza *(m)*. core, corn cob.
gukka *v.* to look.
gummah *(f)*. cucumber.
gummahra *(f)*. cucumbers; pl. of gummah.
gvakkeld *v.* wiggled, wobbled; pp. of vakla.
gvald *(f)*. power, strength.
gvaldich powerful.
gvand *v.* warned; pp. of vanna.
gvandeld *v.* wandered; pp. of vandla.
gvatsht *v.* watched; pp. of vatsha.
gvaxa *v.* grown; pp. of vaxa.
gvayla *v.* to torment.
gvayl-blatz *(m)*. place of torment.
gvayl-bletz *(f)*. places of torment; pl. of gvayl-blatz.
gvayna *v.* to get used to.
gvaynlich customarily.
gveahmd *v.* 1. warmed 2. dewormed.
gveaht *v.* to have shown reluctance; pp. of veaht.
gveahva *(f)*. joints of bones.
gveahva *v.* to squirm.
gveind *v.* wept; pp. of veina.
gveiseld *v.* whitewashed; pp. of veisla.
gvekt *v.* woke; pp. of vekka.
gvesha *v.* washed; pp. of vesha.
gvessaht *v.* watered (such as plants); pp. vessahra.
gvest *v.* was, were, used with "sei" to create past perfect tense; pp. of sei.

gvicht *(f)*. weight.
gvichta *(f)*. weights; pl. of gvicht.
gviddah *(m)*. thunder storm.
gviddah-stoahm *(m)*. thunderstorm (lit.- lightning storm).
gviddah-stoahms *(f)*. thunderstorms (lit.-lightning storms); pl. of gviddah-stoahm.
gvikkeld *v.* wrapped; pp. of vikla.
gvild *(m)*. quilt.
gvilda *v.* to quilt.
gvilds *(f)*. quilts; pl. of gvild.
gvimseld *v.* whimpered; pp. of vimsla.
gvinsht *v.* wished; pp. of vinsha.
gvissa *(neu)*. conscience.
gvissa *v.* shown; pp. of veisa.
gvist *v.* knew, known; pp. of vissa.
gvoahra *v.* worn; pp. of veahra.
gvoaht *v.* waited.
gvohwa *v.* weighed; pp. of veeya.
gvoond *v.* dwelled, where a person used to live; pp. of voona.
gvott *v.* wished; pp. of vodda.
gvunna *v.* 1. won 2. persuaded.
gvunnah-naws nosey, overly curious.
gvunnahrich curious.
gvunnaht *v.* wondered; pp. of vunnahra.
gyammaht *v.* lamented, groaned; pp. of yammahra.
gyawkt *v.* chased; pp. of yawwa.

gyoost *v.* used; pp. of yoosa.

H - h

habb *v.* have; used with the pronoun "ich" - " I ".
haendla *v.* to handle.
haffa *(m).* pot, crock.
haftich hefty.
HAH / Hah *(m).* LORD, (In the Bible whenever the word "LORD" occurs in all capital letters, the name in the orignal Hebrew is "Jehovah").
hahra *(f).* lords.
hakk *(f).* 1. hoe 2. a striking blow 3. an insulting remark.
hakka *(f).* 1. hoe 2. striking blows 3. insulting remarks; pl. of hakk.
hakka *v.* to hoe.
halb half.
halb-nacht *(f).* midnight or half-night.
halda *v.* to keep.
halftah *(m).* halter.
halftahs *(f).* halters; pl. of halftah.
hallich glorious.
hallichkeida *(f).* glories; pl. of hallichkeit.
hallichkeit *(f).* glory.
hals *(m).* 1. neck 2. throat.
hals-dichah *(f).* capes (lit.- neck cloths); pl. of hals-duch.
hals-duch *(neu).* cape (lit.-neck cloth).
halvah half (as used in time, example: "halvah zvay" half-til-two or 1:30).
hamlen *(f).* calves; pl. of hamli.
hamli *(neu).* calf.
hammah *(m).* hammer.
hammahra *v.* to hammer.
hammahs *(f).* hammers; pl. of hammah.
hand *(f).* hand.
handla *v.* 1. to deal with 2. to trade.
hand-lumba *(m).* small towel, hand towel.
hand-shreives *(neu).* handwriting.
hangsht *(m).* stud (horse).
hann *(f).* horn.
hanna *(f).* horns; pl. of hann.
hannaysel *(m).* hornet.
hannaysla *(f).* hornets; pl. of hannaysel.
harf *(f).* harp.
harfa *(f).* harps; pl. of harf.
harf-shpeelah *(m).* harp player; pl. of harfa.
hash *(m).* deer.
hassa *v.* to hate.
hatt hard.
hatt-gukkich ugly, (lit.- hard looking).
hatt-heahrich hard of hearing.

hatt-shaffich hardworking.
hatz *(neu)*. heart.
hatza *(f)*. hearts; pl. of hatz.
hatzlich heartfelt.
haufa many (always preceded by "en") (lit. "a pile of").
haufa / peil *(m)*. pile.
hauptmann *(m)*. captain.
hauptmennah *(f)*. captains; pl. of hauptmann.
haus *(neu)*. house.
haus 1. out here 2. escaped.
haus-dach *(neu)*. house roof.
haus-dechah *(f)*. house roofs; pl. of haus-dach.
haus-faddah *(m)*. the father or master of the house.
haus-feddah *(f)*. fathers or masters of the house; pl. of haus-faddah.
haus-haldah *(m)*. steward, householder.
haus-halding *(neu)*. 1. household 2. stewardship.
haus-haldinga *(f)*. households; pl. of haus-halding.
haus-hohf *(m)*. courtyard.
haus-hohfa *(f)*. courtyards; pl. of haus-hohf.
haus-hohld *(neu)*. household.
haus-hohlda *(f)*. households; pl. of haus-hohld.
haut *(neu)*. skin.
havva *v*. to have.
havvah *(m)*. oats.
havvich "I have".
haws *(m)*. rabbit.
hawsa *(f)*. rabbits; pl. of haws.
hawslen *(f)*. baby rabbits,

bunnies; pl. of hawsli.
hawsli *(neu)*. baby rabbit, bunny.
hay *(f)*. a raised location (always proceeded by "in di").
haych *(f)*. height.
haycha *(f)*. heights; pl. of haych.
haychah higher.
haychsht highest.
hayla *v*. to heal.
haym toward home.
haymedah *(f)*. homes; pl. of haymet.
haymet *(f)*. home.
hays hot.
haysa *v*. 1. to invite 2. to call, name 3. to be called, named.
hayva *v*. to hold.
heah toward here.
heahra *v*. 1. to hear 2. to belong.
heahrich 1. "I hear" 2. "I belong" 3. hearing ability (ex. "hatt-heahrich").
hedda *v*. would have.
hee toward there.
heeda *v*. 1. to beware of 2. to take care of.
heedah *(m)*. one who takes care of.
heet *(f)*. hats; pl. of hoot.
heicha *v*. 1. to listen 2. to obey.
heichlah *(m)*. hypocrite.
Heid *(m)*. Gentile.
Heida *(f)*. Gentiles; pl. of Heid.
heidah *(f)*. skins; pl. of haut.
heidich's used only in the phrase "heidich's dawk" (now-a-days").
heifa *(f)*. piles; pl. of haufa.
heifla *v*. to pile together.

heiflen *(f).* little piles; pl. of
heifli.
heifli *(neu).* little pile.
heila *v.* to weep.
Heiland *(m).* the Savior, Jesus
Christ.
heilich holy, sanctified.
heilicha *v.* to sanctify, to make
holy.
heilsam wholesome.
heisah *(f).* houses; pl. of haus.
heit today.
heiyahra *v.* to marry.
hekk *(f).* a branch or twig.
hekka *(f).* branches or twigs; pl.
of hekk.
hekka-putsha *(m).* clump of
bushes.
helfa *v.* to help.
helfah *(m).* helper.
helft *(f).* half (used as a pronoun,
example: "di annah helft"
the other half).
helfta *(f).* halves; pl. of helft.
hell *(f).* believed by some to be a
fiery place of torment (lit.
"common grave of
mankind").
hell *adj.* 1. light, pale color 2.
used to describe a piercing
quality in noise 3. of light,
very bright illumination.
hell-feiyah *(neu).* believed by
some to be fire in a place of
torment (see - hell).
helling *(f).* light and/or its
properties.
hellish pertaining to the belief by
some in a fiery place of
torment (see - hell).
hels *(f).* 1. necks 2. throats; pl. of
hals.
hemm *(neu).* shirt.
hemmah *(f).* shirts; pl. of hemm.
hend *(f).* hands; pl. of hand.
henka *v.* to hang.
henshing *(m).* glove.
heslich extremely, very.
hetza *v.* to incite.
hexah *(m).* sorcerer.
hexahrei *(neu).* sorcery.
hifda *(f).* hips; pl. of hift.
hift *(f).* hip.
hilf *(f).* help, assistance.
himla *(f).* heavens; pl. of
himmel.
himlish heavenly.
Himmel *(m).* heaven.
Himmel-reich *(neu).* kingdom
of heaven.
Himmels-broht *(neu).*
showbread.
Himmels-grefta *(f).* powers of
heaven.
Himmelshafda *(f).* heavenly
establishments; pl. of
himmelshaft.
Himmelshaft *(f).* heavenly
establishment.
hinkel *(neu).* chicken.
hinkla *(f).* chickens; pl. of hinkel.
hinna located to the back.
hinnahnis *(neu).* hindrance.
hinnahnissa *(f).* hindrance; pl.
of hinnahnis.
hinnahsht farthest to the back,
rear.
hinnahsich backward.

hinna-noch behind (example: running behind on time) lagging, after (example: come after that).

hinnich behind.

hitz *(f)*. heat.

hitza *v*. to heat.

hitzich eager, rarin' to go.

hivlich hilly.

hivvel *(m)*. hill.

hivvela *(f)*. hills; pl. of hivvel.

hoah *(f)*. hair.

hoahrich hairy.

hochtzeidah *(m)*. bridegroom.

hochtzich *(f)*. wedding.

hochtzicha *(f)*. weddings; pl. of hohtzich.

hochtzich-mann *(m)*. bridegroom, the man of the wedding.

hochtzich-maydel *(neu)*. bride.

hochtzich-mayt *(f)*. brides; pl. of hochtzich-maydel.

hochtzich-mennah *(f)*. bridegrooms; pl. of hochtzich-mann.

hoffa *v*. to hope.

hofning *(f)*. hope.

hofninga *(f)*. hopes; pl. of hofning.

hohch 1. high 2. non-Amish.

hohch-engel *(m)*. archangel.

hohch-engela *(f)*. archangels; pl. of hohch-engel.

hohch-gacht highly esteemed.

hohch-geboahra of noble birth.

hohch-gelohbt highly praised.

hohchmeedich proud, haughty.

hohchmoot *(m)*. pride.

hohf *(m)*. yard, lawn.

hohfa *(f)*. yards; pl. of hohf.

hohf-mayah *(m)*. lawnmower.

hohf-mayahs *(f)*. lawnmowers; pl. of hohf-mayah.

hohka *(m)*. hook.

hohla *v*. to fetch.

hohna *(m)*. rooster.

hohtzich-leit *(f)*. people in a wedding party.

hoi *(neu)*. hay.

hoi-shrekk *(m)*. grasshopper.

hoi-shrekka *(f)*. grasshoppers; pl. of hoi-shrekk.

hokka *v*. to sit.

hols *(neu)*. wood.

holsich wooden.

hooshta *(m)*. cough.

hoot *(m)*. hat.

hossa *(f)*. pants.

hott *v*. has.

huah *(f)*. harlot, prostitute.

huahra *(f)*. harlots, prostitutes; pl. of huah.

huahra *v*. to indulge in debauchery.

huahrah *(m)*. one who indulges in debauchery.

huahrarei *(neu)*. prostitution.

humla *(f)*. bumble bees; pl. of hummel.

hummel *(m)*. bumble bee.

hund *(m)*. dog.

hunda *v*. to hunt.

hungah *(m)*. hunger.

hungah-nohda *(f)*. famines; pl. hungahs-noht.

hungahrich hungry.

hungahs-noht *(f)*. famine.

hunna down here.
hunnaht hundred.
hunnich *(m)*. honey.
hupsa *v.* to hop.
hutsh *(m)*. colt.

hutsha *(f)*. colts; pl. of hutsh.
hutshlen *(f)*. foals, baby horses;
   pl. of hutshli.
hutshli *(neu)*. foal, baby horse.

I - i

iahra 1. her, hers 2. their, theirs
   3. to her.
ich the pronoun " I ".
im in the.
imblatz instead, in place of.
imma contraction of "im en" (in
   a).
immah always.
in in.
indressa *(f)*. interest (financial).
ingeyya 1. headed in the
   direction of 2. contrary to
   one's will or desire.
innahlich inward.
innen in a.
inseit inside.
insens-awldah *(m)*. incense
   altar.
insens-awldahra *(f)*. incense
   altars; pl. of insens-awldah.
insens-koblen *(f)*. incense
   cups; pl. of insens-kobli.
insens-kobli *(neu)*. incense cup.
invendich on the inside.
is is.
ivvah 1. over, above 2. past 3.
   again.
ivvah-beeya *v.* to bend over.
ivvah-deenah *(m)*. commanding

officer.
ivvah-dekka *v.* to cover over.
ivvahdemm then, at that time.
ivvah-denka *v.* to think over.
ivvah-dimaws extremely,
   beyond measure.
ivvah-drayya *v.* to turn over.
ivvah-dredda *v.* to trespass.
ivvah-dreddah *(m)*. one who
   trespasses.
ivvah-dredding *(f)*. trespass.
ivvah-dreddinga *(f)*.
   trespasses; pl. of ivvah-
   dredding.
ivvah-gebohwa *v.* bent over;
   pp. of ivvah-beeya.
ivvah-gedekt *v.* covered over;
   pp. of ivvah-dekka.
ivvah-gedenkt *v.* thought over;
   pp. of ivvah-denka.
ivvah-gedrayt *v.* turned over;
   pp. of ivvah-drayya.
ivvah-gedredda *v.* trespassed;
   pp. of ivvah-dredda.
ivvah-gegukt *v.* 1. looked over
   2. overlooked 3. disregarded
   purposely; pp. of ivvah-
   gukka.
ivvah-gevva *v.* to give control of

a matter to another.

ivvah-glaykt *v.* overlayed; pp. of ivvah-layya.

ivvah-gloffa *v.* overflowed, run over; pp. of ivvah-lawfa.

ivvah-glost *v.* having left control of a matter to another; pp. of ivvah-lossa.

ivvah-gmacht *v.* made again, remade; pp. of ivvah-macha.

ivvah-gnumma *v.* 1. having taken over 2. overtaken; pp. of ivvah-nemma.

ivvah-gukka *v.* 1. to look over 2. to overlook 3. to disregard purposely.

ivvah-gvunna *v.* 1. won over, persuaded 2. conquered; pp. of ivvah-vinna.

ivvah-hand *(f).* dominance.

ivvah-hemm *(neu).* over shirt, garment you wear over another garment, over coat.

ivvah-hemmah *(f).* overshirts; pl. of ivvah-hemm.

ivvah-ksenna *v.* overseen; pp. of ivvah-sayna.

ivvah-kumma *v.* to overcome.

ivvah-kummah *(m).* overcomer.

ivvah-lawfa *v.* to run over-overflow.

ivvah-layya *v.* to overlay, cover.

ivvah-lossa *v.* to leave control

of a matter to another.

ivvah-macha *v.* to make again, remake.

ivvah-macht *(f).* supreme power.

ivvah-machta *(f).* supreme powers; pl. of ivvah-macht.

ivvah-mechtich *v.* supremely powerful.

ivvah-meiya day after tomorrow.

ivvah-nacht overnight.

ivvah-nemma *v.* 1. to take over 2. to overtake.

ivvahraus to a great extent.

ivvahrawl everywhere.

ivvah-rekk *(f).* heavy outer coats; pl. of ivvah-rokk.

ivvahrich left over.

ivvah-rokk *(m).* 1. a heavy outer coat 2. a thick outer garment worn for a coat.

ivvah-sayna *v.* to oversee.

ivvah-saynah *(m).* overseer, a person who oversees something.

ivvah-setza *v.* 1. to translate 2. to put in charge.

ivvah-vinna *v.* 1. to win over, persuade 2. to conquer.

K - k

kabb *(f)*. cap, headcovering worn by women.

kabba *(f)*. caps, headcoverings worn by women; pl. of kabb.

kaeffah *(m)*. insect, bug.

kaeffahra *(f)*. insects, bugs; pl. of kaeffah.

kaendeld *v*. handled; pp. of haendla.

kakt *v*. hoed; pp. of hakka.

kalb *(neu)*. calf (as used in the Bible).

kald cold.

kalda *v*. kept; pp. of halda.

kall *(m)*. fellow.

kallich lime (mineral, as in limestone).

kals *(f)*. fellows; pl. of kall.

kamayl *(m)*. camel.

kamayla *(f)*. camels; pl. of kamayl.

kamm *(m)*. comb.

kammah *(f)*. bedroom.

kammaht *v*. hammered; pp. of hammahra.

kandel *(f)*. rain gutter on roof.

kandeld *v*. 1. dealt with 2. traded; pp. of handla.

kanka *v*. hung; pp. of henka.

kann *(f)*. 1. kernel of grain 2. vessel for carrying liquid 3. a tin can.

kann *v*. can, to be able to.

kash *(f)*. cherry.

kasha *(f)*. cherries; pl. of kash.

kashta *(m)*. 1. chest 2. bin.

kast *v*. hated; pp. of hassa.

katt *v*. had; pp. of havva.

katz *(f)*. cat.

katz short.

katza *(f)*. cats; pl. of katz.

katzlich recently, a short time ago.

kaunda *v*. to count.

kawfa *v*. to buy.

kawf-haus *(neu)*. market building, market place, a store, a place where you can buy items.

kawf-heisah *(f)*. market buildings, market places; pl. of kawf-haus.

kawf-leit *(f)*. merchants, people that you can buy item from.

kawla *v*. to call on the phone.

kayfah *(m)*. merchant, a person that you can buy items from.

kayld *v*. healed; pp. of hayla.

kaynich *(m)*. king.

kaynicha *(f)*. kings; pl. of kaynich.

kaynich-eah *(f)*. majesty.

kaynich-reich *(neu)*. kingdom.

kaynich-shteel *(f)*. thrones; pl. of kaynich-shtool.

kaynich-shtool *(m)*. throne, a king's chair where he sits to rule.

kaynichs-sayna *(f)*. princes,

sons of the king; pl. of
kaynichs-sohn.

kaynichs-sohn *(m)*. prince, the
son of the king.

kays *(m)*. cheese.

kaysa *v*. 1. invited 2. named,
called 3. having been named
or called; pp. of haysa.

keah *(f)*. car.

keahb *(f)*. baskets; pl. of koahb.

keahb-foll *(f)*. baskets full; pl.
of koahb-foll.

keahra *(f)*. cars; pl. of keah.

keahra *v*. to sweep.

keaht *v*. 1. heard 2. belonged;
pp. of heahra.

kebb *(f)*. heads; pl. of kobb.

kebba *v*. to behead.

kedda *(f)*. chains; pl. of kett.

kee *(f)*. cows; pl. of koo.

keel cool.

keela *v*. to cool.

keet *v*. 1. taken heed 2. taken
care of; pp. of heeda.

keicht *v*. 1. listened 2. obeyed;
pp. of heicha.

keidel *(m)*. wedge.

keidla *(f)*. wedges; pl. of keidel.

keifeld *v*. piled together; pp. of
heifla.

keild *v*. wept; pp. of heila.

keilicht *v*. sanctified, made holy;
pp. of heilicha.

keishheit *(f)*. chastity.

keiyaht *v*. married; pp. of
heiyahra.

keldah colder.

keldsht coldest.

kellah *(m)*. basement, celler.

kellahs *(f)*. basements, cellers;
pl. of kellah.

kelvah *(f)*. calves; pl. of kalb (as
used in the Bible).

kemma *v*. to comb.

kemmahlen *(f)*. closets; pl. of
kemmahli.

kemmahli *(neu)*. closet.

kemmahra *(f)*. bedrooms; pl.
of kammah.

kemmahrah *(m)*. eunuch.

kend *v*. would be able to.

kenda *v*. could.

kenn none, not any (used with a
noun).

kenna *v*. to recognize or know
someone or something.

kens none, not any.

keshtlich precious.

kesla *(f)*. kettles, pots; pl. of
kessel.

keslen *(f)*. small pots; pl. of kesli.

kesli *(neu)*. small pot.

kessel *(m)*. kettle, pot.

kett *(f)*. chain.

ketzt *v*. incited; pp. of hetza.

kfalla *v*. fallen, fell; pp. of falla.

kfanga *v*. caught; pp. of fanga.

kfast *v*. having filled a container;
pp. of fassa.

kfaydeld *v*. threaded; pp. of
faydla.

kfayld *v*. pp. of fayla.

kfeahbt *v*. colored usually by
using dye; pp. of feahva.

kfeahlich dangerous.

kfeedaht *v*. fed; pp. of feedra.

kfeel *(neu)*. 1. feeling or sensation
2. good or bad will in a

group.

kfeelah *(f)*. feelings or sensations; pl. of kfeel.

kfeeld *v.* felt; pp. of feela.

kfeicht *v.* feared, afraid; pp. of feicha.

kfeild *v.* filed; pp. of feila.

kfeiyaht *v.* fired (lost job); pp. of feiyahra.

kfellich approved of.

kfengnis *(neu)*. jail.

kfengnissa *(f)*. jails; pl. of kfengnis.

kfiaht *v.* led; pp. of fiahra.

kfikkaht *v.* 1. calculated 2. planned on; pp. of fikkahra.

kfild *v.* filled; pp. of filla.

kfingaht *v.* having fingered something, touched with the fingers; pp. of fingahra.

kfircht *v.* feared (as used in the Bible); pp. of firchta.

kfisht *v.* fished; pp. of fisha.

kfladdaht *v.* having flapped vigorously; pp. of fladra.

kflamd *v.* flared up, flamed, blazed; pp. of flamma.

kflikt *v.* mended; pp. of flikka.

kfloaht *v.* floored, surprised; pp. of floahra.

kflochta *v.* woven; pp. of flechta.

kflohwa *v.* flew; pp. of fleeya.

kflucht *v.* swore, cursed; pp. of flucha.

kfoah *(f)*. danger.

kfoahra *(f)*. dangers; pl. of kfoah.

kfoahra *v.* 1. drove 2. rode 3. hauled; pp. of foahra.

kfochta *v.* fought; pp. of fechta.

kfoddaht *v.* 1. required 2. demanded; pp. of foddahra / fodra.

kfolkt *v.* followed; pp. of folya.

kfrays *(neu)*. debris, litter, rubbish.

kfressa *v.* 1. having eaten (animals only) 2. having overeaten 3. having eaten too fast or impolitely 4. devoured; pp. of fressa.

kfroahra *v.* froze; pp. of friahra.

kfrohkt *v.* asked; pp. of frohwa.

kfroit *v.* rejoiced; pp. of froiya.

kfunna *v.* found; pp. of finna.

kfussaht *v.* 1. having filled the air with dust or lint 2. snowed; pp. of fussahra.

kich *(f)*. kitchen.

kicha *(f)*. kitchens; pl. of kich.

kikka *v.* to kick.

kind *(neu)*. child.

kindish childish, silly.

kinnah *(f)*. children; pl. of kind.

kinnah-eahbshaft *(f)*. inheritance given to your children.

kinnah-eahbshafta *(f)*. inheritances given to children; pl. of kinnah-eahbshaft.

kins-kind *(f)*. grandchild.

kins-kinnah *(f)*. grandchildren; pl. of kins-kind.

kisht *(f)*. chest.

kishta *(f)*. chests; pl. of kisht.

kissa *v.* to kiss.

kissi *(neu)*. pillow.

kissis *(f)*. pillows; pl. of kissi.
kitzla *v*. to tickle.
kitzlich ticklish.
kitzt *v*. heated; pp. of. hitza.
klennah *(m)*. calander.
kliah clear.
kliahra *v*. to clear.
klinglich tinkling.
koahb *(m)*. basket.
koahb-foll *(m)*. basket full.
kobb *(m)*. head.
kobb-dichah *(f)*. scarves, lit.
    head cloth; pl. of kobb-
    duch.
kobb-duch *(neu)*. scarf (lit.-
    head cloth).
kobb-feddahsht headfirst.
koblen *(f)*. cups; pl. of kobli.
kobli *(neu)*. cup.
kocha *v*. to cook.
koft *v*. hoped; pp. of hoffa.
kohl *(f)*. coal.
kohla *(f)*. coals; pl. of kohl.
kohld *v*. fetched; pp. of hohla.
kohva *v*. held; pp. of hayva.
kokt *v*. sat; pp. of hokka.
kolfa *v*. helped; pp. of helfa.
kollah *(m)*. color.
kollahra *v*. to color.
kollahs *(f)*. colors; pl. of kollah.
kolva *(m)*. ear or cob of corn.
koo *(f)*. cow.
koon *(m)*. racoon.
koshta *v*. to cost.
koshtaht *(m)*. custard.
koshtboah costly.
kotz *(m)*. vomit.
kotza *v*. to vomit.
krohn *(m)*. crown.

krohna *v*. to crown.
ksaddeld *v*. saddled; pp. of
    sadla.
ksalbt *v*. anointed; pp. of salba.
ksammeld *v*. gathered; pp. of
    samla.
ksawt *v*. said; pp. of sawwa.
ksaykend *v*. blessed; pp. of
    saykna.
ksaykt *v*. sawn; pp. of sayya.
ksayt *v*. sown, as in sown seeds;
    pp. of sayya.
kseddeld *v*. settled; pp. of sedla.
kseend *v*. separated by passing
    through a sieve; pp. of
    seena.
kseikt *v*. taken care of; pp. of
    seiya.
ksenna *v*. seen, saw; pp. of
    sayna.
ksetz *(neu)*. 1. law 2. the Mosaic
    Law.
ksetza *(f)*. laws; pl. of ksetz.
ksetz-brechah *(m)*. breaker of
    the law, one who breaks the
    law.
ksetz-gevvah *(m)*. law giver.
ksetzt *v*. set; pp. of setza.
ksetzt 1. appointed, set 2. heavy-
    set.
ksha *(neu)*. 1. dish 2. harness.
kshaffa created.
kshaft *v*. worked; pp. of shaffa.
ksharra *(f)*. 1. dishes 2.
    harnesses; pl. of ksha.
kshatt *v*. 1. mattered 2. harmed 3.
    scratched over the surface 4.
    scraped or raked; pp. of
    shadda.

(m) = da   (f) = di   (neu) = es   83

kshaufeld *v.* shoveled; pp. of shaufla.

kshauft *v.* sharpened; pp. of shaufa.

kshaumd *v.* foamed; pp. of shauma.

kshawbt *v.* 1. scraped with a scraper 2. to have scaled a fish; pp. of shawva.

kshayft *v.* shaved; pp. of shayfa.

kshayld *v.* peeled; pp. of shayla.

kshebt *v.* scooped or shoveled; pp. of shebba.

ksheft *(neu).* work, deed.

kshefta *(f).* works, deeds; pl. of ksheft.

ksheind *v.* 1. shined 2. appeared, seemed, looked; pp. of sheina.

ksheit reasonable, moderate.

kshemd *v.* 1. having felt embarrassment or shame 2. having felt shy; pp. of shemma.

kshenk *(neu).* gift.

kshenka *(f).* gifts; pl. of kshenk.

kshenkah-geld *(neu).* donation, offering, gifts of money.

kshenkt *v.* 1. given a gift 2. pardoned; pp. of shenka.

kshicht *(f).* 1. happening 2. story.

kshichta *(f).* happenings, stories; pl. of kshicht.

kshiddeld *v.* shaken; pp. of shidla.

kshikt *v.* sent; pp. of shikka.

kshkaeddaht *v.* scattered; pp. of shkaedra.

kshkayt *v.* skated; pp. of shkayda.

kshkibt *v.* skipped; pp. of shkibba.

kshkribbeld *v.* scribbled; pp. of shkribla.

kshkrobt *v.* scrubbed; pp. of shkrobba.

kshlacht *v.* slaughtered or butchered an animal; pp. of shlachta.

kshlaebt *v.* slapped; pp. of shlaebba.

kshlauwa *v.* having hit; pp. of shlauwa.

kshlawdaht *v.* slaugthered; pp. of shlawdra.

kshlayft *v.* dragged; pp. of shlayfa.

kshlecht *(neu).* 1. generation 2. ethnic group.

kshlechtah *(f).* 1. generations 2. ethnic groups; pl. of kshlecht.

kshlekt *v.* licked with the tongue; pp. of shlekka.

kshlibt *v.* slipped; pp. of shlibba.

kshlicha *v.* moved stealthily; pp. of shleicha.

kshlohfa *v.* slept; pp. of shlohfa.

kshlohsa *v.* has hailed; pp. of shlohsa.

kshlossa *v.* locked; pp. of shleesa.

kshlukt *v.* swallowed; pp. of shlukka.

kshmakk *(m).* scent, smell.

kshmakka *(f).* scents, smells; pl.

of kshmakk.

kshmakt *v.* smelled; pp. of
shmakka.

kshmatzt *v.* hurt or pained; pp.
of shmatza.

kshmaycheld *v.* having
flattered or fawned upon,
looked for favor; pp. of
shmaychla.

kshmeild *v.* smiled; pp. of
shmeila.

kshmissa *v.* thrown; pp. of
shmeisa.

kshmohkt *v.* smoked; pp. of
shmohka.

kshmutzt *v.* greased; pp. of
shmutza.

kshnaebt *v.* snapped; pp. of
shnaebba.

kshnauft *v.* breathed; pp. of
shnaufa.

kshnayt *v.* snowed; pp. of
shnayya.

kshneekt *v.* sneaked; pp. of
shneeka.

kshneffeld *v.* whittled; pp. of
shnefla.

kshneikst *v.* snored; pp. of
shneiksa.

kshnidda *v.* having cut; pp. of
shneida.

kshoahra *v.* shorn, to have cut
with a scissors; pp. of
sheahra.

kshohva *v.* pushed or shoved;
pp. of sheeva.

kshokkeld *v.* rocked; pp. of
shokla.

kshossa *v.* shot; pp. of sheesa.

kshpalda *v.* having been split;
pp. of shpalda.

kshpassich strange, unusual.

kshpautzt *v.* spit; pp. of
shpautza.

kshpeaht *v.* 1. spared from
death, pain, etc. 2. lent 3.
had in excess; pp. of
shpeahra.

kshpeeld *v.* played; pp. of
shpeela.

kshpeest *v.* speared; pp. of
shpeesa.

kshpeiaht *v.* felt; pp. of shpiaht.

kshpeit *v.* regretted; pp. of
shpeida.

kshpeld *v.* 1. pinned 2. spelled;
pp. of shpella.

kshpend *v.* spent; pp. of
shpenda.

kshpoaht *v.* having used
sparingly or frugally; pp. of
shpoahra.

kshpott *v.* mocked; pp. of
shpodda.

kshprunga *v.* having run, ran;
pp. of shpringa.

kshpukk *(m).* a spook, believed
to be a ghost.

kshpukka *(f).* spooks, believed
to be ghosts; pl. of kshpukk.

kshpukkich spooky, eerie,
scary.

kshpunna *v.* spun; pp. of
shpinna.

kshraubt *v.* screwed; pp. of
shrauva.

kshrivva *v.* written, wrote; pp.
of shreiva.

kshtambt *v.* stamped, trampled; pp. of shtamba.

kshtanna *v.* stood; pp. of shtay.

kshtatt *v.* stirred; pp. of shtadda.

kshtatzt *v.* stumbled; pp. of shtatza.

kshtauva *v.* died; pp. of shtauva.

kshtaynicht *v.* stoned; pp. of shtaynicha.

kshteaht *v.* started; pp. of shteahra.

kshtebt *v.* stepped; pp. of shtebba.

kshteibaht *v.* 1. braced 2. resisted; pp. of shteibahra.

kshteld *v.* 1. having set or placed an object 2. appointed a date or time; pp. of shtella.

kshtend *v.* beared or suffered; pp. of shtenda.

kshtikt *v.* stuck, adhered; pp. of shtikka.

kshtobt *v.* stopped; pp. of shtobba.

kshtocha *v.* 1. pricked or pierced 2. stung; pp. of shtecha.

kshtoddit *v.* studied; pp. of shtodya.

kshtoft *v.* stuffed; pp. of shtoffa.

kshtohla *v.* stolen; pp. of shtayla.

kshtohsa *v.* 1. cast or thrown 2. thrust 3. taken offense; pp. of shtohsa.

kshtokka *v.* 1. inserted 2. stuck, adhered 3. persevered; pp. of shtekka / shtikka.

kshtolbaht *v.* stumbled; pp. of shtolbahra.

kshtreecha *v.* stroked; pp. of shtreicha.

kshtrekt *v.* stretched; pp. of shtrekka.

kshtribt *v.* stripped; pp. of shtribba.

kshtridda *v.* battled; pp. of shtreida.

kshtrohft *v.* punished; pp. of shtrohfa.

kshtroit *v.* 1. scattered 2. having spread bedding for livestock; pp. of shtroiya.

kshtunka *v.* stunk; pp. of shtinka.

kshveah *(f).* a boil or sore.

kshveahra *(f).* boils or sores; pl. of kshveah.

kshvengd *v.* rinsed; pp. of shvenga.

kshvetz *(neu)* 1. manner of talking 2. rumor.

kshvetzah *(f).* rumors; pl. of kshvetz.

kshvetzt *v.* talked; pp. of shvetza.

kshvilla *v.* to swell.

kshvind quickly.

kshvitzt *v.* perspired; pp. of shvitza.

kshvoahra *v.* 1. vowed, made an oath 2. swore or made a promise; pp. of shveahra.

kshvulla *v.* swollen; pp. of kshvilla.

kshvumma *v.* swum, swam; pp. of shvimma.

kshwoahmd *v.* swarmed; pp. of shwoahma.

ksicht *(neu)*. face.
ksichtah *(f)*. faces; pl. of ksicht.
ksift *v.* sifted; pp. of sifta.
ksindicht *v.* sinned; pp. of
  sindicha.
ksitzt *v.* seated; pp. of sitza.
ksoffa *v.* intoxicated, drunk; pp.
  of saufa.
ksoffaht *v.* suffered; pp. of
  soffahra.
ksoot *v.* 1. suited 2. pleased; pp.
  of sooda.
ksucht *v.* sought; pp. of sucha.
ksukkeld *v.* sucked; pp. of sukla.
ksund healthy.
ksundhayt *(f)*. health.
ksunga *v.* sung; pp. of singa.
kuaht *v.* indulged in

debaucherey; pp. of huahra.
kubbah *(neu)*. copper.
kubbah-shmidda *(f)*.
  coppersmiths; pl. of kubbah-
  shmitt.
kubbah-shmitt *(m)*.
  coppersmith.
kucha *(m)*. cake.
kumma *v.* to come, came.
kumrawda *(f)*. comrades; pl. of
  kumrawt (#1 def.).
kumrawt *(m)*. 1. comrade 2. gear
  wheel.
kumreddah *(f)*. gear wheels; pl.
  of kumrawt (#2 def.).
kunt *v.* hunted; pp. of hunda.
kupst *v.* hopped; pp. of hupsa.
kuss *(m)*. kiss.

L - l

labbich naughty.
lacha *v.* to laugh.
ladann *(f)*. lantern.
ladanna *(f)*. lanterns; pl. of
  ladann.
ladda *(f)*. wood strips; pl. of latt.
lambah *(neu)*. lumber.
lamm *(neu)*. lamb (as used in the
  Bible).
land *(neu)*. land.
landshaft *(neu)*. 1. region 2.
  landscape, topography.
landshafta *(f)*. landscapes; pl. of
  landshaft.
lands-leit *(f)*. native inhabitants,
  people who are native to the

land.
lang long.
langa *v.* to reach.
lanna *v.* 1. to learn 2. to teach.
lanning *(f)*. 1. teaching or
  doctrine 2. education.
lanninga *(f)*. 1. teachings or
  doctrines 2. educations; pl.
  of lanning.
lasht *(f)*. 1. burden 2. reluctance
  to perform a task.
lashta *(f)*. burdens; pl. of lasht.
latt *(f)*. wood strip.
latt a lot, many.
lauda *v.* to sound or appear to
  someone.

laut 1. loud 2. does sound, sounds "Sell laut goot".

lawb *(neu)*. foliage, leaf.

lawb-haus *(neu)*. ceremonial hut built of branches.

lawb-heisah *(f)*. ceremonial huts built of branches; pl. of lawb-haus.

lawda *(f)*. coffins; pl. of lawt.

lawda *(m)*. shelf.

lawda *v.* to load.

lawfa *v.* to walk.

lawt *(f)*. coffin.

lawva *(f)*. leaves; pl. of lawb.

lawyah *(m)*. lawyer.

layb *(m)*. 1. loaf 2. lion.

laydah *(f)*. ladder.

laydich bored, tired of, fed up.

laydra *(f)*. ladders; pl. of laydah.

layna *v.* 1. to borrow 2. to lend.

laynich alone.

layns-leit *(f)*. money lenders, people who lend money.

laysa *v.* to read.

laysah *(m)*. one who reads.

layva *(f)*. lions; pl. of layb #2 def.

layva *(neu)*. life.

layva *v.* to live.

layves-buch *(neu)*. Book of Life.

layves-krohn *(m)*. crown of life.

layves-lang entire life span.

layves-lawf *(m)*. walk of life, conduct.

layves-mawl *(neu)*. nourishment.

layves-zeit *(f)*. lifetime.

layya *v.* to lay.

leah empty.

leahra *v.* 1. to pour 2. to teach.

leahrah *(m)*. 1. teacher 2. preacher.

leahrah emptier.

leahsht emptiest.

lebbish lukewarm.

lechah *(f)*. holes; pl. of loch.

leddah *(neu)*. 1. leather 2. made of leather.

leddich not married, unattached.

leeb dear, beloved, love.

leebensmawl *(neu)*. religious love feast.

leeblich loving.

leedah *(f)*. songs; pl. of leet.

leek *(m)*. lie, untruth.

leet *(neu)*. song.

leeva *v.* to love.

leevah *(m)*. lever.

leevah rather, preferably.

leevahra *(f)*. levers; pl. of leevah.

leevich loving.

leeya *(f)*. lies, untruths; pl. of leek.

leeya *v.* to lie, tell an untruth.

leeyah *(m)*. one who lies, liar.

leffel *(m)*. spoon.

lefla *(f)*. spoons; pl. of leffel.

leflen *(f)*. teaspoons; pl. of lefli.

lefli *(neu)*. teaspoon.

leftz *(f)*. lip.

leftza *(f)*. lips; pl. of left.

leib *(m)*. body.

leiblich pertaining to the body.

leicht *(m)*. funeral.

leicht 1. light weight, not heavy 2. light colored.

leichta *(f)*. funerals; pl. of leicht.
leicht-hatzich lighthearted, unconcerned, insincere.
leicht-leedah *(f)*. funeral-songs; pl. of leicht-leet.
leicht-leet *(neu)*. funeral song.
leida *v*. to suffer.
lein *(f)*. line.
leina *(f)*. lines; pl. of lein.
leit *(m)*. people.
leivah *(f)*. bodies; pl. of leib.
leiya *v*. to lie, assume a prone position.
lemmah *(f)*. lambs (as used in the Bible) ; pl. of lamm.
lendah *(f)*. lands; pl. of land.
leng *(f)*. length.
lengah longer.
lengsht longest.
leshtah-diah *(neu)*. beast that blasphemes.
leshtah-diahra *(f)*. beasts that blaspheme; pl. of leshtah-diah.
leshtah-nayma *(f)*. names of blasphemy; pl. of leshtah-nohma.
leshtah-nohma *(m)*. name of blasphemy.
leshtahra *v*. to blaspheme.
leshtahrah *(m)*. one who blasphemes.
leshtah-vadda *(f)*. words of blasphemy; pl. of leshtah-vatt.
leshtah-vatt *(neu)*. word of blasphemy.
letsht last.
letz wrong.

levendich alive (formal as used in the Bible).
levvah *(f)*. liver.
levvich alive.
licht *(neu)*. light.
lichtah *(f)*. lights; pl. of licht.
licht-ayl *(neu)*. kerosine.
licht-shtaend *(m)*. lightstand.
licht-shtaenda *(f)*. lightstands; pl. of licht-shtaend.
liknah *(m)*. one who lies, liar.
liknah *(f)*. liars; pl. of liknah.
lilya-blumm *(f)*. lily.
lilya-blumma *(f)*. lilies; pl. of lilya-blumm.
lings 1. on or toward the left 2. left-handed.
linnen-duch *(neu)*. linen fabric.
loch *(neu)*. hole.
lohb *(neu)*. praise.
lohb-breef *(m)*. letter of praise.
lohb-breefa *(f)*. letters of praise; pl. of lohb-breef.
lohb-leedah *(f)*. songs of praise; pl. of lohb-leet.
lohb-leet *(neu)*. song of praise.
lohb-opfah *(neu)*. sacrifice of praise.
lohb-opfahra *(f)*. sacrifices of praise; pl. of lohb-opfah.
lohm lame.
lohn *(m)*. wages, recompense.
lohs *(f)*. sow, female pig.
lohs *(neu)*. the portion that is received as a result of drawing lots.
lohs 1. loose 2. (suffix) devoid of, lacking.
lohsa *(f)*. sows, female pigs; pl.

of lohs.

loht *(f)*. load.

lohva *v.* to praise.

lokka *v.* 1. to call an animal 2. to leave someone or something behind (contrast with "falossa").

lossa *v.* to let.

luft *(f)*. air.

luftich airy, breezy.

lumba *(m)*. towel.

lummahrich limber, flexible, limp.

lusht *(f)*. 1. lust 2. desire.

lushta *(f)*. 1. lusts 2. desires; pl. of lusht.

lushta *v.* 1. to lust 2. to desire.

lushtahrei *(f)*. 1. immorality 2. covetousness.

lushtboah lustful.

lushtboahkeit *(f)*. lustfulness.

M - m

ma 1. one (personal pronoun, nom. case) 2. short, unstressed form of "miah" 3. a, an (dative case).

macha *v.* 1. to make 2. to sound 3. used in idioms "uf macha"(to open) "zu macha"(to close) "um macha" (to cut down).

macht *(f)*. power, authority, might.

madda *(f)*. mares, female horses; pl. of mau.

maddah *(m)*. murderer (not common).

maddahrei *(f)*. murderous actions.

maemm *(f)*. mom.

maemma *(f)*. moms; pl. of maemm.

malawn *(f)*. melon.

malawna *(f)*. melons; pl. of malawn.

mammi *(f)*. grandmother, older lady.

mammis *(f)*. grandmothers, older ladies; pl. of mammi.

mandel *(m)*. robe.

mandela *(f)*. robes; pl. of mandel.

mann *(m)*. 1. man 2. husband.

mannich many.

manskal *(m)*. man, male person.

manskals *(f)*. men, male persons; pl. of manskal.

mansleit *(f)*. men folk.

manudda *(f)*. minutes; pl. of manutt.

manutt *(f)*. minute.

matt weak.

mau *(f)*. mare, female horse.

maul *(neu)*. mouth.

maula *v.* to argue.

maulbeahra *(f)*. mulberry.

maul-foll *(neu)*. mouthful.

mavvah *(f)*. foundation of a wall.

mavvahra *(f)*. foundations of walls; pl. of mavvah.

mawda *(f)*. 1. servant maids 2. hired maids; pl. of mawt.

mawk shall, may.

mawla *v.* to grind.

mawna *(f)*. mane.

maws *(f)*. 1. a measure 2. temperance (used in expression "ivvah di maws").

mawt *(f)*. 1. servant maid 2. hired maid.

mawwa *(f)*. stomach.

mawwa *adj.* gaunt, emaciated.

may more.

maydel *(neu)*. girl.

mayl *(neu)*. flour.

mayna *v.* 1. to mean 2. to have an opinion 3. to be conceited "sich mayna".

mayning *(f)*. 1. meaning 2. opinion.

mayninga *(f)*. 1. meanings 2. opinions; pl. of mayning.

mays except.

mayt *(f)*. girls; pl. of maydel.

maytlen *(f)*. little girls; pl. of maytli.

maytli *(neu)*. little girl.

mayya *v.* to mow.

mechta might, would perhaps.

mechtich strong, mighty.

meeklich / mayklich possible, capable of happening or being done.

meel *(f)*. grinding mill.

meela *(f)*. grinding mills; pl. of meel.

meel-shtay *(m)*. grinding wheel, grinding stone.

meet tired.

mei my.

meik *(m)*. mark.

meika *v.* to mark.

meiks *(f)*. marks; pl. of meik.

meil *(f)*. mile.

meila *(f)*. miles; pl. of meil.

meilah *(f)*. mouths; pl. of maul.

meim my (dative case).

mein mine.

meina my (plural).

meind *(f)*. mind, memory.

meinda *v.* 1. to remember 2. to mind, to care.

meishtah *(f)*. master.

meishtahra *(f)*. masters; pl. of meishtah.

meislen *(f)*. mice; pl. of meisli.

meisli *(neu)*. mouse.

meiya tomorrow, morning - as in "da neksht meiya".

meiya-roht red sky in the morning (lit. morning-red).

meiyet *(m)*. morning.

meiyets *(f)*. mornings; pl. of meiyet.

melka *v.* to milk.

mennah *(f)*. 1. men 2. husbands; pl. of mann.

mensh *(m)*. human.

mensha *(f)*. humans; pl. of mensh.

menshlich pertaining to human reasoning.

mensht most.

mesra *(f)*. knives; pl. of messah.

messa *v.* to measure.

messah *(neu)*. knife.
miah 1. we 2. me (dative case).
mich me.
mich-selvaht myself.
middawk *(f)*. noon period, mid-
day.
middawk *(neu)*. noon meal,
lunch.
middelsht middle, most
centered.
midna contraction of "mitt eena"
(with them).
miklen *(f)*. gnats, very small
flies; pl. of mikli.
mikli *(neu)*. gnat, very small fly.
millich *(f)*. milk.
mint-blansa *(f)*. mint plant.
misht *(f)*. 1. manure.
misht *v.* must ("du misht").
missa *v.* must ("miah missa").
mista *v.* would have to.
mitt with.
mitt-dayl *(neu)*. similar fate or
portion.
mitt-dayla *v.* to share.
mitt-daylah *(m)*. 1. one who
shares the same fate 2. one
who shares.
mitt-daylich willing to share.
mitt-deenah *(m)*. fellow servant
or minister.
mitt-eahvah *(m)*. fellow heir.
mitt-eldishtah *(m)*. fellow
elder.
mitt-eldishti *(f)*. fellow elders;
pl. of mitt-eldishtah.
mitt-gedayld *v.* shared; pp. of
mitt-dayla.
mitt-glidda *v.* sympathized; pp.

of mitt-leida.
mitt-gnecht *(m)*. fellow servant
or slave.
mitt-gnechta *(f)*. fellow
servants; pl. of mitt-gnecht.
mitt-helfah *(m)*. fellow helper.
mitt-leida *v.* to sympathize.
mitt-nacht *(f)*. midnight.
mitt-nannah all together.
mitt-shtreidah *(f)*. fellow
soldier.
mitvoch *(m)*. Wednesday (lit.-
mid-week).
mitvocha *(f)*. Wednesdays; pl. of
mitvoch.
mohl *(neu)*. one repetition, one
time.
moll once, once upon a time.
moonada *(f)*. months; pl. of
moonet.
Moondawk *(m)*. Monday.
Moondawks / Moondawwa
(f). Mondays; pl. of
Moondawk.
moonet *(m)*. month.
moot *(f)*. 1. mood 2. enthusiasm 3.
courage.
moshmalawn *(f)*. cantaloupe,
muskmelon.
moshmalawna *(f)*. cantaloupes,
muskmelons; pl. of
moshmalawn.
moshtaht *(m)*. mustard.
muddah *(f)*. mother.
muddahra *(f)*. mothers; pl. of
muddah.
muddahs-leib *(f)*. womb.
muddahs-leivah *(f)*. wombs;
pl. of muddah-leib.

mukk *(f)*. fly.
mukka *(f)*. flies; pl. of mukk.
mushtah *(neu)*. pattern.
mushtahra *(f)*. patterns; pl. of

mushtah.
muss *v*. must ("Ich muss").

N - n

na 1. contraction of "eena" (them) 2. a, an (dative case).
nacht *(f)*. night.
nachtmawl *(neu)*. religious communion meal.
nachts at night.
nadda northward, going in the northern direction.
naddish foolish.
nadiahlich 1. carnal, not spiritual 2. natural.
naduah *(m)*. 1. temperament, disposition 2. carnal nature.
naduaht natured, having the disposition of.
naett not.
nah *(m)*. fool.
nakkel / nawwel *(m)*. nail ("nawwel" - common pronunciation).
nakkel-loch *(neu)*. nail hole.
nakkich naked, without clothes.
nakla *v*. to nail.
nambah *(m)*. number.
nambahs *(f)*. numbers; pl. of nambah.
nannah each other.
narra *(f)*. fools; pl. of nah.
nasht *(m)*. branch.
nass wet.

natt *(f)*. north.
natt-eest northeast.
natt-vest northwest.
nau now.
naus toward an outer location.
naws *(f)*. nose.
naws-lechah *(f)*. nostrils; pl. of naws-loch.
naws-loch *(neu)*. nostril.
nay no.
naychah nearer.
nayksht near.
naykshtisht nearest.
nayma *(f)*. names; pl. of nohma.
nayma *v*. to name.
naymlich namely.
nays *(f)*. noses; pl. of naws.
naytz *(m)*. thread.
naytza *(f)*. threads; pl. of naytz.
nayva located at the side.
nayvich beside.
nayya *v*. to sew.
necht *(f)*. nights; pl. of nacht.
nee never (not used alone).
neemols never, not even once.
nee-naett never (used alone).
nei 1. toward an inner location 2. new.
nei-gmacht *v*. 1. made new, renewed 2. built-in.

nein nine.
neina-neintzich ninety-nine.
neind ninth.
neintzich ninety.
neiya new.
neiyetz nowhere.
nekkel / nayyel *(f)*. nails ("nayyel" - common pronunciation).
nekkel-lechah *(f)*. nail holes; pl. of nakkel-loch.
neksht next.
nemma *v.* to take.
nesht *(f)*. branches; pl. of nasht.
nesht *(neu)*. nest.
neshtah *(f)*. nests; pl. of nesht.
nett *(neu)*. net.
netts *(f)*. nets; pl. of nett.
nevlich foggy.
nevvel *(m)*. fog.
niddah low.
niddahrah / nidrah lower ("nidrah" - common pronunciation).
niddahsht lowest.
nientzay ninteen.
nimmand no one.
nimmi no longer, no more.
nivvah toward a location over there.
nix nothing.
no then.
noch 1. yet 2. after 3. another.
nochamohl again.
nochbah *(m)*. neighbor.
nochbahshaft *(f)*. neighborhood.
nochbahshafta *(f)*. neighborhoods; pl. of nochbahshaft.

nochbra *(f)*. neighbors; pl. nochbah.
nochmiddawk in the afternoon.
nohch after, behind, following.
nohch-folya *v.* to follow.
nohch-folyah *(m)*. follower, disciple.
nohch-gmacht *v.* 1. imitated, followed an example 2. followed; pp. of nohch-macha.
nohch-kfolkt *v.* followed; pp. of nohch-folya.
nohch-macha *v.* 1. to imitate, follow an example 2. to follow.
nohch-machah *(m)*. one who follows an example.
nohda *(f)*. 1. necessities 2. seams; pl. of noht.
nohdel *(f)*. needle.
nohdla *(f)*. needles; pl. of nohdel.
nohdvendich necessary.
nohma *(m)*. name.
noht *(f)*. 1. necessity 2. seam.
noodel *(m)*. noodle.
noodla *(f)*. noodles; pl. of noodel.
nuff toward a higher location.
nuftzus upwards.
nunnah toward a lower location.
nunnah-bezawling *(f)*. down payment.
nunnah-bezawlinga *(f)*. down payments; pl. of nunnah-betzawling.

nunnah-glawda *v.* loaded down, burdened; pp. of nunnah-lawda.

nunnah-grand *v.* 1. run down, having become decrepit 2. run down, slandered; pp. of nunnah-ranna.

nunnah-lawda *v.* to load down, burden.

nunnah-ranna *v.* 1. to run down, become decrepit 2. to run down, slander.

O - o

oah *(neu).* ear.

oahm *(m).* arm.

oahm poor.

oahma-geld *(neu).* funds for charity, money for the poor.

oahmoot *(f).* 1. poverty 2. pitiful condition.

oahra *(f).* ears; pl. of oah.

oahrich *(f).* ark.

oahrich very.

oahrichs *(f).* arks; pl. of oahrich.

obsht *(neu).* fruit (not as comman).

offa *(m).* oven, stove.

offa-rau *(neu).* stovepipe.

offenboahring *(f).* 1. revelation 2. Revelation (book of the Bible).

offenboahringa *(f).* revelations; pl. of offenboahring.

oft often, frequent.

ohbayda *v.* to worship.

ohbeeda *v.* to offer.

ohbinna *v.* to tie to a fixed object, to tether.

ohbringa *v.* to incur.

ohdenka *v.* to estimate, esteem.

ohdenkes *(neu).* a remembrance, souvenir.

ohdreffa *v.* to meet.

ohdu *v.* to dress, to put clothes on, to put on.

ohfang *(m).* beginning.

ohfanga *(f).* beginnings; pl. of ohfang.

ohfanga *v.* to begin.

ohften *(f).* breath.

ohganga *v.* 1. happened, occurred 2. ignited 3. lit up; pp. of ohgay.

ohgay *v.* 1. to happen or occur 2. to ignite 3. to light.

ohgebayda *v.* worshipped; pp. of ohbayda.

ohgebodda *v.* offered; pp. of ohbeeda.

ohgebrocht *v.* incurred; pp. of ohbringa.

ohgebunna *v.* tied to a fixed object, tethered; pp. of ohbinna.

ohgedroffa *v.* met; pp. of ohdreffa.

ohgedu *v.* put on, having put clothes on, dressed; pp. of ohdu.

ohgeglawkt *v.* accused; pp. of ohglawwa.

ohgeglobt *v.* knocked, requested entrance; pp. of ohglobba.

ohgegmohnd *v.* reminded; pp. of ohgmohna.

ohgegukt *v.* looked at; pp. of ohgukka.

ohgezowwa *v.* 1. having put on or donned (clothing) 2. stretched over a frame 3. having drawn moisture; pp. of ohzeeya.

ohglawwa *v.* to accuse.

ohglaykt *v.* laid on (hands or clothes); pp. of ohlayya.

ohglobba *v.* to knock on a door, request entrance.

ohglost *v.* 1. pretended, let on 2. left on (light, clothes, etc.); pp. of ohlossa.

ohgmacht *v.* 1. having lit a fire or lamp 2. switched on a light 3. gained another's favor; pp. of ohmacha.

ohgmohna *v.* to remind.

ohgnaymd *v.* 1. well accepted 2. highly honored.

ohgnumma *v.* 1. accepted 2. adopted 3. endured patiently; pp. of ohnemma.

ohgraykt *v.* touched (not common); pp. of ohrayya.

ohgroofa *v.* called upon; pp. of ohroofa.

ohgukka *v.* to look at.

ohgunnish envious.

ohgunsht *(m).* envy.

oh'halda *v.* to continue.

oh'hayva *v.* to adhere to steadfastly.

oh'heicha *v.* to listen to obediently.

oh'henka *v.* to hang onto.

ohkalda *v.* continued; pp. of oh'halda / onhalda.

ohkanka *v.* hung onto; pp. of oh'henka.

ohkeicht *v.* listened to obediently; pp. of oh'heicha.

ohkfanga *v.* began; pp. of ohfanga.

ohkohva *v.* adhered to steadfastly; pp. of oh'hayva.

ohksenna *v.* esteemed, rated; pp. of ohsayna.

ohkshikt *v.* acted or behaved; pp. of ohshikka.

ohkshpritzt *v.* having sprinkled or sprayed an object with liquid; pp. of ohshpritza.

ohkshtokka *v.* 1. having lit a fire of lamp 2. infected another with a contagious sickness; pp. of ohshtekka.

ohlayya *v.* to lay on - hands or clothes.

ohlossa *v.* 1. to pretend 2. to leave on (a light, clothes, etc.).

ohmacha *v.* 1. to light a fire or lamp (to make or turn on) 2. to switch on a light 3. to gain another's favor.

ohnemma *v.* 1. to accept 2. to adopt 3. to endure patiently.

ohrayya *v.* to touch (not common).

ohroofa *v.* to call upon.

ohsayna *v.* to esteem, to rate.

ohshikka *v.* to act or behave.

ohshpritza *v.* to sprinkle or spray an object with liquid.

Ohshtah 1. Passover 2. a holiday that some religions celebrate - Easter.

Ohshtah-fesht *(neu).* Passover feast.

Ohshtah-lamm *(neu).* sacrificial Passover lamb.

ohshtekka *v.* 1. to light a fire or lamp (to light with a matchstick) 2. to infect another with a contagious sickness, exposed to.

ohveda *(f).* evenings; pl. of ohvet.

ohvet *(m).* evening.

ohvet-essa *(neu).* evening meal.

ohvet-roht evening red.

ohzeeya *v.* 1. to put on, to don 2. to stretch over a frame 3. to draw moisture.

oi *(neu).* egg.

oiyah *(f).* eggs; pl. of oi.

onhalda *v.* to continue.

oowah *(f).* clock.

oowahra *(f).* clocks; pl. of oowah.

opfah *(neu).* sacrifice.

opfah-awldah *(m).* altar used to sacrifice upon.

opfah-awldahra *(f).* altars used to sacrifice upon; pl. of opfah-awldah.

opfah-lamm *(neu).* sacrificial lamb.

opfah-lemmah *(f).* sacrificial lambs; pl. of opfah-lamm.

opfahra *(f).* sacrifices; pl. of opfah.

opfahra *v.* to sacrifice.

ovva located above.

ovva-druff on top.

ovva-heah from above.

ovvahrichkeida *(f).* governments; pl. of ovvahrichkeit.

ovvahrichkeit *(f).* government.

ovvich above.

ox *(m).* ox.

oxa *(f).* oxen; pl. of ox.

P - p

paddah *(neu).* powder.

palma *(f).* palm tree.

pann *(f).* pan, skillet.

panna *(f).* pans, skillets; pl. of pann.

pannakuch *(f).* pancake.

pannakucha *(f).* pancakes; pl. of pannakuch.

(m) = da   (f) = di   (neu) = es   97

paradees *(f)*. paradise.
pashing *(m)*. peach.
patiklah 1. particular 2.
    especially.
pawda *(f)*. paths; pl. of pawt.
pawt *(f)*. path.
paydahli *(neu)*. parsley.
paynd *(f)*. paint.
payndah *(m)*. painter.
paytsh *(neu)*. page.
paytshes *(f)*. pages; pl. of
    paytsh.
pedla *v*. to peddle.
peepsa *v*. to peep.
peffah *(f)*. pepper.
peffahra *(f)*. peppers; pl. of
    peffah.
peif *(f)*. 1. whistle 2. flute
    (musical instrument) 3. pipe
    used to smoke tobacco.
peifa *v*. to whistle.
peifah *(m)*. one who whistles or
    plays a flute.
peif-shpeelah *(m)*. flute or
    musical pipe player.
peil / haufa *(m)*. pile.
peila *v*. to pile.
petza *v*. to pinch.
pikk *(f)*. pig.
pikka *v*. to pick, to choose.
pikkah *(m)*. beak or bill of a
    bird.
piklen *(f)*. piglets; pl. of pikli.
pikli *(neu)*. piglet.
piks *(f)*. pigs; pl. of pikk.
piktah *(neu)*. picture.
piktahs *(f)*. pictures; pl. of
    piktah.
pinklich in great detail.

pishpahra *v*. to whisper.
pitshah *(m)*. pitcher.
poah pair, couple.
poahbes deliberately, on
    purpose.
poahtsh *(f)*. porch.
poahtsha *(f)*. porches; pl. of
    poahtsh.
pobbi *(m)*. puppy.
pobbis *(f)*. puppies; pl. of pobbi.
poddel *(m)*. puddle.
podla *(f)*. puddles; pl. of poddel.
poffa *v*. to puff.
poffich puffy.
pokk *(f)*. pimple.
pokka *(f)*. pimples; pl. of pokk.
pokkich pimply.
poshta *(m)*. post, pillar.
preeshtah-adning *(f)*. division
    of priests.
preeshtah-adninga *(f)*.
    divisions of priests; pl. of
    preeshtah-adning.
preeshtahshaft *(f)*. priesthood.
preeshtahshafta *(f)*.
    priesthoods; pl. of
    preeshtahshaft.
preeshtahtum *(neu)*.
    priesthood.
preeshtahtumma *(f)*.
    priesthoods; pl. of
    preeshtahtum.
preisa *v*. to praise.
pshuldicha *v*. to accuse.
pshuldicht *v*. accused; pp. of
    pshuldicha.
psuch *(f)*. visitor, guest,
    company.
psucha *v*. to visit.

psuch-leit *(f)*. visitors, people visiting , guests, company.
psunna disposed, minded.
pund *(f)*. pound.

punka *(m)*. point.
pusha *v.* to push.

R - r

rabla *v.* to rattle.
rablen *(f)*. rattles used by baby; pl. of rabli.
rabli *(neu)*. a babys rattle.
rablich noisy, rattling (common use).
radda *(f)*. rats; pl. of ratt.
raekkeda *(f)*. noises (common use); pl. of raekket.
raekket *(f)*. noise (common use).
ratt *(f)*. rat.
rauda-shtekk *(f)*. herb plants; pl. of rauda-shtokk.
rauda-shtokk *(m)*. herb plant.
raulich mischievous.
raus out of.
raus-groofa *v.* called out of; pp. of raus-roofa.
rausha *v.* to make a rushing sound.
raus-roofa *v.* to call out of.
rawm *(m)*. cream.
rawsa *v.* 1. to move energetically 2. to rave 3. to rant or rage.
rawsich 1. energetic 2. raging, uncontrolled.
rawt *(neu)*. wheel.
rawva *v.* to rob.
rawvah *(m)*. robber.
rawvahrei *(f)*. thievery.

raydla *(f)*. measles.
recha *v.* to rake.
recht correct, right (answer).
rechts right (direction).
reddah *(f)*. wheels; pl. of rawt.
reddich *(f)*. radish.
rei in from outside.
reich *(neu)*. kingdom.
reich rich.
reicha *(f)*. kingdoms; pl. of reich.
reichheida *(f)*. richeses; pl. of reichheit.
reichheit *(f)*. riches.
reichlich richly.
reichlichkeida *(f)*. richnesses; pl. of reichlichkeit.
reichlichkeit *(f)*. richness.
reichtum *(neu)*. riches.
reid *(m)*. ride.
reida *v.* to ride.
reidah *(m)*. rider.
reidahs *(f)*. riders; pl. of reidah.
reids *(f)*. rides; pl. of reid.
rein pure.
reinicha *v.* to cleanse, purify.
reiniching *(f)*. purification.
reinichkeit *(f)*. purity.
reisa *v.* to tear.
reiva *v.* 1. to rub 2. to tease.
rekk *(f)*. dresses; pl. of rokk.

(m) = da   (f) = di   (neu) = es   99

renna *v.* to shove or poke.
resayda *(f).* recipes; pl. of resayt.
resayt *(f).* recipe.
revvah *(f).* river.
revvahra *(f).* rivers; pl. of revvah.
reyyah / reyya *(m).* rain.
reyyah-boh *(m).* rainbow.
reyyahra *v.* to rain.
reyyahrich rainy.
riahra *v.* to stir.
richta *v.* to judge.
richtah *(m).* judge.
richtah-dawk *(m).* day of judgement.
richtah-dawwa *(f).* days of judgement; pl. of richtah-dawk.
richtah-shteel *(f).* judgement seats; pl. of richtah-shtool.
richtah-shtool *(m).* judgement seat.
richt-haus *(neu).* judgement hall.
richt-heisah *(f).* judgement halls; pl. of richt-haus.
richtichkeit *(f).* judgement.
richts-blatz *(m).* place of judgement.
richts-bletz *(f).* places of judgement; pl. of richts-blatz.
rind *(neu).* heifer, female milk cow.
rinna *v.* to leak.
rinnah *(f).* heifers, female milk cows; pl. of rind.
rinnich leaky.
rishta *v.* to prepare.

risht-dawk *(m).* day of preparation.
risht-dawwa *(f).* days of preparation; pl. of risht-dawk.
rivvah toward here.
robba *v.* to pluck, to pick (as in pick fruit from a tree).
robbah rubber.
roff rough.
roh raw.
rohda *v.* 1. to advise 2. to counsel 3. to vote.
roht red.
roht-reeb *(f).* redbeet.
roht-reeva *(f).* redbeets; pl. of roht-reeb.
roi *(f).* row.
rokk *(m).* dress.
rokka *(f).* rye.
rolla *v.* to roll.
rollah *(m).* roller.
rollahs *(f).* rollers; pl. of rollah.
roo *(f).* rest.
rooda *(f).* rods, staffs; pl. of root.
roof *(m).* call.
roofa *(f).* calls; pl. of roof.
roofa *v.* to call.
roolah *(m).* 1. ruler (king) 2. ruler (tape measure).
roolahs *(f).* 1. rulers (kings) 2. rulers (tape measures) ; pl. of roolah.
rooshta *v.* to roost.
root *(f).* rod, staff.
roowa *v.* to rest.
roowich calm.
rosht *(m).* rust.
roshtich rusty.

ruff up from below.
ruich quiet, restful.
rumm around.
rumm-heah in the general vicinity.

rund round.
runnah down from above.
runsel *(m)*. wrinkle.
runsla *(f)*. wrinkles; pl. of runsel.

S - s

s / es contraction of 1. it 2. the (neuter form) 3. that, who, which (relative pronoun) 4. there (pronoun used to start a sentence or clause) example: " 'S is feel eahvet fa du.".

sach *(f)*. 1. thing 2. matter.

sacha *(f)*. 1. things 2. matters; pl. of sach.

sadda 1. kinds, types; pl. of satt 2. sort of, kinda.

saddel *(m)*. saddle.

sadla *(f)*. saddles; pl. of saddel.

sadla *v.* to saddle.

saft *(f)*. 1. sap 2. juice.

safta *(f)*. juices; pl. of saft.

sakk *(m)*. sack, bag, pocket.

sakk-dichah *(f)*. sack cloths; pl. of sakk-duch.

sakk-duch *(neu)*. sackcloth.

sakk-glaydah *(f)*. garments made of sackcloth; pl. of sakk-glayt.

sakk-glayt *(neu)*. garment made of sackcloth.

sakk-messah *(neu)*. pocketknife.

salawt *(neu)*. lettuce.

salba *v.* to anoint.

salba-ayl *(neu)*. oil used for anointing.

sals *(m)*. salt.

salsich salty.

samla *v.* to gather.

samling *(f)*. 1. a gathering 2. a collection.

samlinga *(f)*. gatherings; pl. of samling.

samm some.

samm-vayk someway, somehow.

samm-zeit sometime.

Samshdawk *(m)*. Saturday.

sand *(m)*. sand.

sanda *(f)*. sands; pl. of sand.

sandich sandy.

sanftmeedich gentle, meek.

sanftmeedichkeit *(f)*. meekness.

sanftmoot *(f)*. meekness.

satan *(m)*. Satan.

satt 1. kind, type of 2. satiated, full.

sau *(f)*. pig, hog, swine.

sauda south.

saufa *v.* 1. to drink (only used with animals) 2. to drink

alcoholic beverages to an
excess.

saufahrei *(f)*. drunkenness.

saund *(m)*. sound, noise.

saund 1. in good condition,
sound 2. doctrinally correct.

saunds *(f)*. sounds; pl. of saund.

saut *(f)*. the south.

saut-eest southeast.

saut-vest southwest.

sauvah clean.

savvah sour.

savvah-dayk *(m)*. sourdough,
leaven.

savvah-dayka *(f)*. sourdoughs;
pl. of savvah-dayk.

sawwa *v*. to say.

sawwich "I say".

say *(m)*. sea.

sayf *(f)*. 1. soap 2. safe, vault.

sayf safe, not dangerous.

sayfa *(f)*. 1. soaps 2. safes,
vaults; pl. of sayf.

sayk *(f)*. 1. sake, intent 2. saw.

saykna *v*. to bless.

sayks *(f)*. sakes; pl. of sayk.

sayl *(f)*. soul.

sayla *(f)*. souls; pl. of sayl.

saylich 1. blessed, happy 2.
saved.

saylichkeit *(f)*. salvation.

saym same.

sayna *v*. to see.

sayya *(f)*. 1. seas; pl. of say 2.
saws; pl. of sayk.

sayya *(m)*. blessing.

sayya *v*. 1. to saw, 2. to sow
seed.

sayyah *(m)*. sower.

seahsht first, preceding others.

sechtzay sixteen.

sechtzich sixty.

sedda should.

sedla *v*. to settle.

see she, her.

seel *(m)*. seal.

seels *(f)*. seals; pl. of seel.

seena *v*. to separate by passing
through a sieve.

sees sweet.

sei *(f)*. pigs, hogs, swine; pl. of
sau.

sei *v*. to be.

sei his, hers, its (possessive
pronoun, used with a noun).

seida made of silk.

seidah *(neu)*. cider.

seida-shpekk *(neu)*. bacon.

sei-flaysh *(neu)*. pork.

sei-heedah *(m)*. swineherder.

seik *(f)*. worry.

sein his, hers (possessive
pronoun, used without a
noun).

seind *v*. to be (future tense).

seit *(f)*. side; pl. seida/seits.

seiya *(f)*. worries; pl. of seik.

seiya *v*. 1. to ensure 2. to take care
of.

sekk *(f)*. sacks, bags, pockets; pl.
of sakk.

selayva ever.

selayva-naett never.

sell 1. that (demonstrative) 2.
that (used with neuter
noun).

sella should be, supposed to.

sellah 1. that (used with

masculine noun) 2. that one.
selli　1. those 2. that (used with feminine noun).
selvaht　1. self 2. alone.
sens　*(f)*. sickle, sythe.
setza　*v.* 1. to set or adjust 2. to appoint 3. to set one's mind upon 4. to set one's confidence upon.
sex　six.
sext　sixth.
shadda　*(m)*. 1. shadow 2. shade.
shadda　*v.* 1. to matter 2. to harm 3. to scratch over the surface 4. to scrape or rake.
shaffa　*v.* to work.
shaffich　industrious.
shand　*(f)*. 1. disgrace, shame 2. abomination.
shanda　*(f)*. 1. disgraces, shames 2. abominations; pl. of shand.
shandlich　disgraceful, abominable.
shank　*(m)*. cabinet.
shanshtah　*(m)*. chimney.
shanshtahs　*(f)*. chimneys; pl. of shanshtah.
shatz　*(m)*. apron.
shatza　*(f)*. aprons; pl. of shatz.
shauf　sharp.
shaufa　*v.* to sharpen.
shaufel　*(f)*. shovel.
shaufla　*(f)*. shovels; pl. of shaufel.
shaufla　*v.* to shovel.
shaum　*(m)*. foam.
shauma　*v.* to foam.
shaumich　foamy.

shawb　*(m)*. 1. moth 2. fish scale.
shawda　*(m)*. harm, danger.
shawl　*(f)*. 1. peel, shell, crust 2. outer covering.
shawla　*(f)*. 1. peelings, shells, crusts 2. outer coverings; pl. of shawl.
shawva　*(f)*. 1. moths 2. fish scales; pl. of shawb.
shawva　*v.* 1. to scrape off with a scraper 2. to scale a fish.
shay　1. nice 2. pretty beautiful.
shayfa　*v.* to shave.
shayheit　*(f)*. prettiness.
shayla　*v.* to peel.
sheah　*(f)*. scissors.
sheahra　*v.* to cut with a scissors.
shebba　*v.* to scoop or shovel.
shebbah　*(m)*. scoop, dipper.
sheesa　*v.* to shoot.
sheeva　*v.* to push or shove.
sheffa　*(f)*. pod.
shein　*(m)*. appearance, similitude.
sheina　*v.* 1. to shine 2. to appear.
sheinich　shiny.
sheiyah　*(f)*. barn.
sheiyahra　*(f)*. barns; pl. of sheiyah.
shemma　*v.* 1. to feel embarrassment or shame 2. to feel shy.
shemmich　shy, bashful.
shenka　*v.* 1. to give a gift 2. to pardon.
shennah　nicer, prettier.
shensht　nicest, prettiest.
shiah　*(f)*. portion or share.
shiah / fasht　almost, nearly.

shiahra *(f)*. portions or shares; pl. of shiah.
shiblen *(f)*. lambs; pl. of shibli.
shibli *(n)*. lamb.
shidla *v.* to shake.
shidlich shaky.
shiff *(neu)*. ship.
shiffah *(f)*. ships; pl. of shiff.
shiff-gnecht *(m)*. sailor.
shiff-gnechta *(f)*. sailors; pl. of shiff-gnecht.
shiff-leit *(f)*. the crew of a ship.
shiff-meishtah *(m)*. shipmaster, captain.
shiff-meishtahra *(f)*. shipmasters, captains; pl. of shiff-meishtah.
shikka *v.* to send.
shiklich appropriate, suitable, proper.
shisla *(f)*. large bowls, serving bowls; pl. of shissel.
shissel *(f)*. large bowl, serving bowl.
shkaedra *v.* to scatter.
shkayda *v.* to skate.
shkibba *v.* to skip.
shkoll *(m)*. skull.
shkoll-blatz *(m)*. the skull place.
shkols *(f)*. skulls; pl. of shkoll.
shkraebb *(neu)*. scrap.
shkribla *v.* to scribble.
shkrobba *v.* to scrub.
shkvall *(m)*. squirrel.
shlabb *(f)*. a person that is sloppy.
shlabb *(neu)*. slop, food scraps and kitchen waste fed to pigs.

shlabbich sloppy.
shlacht *(f)*. slaughter.
shlachta *(f)*. slaughters; pl. of shlacht.
shlachta *v.* to slaughter or butcher an animal.
shlacht-dawk *(m)*. day of slaughter.
shlacht-dawwa *(f)*. days of slaughter; pl. of shlacht-dawk.
shlaebba *v.* to slap.
shlang *(f)*. snake.
shlanga *(f)*. snakes; pl. of shlang.
shlauwa *v.* to hit.
shlawdra *v.* to slaughter or murder.
shlawdra *v.* to slaugther.
shlay *(f)*. sleigh.
shlayfa *v.* to drag.
shlayfah *(m)*. one who sleeps.
shlayfahrich sleepy.
shlechsht the worst.
shlecht 1. bad 2. sick.
shlechtah worse.
shleesa *v.* to lock.
shleicha *v.* to move stealthily.
shleimich slimy.
shlekka *v.* to lick with the tongue.
shlibba *v.* to slip.
shlibbah *(m)*. slipper.
shlibbich slippery.
shlichtich 1. crafty, dishonest 2. secretly.
shlichtichkeit *(f)*. craftiness.
shlidda *(m)*. sled.
shliffah *(m)*. splinter.
shliffahra *(f)*. splinters; pl. of

shliffah.

shlimm terrible, awful.

shlisla *(f)*. keys; pl. of shlissel.

shlissel *(m)*. key.

shlitz *(m)*. slit.

shlitzoahrich deceitful.

shlobb *(m)*. bow (of string or ribbon).

shloh slow.

shlohf *(m)*. sleep.

shlohfa *v*. to sleep.

shlohf-haus *(neu)*. inn, hotel.

shlohf-heisah *(f)*. inns, hotels; pl. of shlohf-haus.

shlohsa *(f)*. hailstones.

shlohsa *v*. to hail.

shloss *(f)*. lock.

shlossa *(f)*. locks; pl. of shloss.

shlukka *v*. to swallow.

shmakka *v*. to smell.

shmakkich smelly.

shmatz *(m)*. pain.

shmatza *(f)*. pains; pl. of shmatz.

shmatza *v*. to hurt.

shmawl narrow (common use).

shmaychla *v*. to flatter or fawn upon, to seek favor.

shmeaht smart.

shmeil *(m)*. smile.

shmeila *v*. to smile.

shmeilich smiley.

shmeisa *v*. to throw.

shmiah *(f)*. 1. salve 2. ointment 3. any substance with a glutinous or viscous consistency.

shmiahra *(f)*. salves, ointments; pl. of shmiah.

shmidda *(f)*. smiths; pl. of shmitt.

shmitt *(m)*. smith.

shmohk *(m)*. smoke.

shmohka *v*. to smoke.

shmohkich smoky.

shmohk-shtaekk *(m)*. smoke stack.

shmukk *(m)*. adornment.

shmutz *(m)*. grease.

shmutza *v*. to grease.

shmutzich greasy.

shnaebba *v*. to snap.

shnaufa *v*. to breath.

shnautzah *(m)*. mustache.

shnavvel *(m)*. bill, beak on a bird.

shnay *(m)*. snow.

shnayya *v*. to snow.

shnayyich snowy.

shneeka *v*. to sneak.

shnefla *v*. to whittle.

shneida *v*. to cut.

shneiksa *v*. to snore.

shnell quickly.

shnohk *(f)*. mosquito.

shnohka *(f)*. mosquitos; pl. of shnohk.

shnokk cute, adorable.

shnoot *(f)*. snout.

shnuah *(m)*. string.

shnubb-dichah *(f)*. handkerchiefs; pl. of shnubb-duch.

shnubb-duch *(n)*. handkerchief.

shohf *(m)*. sheep.

shohf-doah *(neu)*. door of a sheepfold (lit. sheep door).

shohf-doahra *(f)*. doors of a

sheepfold (lit. sheep doors); pl. of shohf-doah.

shohf-haut *(f)*. sheepskin.

shohf-heedah *(m)*. shepherd.

shohf-heidah *(f)*. sheepskins; pl. of shohf-haut.

shohf-shtall *(m)*. sheepfold.

shohf-shtell *(f)*. sheepfolds; pl. of shohf-shtall.

shohm *(m)*. shame, disgrace.

shohs *(f)*. lap.

shohsa *(f)*. laps; pl. of shohs.

shokkel-shteel *(f)*. rocking chairs; pl. of shokkel-shtool.

shokkel-shtool *(m)*. rocking chair.

shokla *v*. to rock.

shoo *(m)*. shoe.

shoo-bendel *(m)*. shoestring.

shoo-bendela *(f)*. shoestrings; pl. of shoo-bendel.

shool *(f)*. school.

shoola *(f)*. schools; pl. of shool.

shoolah *(m)*. student in school.

shool-meishtah *(m)*. schoolmaster, school teacher.

shpadda *(m)*. rafter.

shpalda *v*. to split.

shpalding *(f)*. schism.

shpaldinga *(f)*. schisms; pl. of shpalding.

shpatz *(f)*. sparrow.

shpatza *(f)*. sparrows; pl. of shpatz.

shpautz *(m)*. spit.

shpautza *v*. to spit.

shpaydah later.

shpeahra *v*. 1. to spare from

death, pain, distress, expense, etc. 2. to lend 3. to have in excess.

shpeddah *(f)*. mockers; pl. of shpoddah.

shpeela *v*. to play.

shpees *(m)*. spear.

shpeesa *(f)*. spears; pl. of shpees.

shpeesa *v*. to spear.

shpeichah *(m)*. upstairs, second floor.

shpeichahra *(f)*. upstairs, second floors; pl. of shpeichah.

shpeida *v*. to regret.

shpeis *(f)*. food (used in the Bible).

shpeisa *(f)*. foods; pl. of shpeis (used in the Bible).

shpeisich spicy.

shpell *(f)*. pin.

shpella *(f)*. pins; pl. of shpell.

shpella *v*. 1. to pin 2. to spell.

shpenda *v*. to spend.

shpiah *(m)*. spear.

shpiahra *v*. to feel.

shpiahs *(f)*. spears; pl. of shpiah.

shpikkel *(m)*. mirror.

shpikla *(f)*. mirrors; pl. of shpikkel.

shpinn *(m)*. spider.

shpinna *(f)*. spiders; pl. of shpinn.

shpinna *v*. to spin.

shpitza *(m)*. point.

shpitzich pointy, coming to a point.

shpoahra *v*. to use sparingly or frugally.

shpodda *v.* to mock.
shpoddah *(m).* mocker.
shpoht late.
shpoht-yoah *(neu).* fall, autumn, season late in the year.
shpoola *(m).* spool.
shprau *(neu).* chaff.
shprich-vadda *(f).* proverbs; pl. of shprich-vatt.
shprich-vatt *(neu).* proverb.
shpringa *v.* to run.
shpritza *v.* to sprinkle or spray.
shprohch *(f).* language.
shprohcha *(f).* languages; pl. of shprohch.
shraub *(f).* screw.
shrauva *(f).* screws; pl. of shraub.
shrauva *v.* to screw.
shrayks on a slant or uneven, on an angle.
shreinah / zimmah *(m).* carpenter.
shreinra *v.* to work as a carpenter.
shreiva *v.* to write.
shreivah *(m).* writer.
shreives *(neu).* written document.
shreklich scary, terrifying, awful.
Shrift *(f).* Scripture.
Shrifta *(f).* Scriptures; pl. of Shrift.
shrift-geleahrah *(m).* scribe.
shritt *(m).* stride.
shtaend *(m).* platform or stand.
shtaends *(f).* platforms or

stands; pl. of shtaend.
shtall *(m).* 1. stall 2. building that shelters one kind of animal 3. section of a barn used for storing hay, grain, etc.
shtamba *v.* to stamp, to trample.
shtamm *(m).* 1. stem of a plant 2. trunk of a tree 3. family, race.
shtandhaftich steadfast, faithful.
shtandhaftichkeit *(f).* steadfastness, faithfulness.
shtann *(f).* 1. star 2. forehead.
shtanna *(f).* 1. stars 2. foreheads; pl. of shtann.
shtarra / shtadda *v.* to stir.
shtatt *(f).* town.
shtatt-richtah *(m).* magistrate.
shtatza *v.* to stumble.
shtaut strong, sturdy.
shtauva *v.* to die.
shtawb *(m).* dust.
shtawl *(neu).* steel.
shtawlich made of steel.
shtawvich dusty.
shtay *(m).* stone.
shtaya *v.* to stand.
shtayk *(f).* set of stairs, stairway.
shtayla *v.* to steal.
shtaylah *(m).* theif.
shtaylahrei *(f).* thievery.
shtaynich 1. made of stone 2. rocky.
shtaynicha *v.* to stone.
shtaynlen *(f).* little stone, pebbles; pl. of shtaynli.

shtaynli *(neu)*. little stone, pebble.

shtay-tablet *(neu)*. stone tablet.

shtay-tablets *(f)*. stone tablets; pl. of shtay-tablet.

shtayya *(f)*. sets of stairs, stairways; pl. of shtayk.

shteahblich able to die, subject to death, mortal.

shteahm *(f)*. storms; pl. of shtoahm.

shteahmich stormy.

shteahra *v.* to start.

shteahva *v.* to die.

shtebb *(m)*. step.

shtebba *v.* to step.

shtebs *(f)*. steps; pl. of shtebb.

shtecha *v.* 1. to prick or pierce 2. to sting.

shtechah *(m)*. 1. stinger 2. sharp pointed instrument that pierces.

shtedlen *(f)*. towns, villages; pl. of shtedli.

shtedli *(neu)*. town, village.

shteeb steep.

shteech *(m)*. a sting (example: a bee sting).

shteef-maemm *(f)*. stepmother.

shteef-maemma *(f)*. stepmothers; pl. of shteef-maemm.

shteel *(f)*. chairs, thrones; pl. of shtool.

shteelen *(f)*. stools; pl. of shteeli.

shteeli *(neu)*. stool.

shteem *(m)*. steam.

shteemah *(m)*. steamer.

shteibahra *v.* 1. to brace 2. to resist.

shteibahrich stubborn, obstinate.

shteif stiff.

shteik 1. fast 2. strong.

shteil *(m)*. style.

shtekk *(f)*. 1. plants 2. walking sticks, canes; pl. of shtokk.

shtekka *(m)*. stick.

shtekka *v.* 1. to insert 2. to stick, adhere.

shteklen *(f)*. 1. small plants 2. small sticks; pl. of shtekli.

shtekli *(neu)*. 1. small plant 2. small stick.

shtell *(f)*. 1. stalls 2. buildings that shelter one kind of animal; pl. of shtall.

shtella *v.* 1. to set or place an object 2. to appoint a date or time.

shtemm *(f)*. 1. stems of plants 2. tree trunks; pl. of shtamm.

shtenda *v.* to bear or suffer.

shtengel *(m)*. 1. stem 2. rhubarb.

shtett *(f)*. towns; pl. of shtatt.

shtiah-beaht *(f)*. rudders (lit.- steering boards).

shtiah-boaht *(neu)*. rudder (lit.- steering board).

shtiah-mann *(m)*. pilot.

shtiah-mennah *(f)*. pilots; pl. of shtiah-mann.

shtiffel *(m)*. boot.

shtikk *(neu)*. 1. piece 2. a small distance.

shtikka *v.* 1. to stick, adhere 2. to

persevere.

shtikkah *(f)*. pieces; pl. of shtikk.

shtill still, quiet.

shtimm *(f)*. voice.

shtimma *(f)*. voices; pl. of shtimm.

shtinka *v.* to stink.

shtoah *(m)*. store.

shtoah-haus *(neu)*. storehouse.

shtoah-heisah *(f)*. storehouses; pl. of shtoah-haus.

shtoahm *(m)*. storm.

shtoahra *(f)*. stores; pl. of shtoah.

shtoahri *(f)*. story.

shtoahris *(f)*. stories; pl. of shtoahri.

shtobba *v.* to stop.

shtodya *v.* to study.

shtoffa *v.* to stuff.

shtoffich stuffy.

shtohsa *v.* 1. to cast or throw 2. to thrust 3. to take offense.

shtokk *(m)*. 1. plant 2. walking stick, cane.

shtolbah-blakk *(m)*. stumbling block.

shtolbah-blaks *(f)*. stumbling blocks; pl. of shtolbah-blakk.

shtolbahra *v.* to stumble.

shtolbah-shtay *(m)*. stumbling stone.

shtols 1. proud 2. stubborn.

shtool *(m)*. chair, throne.

shtraebb *(m)*. strap.

shtraebs *(f)*. straps; pl. of shtraebb.

shtraych *(m)*. 1. stripe or streak 2. strike or blow 3. stroke, attack of paralysis 4. a period of time.

shtrayma *(m)*. stripe.

shtreicha *v.* to stroke.

shtreida *v.* to battle.

shtrekka *v.* to stretch.

shtreng strict.

shtribb *(m)*. strip.

shtribba *v.* to strip.

shtribs *(f)*. strips; pl. of shtribb.

shtrichlen *(f)*. small strokes; pl. of shtrichli.

shtrichli *(neu)*. 1. a small stroke 2. a small caress.

shtrikk *(m)*. rope.

shtrikka *(f)*. ropes; pl. of shtrikk.

shtrimb *(f)*. socks; pl. of shtrumb.

shtroh *(neu)*. straw.

shtrohf *(m)*. punishment.

shtrohfa *(f)*. punishments; pl. of shtrohf.

shtrohfa *v.* to punish.

shtrohf-dawk *(m)*. day of punishment.

shtrohf-dawwa *(f)*. days of punishment; pl. of shtrohf-dawk.

shtrohf-zeida *(f)*. times of punishment; pl. of shtrohf-zeit.

shtrohf-zeit *(f)*. time of punishment.

shtrohs *(f)*. street.

shtrohsa *(f)*. streets; pl. of shtrohs.

shtrohsa-ekk *(neu)*. corner of a street.

shtrohsa-ekkah *(f)*. corners of a street; pl. of shtrohsa-ekk.

shtrohsa-leng *(f)*. length of a street.

shtroiya *v.* 1. to scatter 2. to spread bedding for livestock.

shtrumb *(m)*. sock.

shtubb *(f)*. room.

shtubba *(f)*. rooms; pl. of shtubb.

shtubbel *(m)*. stubble.

shtubla *(f)*. stubbles; pl. of shtubbel.

shtumb dull, not sharp.

shtumba *(m)*. stump.

shtund *(f)*. hour.

shtunda *(f)*. hours; pl. of shtund.

shuah sure.

shubkaych *(m)*. wheelbarrow.

shubkaycha *(f)*. wheelbarrows; pl. of shubkaych.

shublawda *(f)*. drawers; pl. of shublawt.

shublawt *(f)*. drawer.

shuld *(f)*. 1. fault, blame 2. debt.

shulda *(f)*. 1. faults, blames 2. debts; pl. of shuld.

shuldah *(m)*. shoulder.

shuldich 1. at fault, blameworthy 2. indebted to, under obligation.

shuldichkeit *(f)*. obligation.

shuldlohs blameless.

shuldra *(f)*. shoulders; pl. of shuldah.

shulkichkeida *(f)*. obligations; pl. of shuldichkeit.

shund already.

shunsht 1. otherwise 2. in addition, else.

shvach weak.

shvachheida *(f)*. weaknesses; pl. of shvachheit.

shvachheit *(f)*. weakness.

shvadda *(f)*. swords; pl. of shvatt.

shvadda-shnitt *(m)*. 1. edge of a sword 2. cut made by a sword.

shvalma *(f)*. swallow (kind of bird).

shvans *(m)*. tail.

shvatt *(neu)*. sword.

shvatz black.

shveah heavy.

shveahra *v.* 1. to vow, make an oath 2. to swear, make a promise.

shvechah weaker.

shvechsht weakest.

shvenga *v.* to rinse.

shvens *(f)*. tails; pl. of shvans.

shveshtah *(f)*. sister.

shveshtra *(f)*. sisters; pl. of shveshtah.

shvetza *v.* to talk.

shvetzah *(m)*. talker.

shvetzich talkative.

shvevvel *(neu)*. sulphur.

shviah-dochtah *(f)*. daughter-in-law.

shviah-dochtahra *(f)*. daughters-in-law; pl. of shviah-dochtah.

shviah-muddah *(f)*. mother-in-law.

shviah-muddahra *(f)*. mothers-in-law.

shvimma *v*. to swim.

shvitz *(m)*. sweat.

shvitza *v*. to sweat.

shvitzich sweaty.

shwoahm *(m)*. swarm.

shwoahma *v*. to swarm.

si they, them.

sich self (reflexive).

sichel *(f)*. 1. sickle 2. blade or shoot on a plant.

sichla *(f)*. sickles; pl. of sichel.

sich-selvaht himself, herself, itself.

siddah since.

siffah *(m)*. alcoholic.

sifta *v*. to sift.

sikkeah *(f)*. cigar.

sikkeahra *(f)*. cigars; pl. of sikkeah.

silvah silver.

silvahrich silvery.

silvah-smitt *(m)*. silversmith.

sind *(f)*. sin, transgression.

sinda *(f)*. sins, transgressions; pl. of sind.

sindah *(m)*. sinner.

sindfloot *(f)*. deluge, global flood in Noah's day that God used to destroy the wicked inhabitants of the earth (lit. sin-flood).

sindfol sinful.

sindicha *v*. to sin.

sindlich sinful.

sind-opfah *(neu)*. sin offering, sacrificial offering for sin.

sind-opfahra *(f)*. sin offerings, sacrificial offerings for sin; pl. of sind-opfah.

singa *v*. to sing.

singah *(m)*. singer.

sinn *v*. are "miah sinn" , "si sinn".

sitz *(m)*. seat.

sitza *(f)*. seats; pl. of sitz.

sitza *v*. to seat.

sivva seven.

sivveda the seventh one.

sivvet seventh.

sivvetzay seventeen.

sivvetzich seventy.

so 1. so 2. therefore.

soah sore.

sobbah *(neu)*. supper.

sobbahs *(f)*. suppers; pl. of sobbah.

soffahra *v*. to suffer.

sohbah sober.

sohma *(m)*. seed.

sohwich suchlike.

soll *v*. shall, should.

sooda *v*. 1. to suit 2. to please.

subb *(f)*. soup.

subba *(f)*. soups; pl. of subb.

sucha *v*. to seek.

sukla *v*. to suck.

summah *(m)*. summer.

summahra *(f)*. summers; pl. of summah.

Sundawk *(m)*. Sunday.

Sundawks / Sundawwa *(f)*. Sundays; pl. of Sundawk.

sunn *(f)*. sun.

sunna *(f)*. suns; pl. of sunn.

sunnich sunny.
sunn-shein sunshine.
sunn-sheinich sunshiny.

sunn-uf sun-up.
sunn-unnah sundown.

T - t

taena *v.* to tan (example - animal hide, leather).
taenah *(m).* tanner.
tamaeddes *(f).* tomato, tomatoes.
tavvah *(m).* tower.
tax-dish *(m).* tax collector's desk (lit.- tax table).
taxdisha *(f).* tax collector's desks (lit.- tax tables).
tax-einemmah *(m).* tax collector.
tay *(m).* tea.
tayb *(neu).* tape.
tayba *v.* to tape.
tayklich daily (as used in the Bible).
taysta *v.* to taste.
teetsha *v.* to teach.
teetshah *(m).* teacher.
teetshahs *(f).* teachers; pl. of teetshah.
teidna *v.* to tighten.
teil *(m).* tile.
teils *(f).* tiles; pp. of teil.
teit tight.
teiyah *(m).* tire.
tempel *(m).* temple.
tempel-box *(f).* treasury (lit.- temple box).
tempel-boxa *(f).* treasuries (lit.- temple boxes).

tempel-broht *(neu).* ceremonial showbread (lit.- temple bread).
tempel-fesht *(neu).* feast of dedication (lit.- temple feast).
tempel-feshta *(f).* feasts of dedication (lit.- temple feasts).
tempels *(f).* temples; pl. of tempel.
tempta *v.* to tempt (informal).
tent-tempel *(m).* tabernacle (lit.- tent temple).
tent-tempels *(f).* tabernacles; pl. of tent-tempel.
Teshtament *(neu).* Testament.
Teshtamenta *(f).* Testaments; pl. of Teshtament.
Teshtamentah *(f).* Testaments; pl. of Teshtament.
tieyahs *(f).* tires; pl. of teiyahs.
toff tough.
totsha *v.* to touch (common use).
totshich touchy.
traektah *(m).* tractor.
traektahs *(f).* tractors; pl. of traektah.
traesha *v.* to trash.
traeshich trashy.
trayda *v.* to trade (common

use).
trayna *v.* to train.
trikka *v.* to trick.
trikkah *(m).* trigger.
trikkich tricky.
tshaett decent, proper.
tshaub *(m).* job, occupation.
tshawwa *v.* to chew.
tshaynsha *v.* to change.

tsheah *(m).* jar.
tsheahs *(f).* jars; pl. of tsheah.
tsheahtsha *v.* to charge.
tsheeda *v.* to cheat.
tsheins *(m).* chance,
    opportunity.
tshumba *v.* to jump.
tshumbich jumpy, skittish.

U - u

uahsach *(f).* reason, cause.
uahsacha *(f).* reasons, causes;
    pl. of uahsach.
uf 1. on, upon 2. open 3. up 4.
    (separable prefix) on,
    ongoing, continuous, open,
    up.
ufdekka *v.* to uncover.
uffana *(neu).* a wide unobstructed
    space.
uffashtayung *(f).* resurrection.
uffashtayunga *(f).*
    resurrections; pl. of
    uffahshtayung.
uffaykna *v.* to admit.
ufgaykend *v.* admitted; pp. of
    uffaykna.
ufgedekt *v.* uncovered; pp. of
    ufdekka.
ufglicht *v.* lit up; pp. of uflichta.
ufgmacht *v.* opened; pp. of
    ufmacha.
ufgmundaht *v.* encouraged;
    pp. of ufmundahra.
ufgriaht *v.* stirred up; pp. of

ufriahra.
ufgrohmd *v.* tidied up; pp. of
    ufrohma.
uf-kshtanna *v.* stood up, got up;
    pp. of uf-shtay.
ufkshtohsa *v.* burped; pp. of
    ufshtohsa.
uflichta *v.* to light up.
ufmacha *v.* to open.
ufmundahra *v.* to encourage.
ufriahra *v.* to stir up.
ufrichtich upright, honest.
ufrichtichkeit *(f).* uprightness,
    honesty.
ufrohma *v.* to tidy up.
ufruah *(m).* tumult.
ufruahra *(f).* tumults; pl. of
    ufruah.
uf-shtay *v.* to stand up, to get
    up.
ufshtohsa *v.* to burp.
um 1. (separable prefix) down,
    dead, around 2.
    approximately, about 3.
    around.

(m) = da   (f) = di   (neu) = es   113

umbringa *v.* to kill.

umgebrocht *v.* killed; pp. of umbringa.

umkumma *v.* to die in an accident.

ummechtich unconscious as a result of fainting.

ummeeklich impossible.

ummens *(f).* ant.

ummensa *(f).* ants; pl. of ummens.

umshmeisa *v.* 1. to upset, capsize 2. to overthrow.

umshtand *(m).* circumstance.

umshtenda *(f).* circumstances; pl. of umshtand.

un   and.

una   contraction of "un en".

unadlich lawless.

unadning *(f).* disorder.

unaydich unnecessary.

unaynich not in unity, in disagreement.

unaynichkeida *(f).* disunities; pl. of unaynichkeit.

unaynichkeit *(f).* disunity.

unbamhatzich merciless.

unbegreiflich astonishing, incomprehensible.

unbekand unknown.

unbekimmaht unconcerned.

unbeshneiding *(f).* uncircumcision.

unbeshnidda uncircumcised.

undankboah unthankful.

uneahlich dishonest.

unfagenglich imperishable.

unfahoft unexpected.

unfaseikt 1. not taken care of 2.

unaccomplished.

unfashendlich 1. without understanding 2. intemperate.

unfashtendlichkeit *(f).* 1. state of being without understanding 2. intemperance.

unfruchtboah unfruitful.

ungeboahra unborn.

ungeglayt unclothed.

ungehorsam disobedient.

ungeishtlich not holy, not spiritual.

ungerecht not right.

ungerechtich unrighteous.

ungerechtichkeit *(f).* unrighteousness.

ungetlich ungodly.

ungetlichkeit *(f).* ungodliness.

ungland 1. not taught 2. lacking in social graces.

unglawva *(m).* unbelief, disbelief.

unglawvich unbelieving.

unglikk *(neu).* misfortune.

ungliklich unfortunate.

Ungreeyish not of Greek nationality.

unksavvaht unleavened.

unksheit 1. not sensible 2. risky, foolhardy.

unkshikt 1. improper 2. not talented.

unkshrunka not preshrunk.

unna located down below, at the bottom.

unnah 1. under 2. (prefix) under.

unnah-gnumma *v.* undertaken,

attempted; pp. of unnah-
nemma.

unnah-hauptmann *(m)*.
centurion (lit.- under
captain).

unnah-hauptmennah *(f)*.
centurions, (lit. under
captains); pl. of unnah-
hauptmann.

unnah-ksucht *v.* examined,
searched out; pp. of unnah-
sucha.

unnah-nemma *v.* to undertake,
to attempt.

unnahs-evvahsht upside
down.

unnahshidda *(f)*. differences;
pl. of unnahshitt.

unnahshidlich 1.
distinguishable 2. various 3.
changeable.

unnahshitt *(m)*. difference.

unnah-sucha *v.* to examine,
search out.

unni 1. without 2. unless.

unnich under.

unrein impure.

unreinichkeit *(f)*. impurity.

unroo *(f)*. unrest.

unruich restless.

uns us.

unsah our.

unsauvah unclean.

unshiklich improper.

unshprechlich too magnificent
to express in words.

unshtandhaftich unstable.

unshtrayflich blameless (lit.-
not punishable).

unshuldich innocent.

unshuldichkeit *(f)*. innocence.

unveahdich unworthy.

unvillich unwilling, reluctant.

unvoahret *(f)*. untruth,
falsehood.

unzucht *(f)*. licentiousness,
unrestrained, go beyond the
proper bounds or limits.

V - v

vadda *(f)*. words; pl. of vatt.

vadda *v.* to become.

vaddawks everyday, during the
week (informal) (Example:
"vaddawks
glaydah" - everyday
clothing).

vakkah awake.

vakla *v.* to wiggle, to wobble.

vaklich wiggly, wobbly.

valfish *(m)*. whale.

vammes *(m)*. coat.

vand *(f)*. wall.

vanda *(f)*. walls; pl.of vand.

vandla *v.* to wander.

vann 1. when 2. if.

vann one pronoun.

vanna *v.* to warn.

vann-evvah whenever.

vanning *(f)*. warning.

(m) = da   (f) = di   (neu) = es   115

vanninga *(f)*. warnings; pl. of vanning.

vans ones; pl. of pronoun vann.

vasht *(f)*. sausage.

vass 1. what 2. that, which, who (relative pronoun).

vassah *(neu)*. water, body of water.

vassah-lechah *(f)*. watering holes; pl. of vassah-loch.

vassah-loch *(neu)*. 1. watering hole 2. mud puddle.

vassah-pabla *(f)*. chicken pox.

vassahra *(f)*. waters; pl. of vassah.

vassah-shpring *(f)*. spring of water.

vassah-shpringa *(f)*. water springs.

vassah-sucht *(f)*. dropsy.

vass-evvah whatever.

vatsh *(f)*. 1. the period during which a guard is on duty 2. watch, timepiece.

vatsha *(f)*. watches; pl. of vatsh.

vatsha *v*. to watch.

vatt *(neu)*. word.

vatzel *(f)*. root.

vatzla *(f)*. roots; pl. of vatzel.

vauwa *(m)*. large wagon.

vaxa *v*. to grow.

vay *(f)*. woe.

vay painful, sore.

vayda *(f)*. pastures; pl. of vayt.

vay-du *v*. to hurt.

vay-gedu *v*. hurt; pp. of vay-du.

vayk *(m)*. 1. way 2. road.

vayklen *(f)*. little wagons; pl. of vaykli.

vaykli *(neu)*. little wagon.

vayks 1. ways 2. (a suffix of adverbs) "shtikk vayks" (part ways).

vaysa *(neu)*. unnecessary fuss or display.

vayt *(f)*. pasture.

vaytza *(m)*. wheat.

vayya *(f)*. 1. ways 2. roads; pl. of vayk.

vayya *(f)*. woes, pl. of vay.

vayyich soft.

vayyichah softer.

vayyich-hatzich softhearted.

vayyichsht sortest.

veah who.

veah-evvah whoever.

veahm *(f)*. worms; pl. of voahm.

veahma *v*. 1. to warm 2. to deworm.

veahmah warmer.

veahmsht warmest.

veahra *v*. would be.

veahra *v*. to wear.

veaht *(f)*. worth, value.

veaht *v*. to show reluctance.

veahtfol worthy.

veahtfollich worthwhile.

vedda *v*. would want.

veddah *(neu)*. weather.

veddah contracting against.

veddah-glaycht *v*. when lightning has flashed; pp. of veddah-laych.

veddah-laych *(m)*. lightning.

veddah-laycha *(f)*. lightning flashes.

veddah-laycha *v*. to flash lightning.

veecha *(m).* wick on a lamp.
veesht bad, awful, evil.
veeshtahlich wickedly.
veetz *(neu).* weeds.
veeya *v.* to weigh.
vei *(m).* wine.
vei why (preface to a mark).
veib *(neu).* woman, wife (not common).
veibsleit *(f).* women, female persons.
veibsmensh *(neu).* woman, female person.
veida-bohm *(m).* willow tree.
veidah further.
vei-drayk *(f).* wine vats; pl. of vei-drohk.
vei-drohk *(m).* wine vat.
vei-goahra *(m).* vineyard.
veiklich truly.
veil 1. while 2. because 3. a little while.
veina *v.* to weep.
vei-press *(f).* winepress.
vei-presses *(f).* winepresses; pl. of vei-press.
veis *(f).* tune.
veis white.
veisa *(f).* tunes; pl. of veis.
veisa *v.* to show.
vei-sakk *(m).* wineskin.
vei-saufah *(m).* wine drinker.
vei-sekk *(f).* wineskins; pl. of vei-sakk.
veisheit *(f).* wisdom.
vei-shtekk *(f).* grapevines, pl. of vei-shtokk.
vei-shtokk *(m).* grapevine (lit. wine plant).

veising *(f).* revelation, showing.
veisinga *(f).* revelations, showings; pl. of veising.
veisla *v.* to whitewash.
veit far.
veitsht furthest.
veivah *(f).* women, wives (not common).
vekk away.
vekka *v.* to wake up.
veld *(f).* world.
velda *(f).* worlds; pl. of veld.
veldlich worldly.
velf *(f).* wolfs.
velk wilted.
vell *(f).* wave of water.
vell well (preface to a remark).
vella *(f).* waves of water; pl. of vell.
vella *v.* to want, ("want" used with "we", "they").
vellet *v.* want (only used with "you all").
vels which one.
velshkan *(neu).* corn.
vemm whom.
vemm sei whose.
vemmes *(f).* coats; pl. of vammes.
vennich 1. a little 2. few.
vennichah less.
vennichsht least.
verk *(neu).* work, accomplishment.
verka *(f).* works, accomplishments; pl. of verk.
vesh *(f).* laundry.
vesha *v.* to wash.

vesh-lumba *(m)*. washcloth.
veshp *(f)*. wasp.
veshpa *(f)*. wasps; pl. of veshp.
vesh-shisla *(f)*. washbowls; pl. of vesh-shissel.
vesh-shissel *(f)*. washbowl.
vessahra *v*. to water (such as plants).
vest west.
vexel *(m)*. 1. monetary change 2. trade.
veyyich / veyya about, concerning.
vi 1. how 2. as, like 3. than.
vichtich weighty, important.
viddah 1. again 2. against, opposed to.
viddah bat *(neu)*. argument, verbal opposition.
viddah bat-haddah *(m)*. a person given to arguing.
viddah-chrishta *(f)*. antichrists; pl. of viddah-chrisht.
viddah-christ *(m)*. antichrist.
viddah-shtand *(m)*. defense, opposition.
viddah-shteit *(m)*. opposition.
vikla *v*. to wrap.
vild wild.
vildahnis *(f)*. wilderness.
vildahnissa *(f)*. wildernesses; pl. of vildahniss.
vill *v*. want (only used with "I", "he", "she", "it").
villa *(m)*. 1. the power to make choices 2. desire 3. a will, document of direction after death.

villich willing.
villichlich willingly.
vimsla *v*. to whimper.
vind *(m)*. wind.
vinda *(f)*. winds; pl. of vind.
vindah *(m)*. winter.
vindel *(f)*. diaper.
vindel-shpell *(f)*. safty pin.
vindich windy.
vindla *(f)*. diapers; pl. of vindel.
vindla-dichah *(f)*. diaper cloths; pl. of vindla-duch.
vindla-duch *(neu)*. diaper cloth.
vindra *(f)*. winters; pl. of vindah.
vind-shteahm *(f)*. windstorms; pl. of vind-shtoahm.
vind-shtoahm *(m)*. windstorm.
vinsha *v*. to wish, example: "We wish you the best.".
vislen *(f)*. weasels; pl. of visli.
visli *(neu)*. weasel.
vissa *v*. to know information or facts.
vissaheit *(f)*. knowledge.
vista *v*. would know.
vitt *v*. want (only used with "you").
vitt-fraw *(f)*. widow.
vitt-mann *(m)*. widower.
vitt-mennah *(f)*. widowers; pl. of vitt-mann.
vitt-veib *(neu)*. widow.
vitt-veivah *(f)*. widows; pl. of vitt-fraw; vitt-veib.
vo 1. where 2. that, which, who (relative pronoun) 3. when (conjunction).
voah *v*. was.

voah true-.
voahhaftich 1. truly, certainly 2. genuine 3. faithful.
voahheit *(f)*. truth.
voah-ksawt *v.* to have a fortune told; pp. of voah-sawwa.
voahlich truly.
voahm *(m)*. worm.
voahm *adj.* warm.
voahra *v.* to wait.
voahra *v.* were.
voahret *(f)*. truth.
voahrich I was.
voah-sawwa *v.* to tell a fortune.
voah-sawwah *(m)*. fortune teller.
voahtz *(f)*. wart.
voahtza *(f)*. warts; pl. of voahtz.
voch *(f)*. week.
vocha *(f)*. weeks; pl. of voch.
vodda *v.* to wish, example: "I wish it was warm.".
vo-evvah wherever.
vo-heah why, wherefore.
vohk *(f)*. scales used to weigh.
vohl-kfalla *(neu)*. good will, pleasure.
vohlusht *(f)*. 1. fleshly pleasure 2. fleshly desire.

vohlushta *(f)*. 1. fleshly pleasures 2. fleshly desires; pl. of vohlusht.
vohning *(f)*. dwelling, abode.
vohninga *(f)*. dwellings, abodes; pl. of vohning.
vohwa *(f)*. scales used to weigh; pl. of vohk.
volf *(m)*. wolf.
volk *(f)*. cloud.
volka *(f)*. clouds; pl. of volk.
volkich cloudy.
voll of course, certainly.
voona *v.* to dwell, where a person lives.
voon-blatz *(f)*. dwelling place.
voon-bletz *(f)*. dwelling places; pl. of voon-blatz.
vull *(f)*. wool.
vullich wooly.
vulli-veahm *(f)*. catapillers; pl. of vulli-voahm.
vulli-voahm *(m)*. catapiller.
vundahboah amazing.
vundahboahlich amazingly.
vunnah *(m)*. marvel, wonder.
vunnahra *v.* to wonder.
vunnahs *(f)*. marvels, wonders; pl. of vunnah.

Y - y

yacht *(f)*. noise.
yachtich noisy.
yammahlich lamentable, wretched.

yammahra *v.* to lament to groan.
yatchta *(f)*. noises; pl. of yacht.
yau yes.

(m) = da   (f) = di   (neu) = es   119

yawwa *v.* to chase.
yaydah each.
yeahs-dawk *(m).* birthday.
yeahs-dawwa *(f).* birthdays; pl. of yeahs-dawk.
yiddish Jewish.
yingah *(m).* disciple.
yingah younger.
yingsht youngest.
yo 1. yes, only used when contradicting a negative statement 2. by all means be very careful.
yoah *(neu).* year.
yoahra *(f).* years; pl. of yoah.
yoaht *(m).* yard (36 inches).

yoaht-shtekka *(m).* yardstick.
yoch *(neu).* yoke.
yocha *(f).* yokes; pl. of yoch.
yoosa *v.* to use.
yudda *(f).* Jews; pl. of yutt.
yudda-council *(f).* Jewish council.
yudda-gmay *(f).* Jewish church.
yudda-gmayna *(f).* Jewish churches; pl. of yudda-gmay.
yung young.
yusht only, just.
yutt *(m).* Jew.

Z - z

zabbahrah *(m).* sorcerer.
zammah together.
zang *(f).* pliers.
zank *(m).* strife, arguing.
zanka *v.* to scold.
zann *(m).* anger.
zannich furious.
zarra / zadda *v.* 1. to tease 2. to argue.
zaufa *v.* to bicker.
zay *(f).* teeth.
zaycha *(m).* 1. miracle or special sign 2. pointer of a clock or meter.
zaycha-shaffah *(m).* worker of miracles.
zaycha-sheffah *(f).* miracle workers; pl. of zaycha-

shaffah.
zayl *v.* will, shall.
zayla *v.* to count.
zaym *(f).* bridles; pl. of zohm.
zebba *v.* to braid.
zeeya *v.* 1. to pull 2. to move to another residence.
zeida *(f).* times; pl. of zeit.
zeidich ripe.
zeiknis *(neu).* witness, testimony.
zeit *(f).* time.
zeitlang homesick.
zeitlich timely.
zeiya *v.* to witness, to testify.
zeiyah *(m).* one who testifies, a witness.
zenglen *(f).* small pliers; pl. of

zengli.
zengli *(neu).* small pliers.
zeyya ten.
zeyydel *(neu).* one tenth.
zeyyet tenth.
ziddahra *v.* to shiver or tremble.
zimmah / shreinah *(m).*
    carpenter.
zimmahra *v.* to work as a
    carpenter.
zoddel *(m).* rag.
zodla *(f).* rags; pl. of zoddel.
zodlich ragged, unkept.
zoh *(m).* tooth.
zohm *(m).* bridle.
zohm tame.
zohma *v.* to tame.
zoll *(f).* inch, inches.
zrikk 1. toward a former place
    or state, back 2. return or
    reply.
zrikk-bezawlah *(m).* 1. one
    who revenges 2. one who
    pays back.
zrikk-kshtohsa *v.* rejected; pp.
    of zrikk-shtohsa.
zrikk-shtohsa *v.* 1. to cast
    back 2. to reject.
zu 1. to 2. too, in excess
    3. closed.

zu-dekka *v.* to cover.
zufridda content.
zu-gedekt *v.* covered; pp. of zu-
    dekka.
zukkah *(m).* sugar.
zumma contraction of "zu en"
    (to a).
zung *(f).* 1. tongue 2. language.
zunga *(f).* 1. tongues 2.
    languages; pl. of zung.
zvansich twenty.
zvay two.
zvayk 1. tidy 2. in order 3.
    onward along - example:
    zvayk kumma (get along).
zvay-ksichtich two-faced,
    deceitful.
zvay-shneidich having two
    cutting edges.
zveicha *v.* to graft.
zveifla *v.* to doubt.
zvelf twelve.
zvelft twelfth.
zvett second.
zvilling *(m).* twins.
zvinga *v.* to compel.
zvisha in between.
zvishich between.
zvivla *(f).* onions; pl. of zvivvel.
zvivvel *(f).* onion.

ENGLISH

to

PENNSYLVANIA GERMAN

(m) = da   (f) = di   (neu) = es

A - a

a   1. en   2. ma *(dative case)*
ability *(f)*. famayya.
abode *(f)*. vohning.
abodes *(f)*. vohninga.
abominable shandlich.
abomination *(f)*. shand.
abominations *(f)*. shanda.
about - veyyich / veyya.
about it - diveyya.
above - ovvich.
abuse *v.* byoosa.
abused *v.* gebyoost.
accept *v.* ohnemma.
accept counsel *v.* abnemma.
accepted *v.* ohgnumma.
accepted counsel *v.* abgnumma.
accepted (well) *v.* ohgnaymd.
accidental death *v.* umkumma.
accomplish *v.* faddi-bringa.
accomplished *v.* faddi-gebrocht.
accomplishment *(neu)* verk.
accomplishments *(f)* verka.
according to - demnohch.
according to - dinohch.
accountable - fa'andvadlich.
accusation *(f)*. glawk.
accusations *(f)*. glawwa.
accuse *v.* faglawwa.
accuse *v.* fashuldicha.
accuse *v.* ohglawwa.
accuse *v.* pshuldicha.
accused *v.* faglawkt.
accused *v.* fashuldicht.
accused *v.* ohgeglawkt.
accused *v.* pshuldicht.
acre *(m)*. akka / akkah.
across - drivvah.
act *v.* ohshikka.
act (of bragging) *(neu)*. gebraekk.
act (of serving God) *(m)*. Gottes-deensht.
act (overly concerned or surprised) *v.* fakeffahra.
acted *v.* ohkshikt.
acted (overly concerned or surprised) *v.* fakeffaht.
Acts of the Apostles *(f)*. Apostelgeschichte.
adhere *v.* babba.
adhere *v.* shtekka.
adhere *v.* shtikka.
adhere to (steadfastly) *v.* oh'hayva.
adhered *v.* gebabt.
adhered *v.* kshtikt.
adhered *v.* kshtokka.
adhered to (steadfastly) *v.* ohkohva.
adjourn *v.* ausgay.
adjourn *v.* auslossa.
adjourned *v.* ausganga.
adjourned *v.* ausglost.
adjust *v.* setza.
admit *v.* uffaykna.

admitted *v.* ufgaykend.
admonish *v.* famohna.
admonished *v.* famohnd.
admonition *(f).* famohning.
admonitions *(f).* famohninga.
adopt *v.* ohnemma.
adopted *v.* ohgnumma.
adorable - shnokk.
adornment *(m).* shmukk.
adulterous - aybrechich.
adultery *(neu).* aybruch.
adultries *(f).* aybrucha.
advance *(m).* fattshritt.
advances *(f).* fattshridda.
advise *v.* rohda.
advised *v.* grohda.
adze *(m).* dexel.
adzes *(f).* dexla.
affliction *(neu).* bedreebnis.
afflictions *(f).* bedreebnisa.
afraid *v.* kfeicht.
after hinna-noch
    (example: to come after that)
after - noch.
after - nohch.
after all - doch.
afternoon - nochmiddawk.
afterward - dinohch.
again - ivvah.
again - nochamohl.
again - viddah.
against - geyya / gayya.
against - digeyya / digayya.
against - geyyich / gayyich.
age *(f).* eld.
age *v.* fa'elda.
aged - eldlich.
aged *v.* fa'eld.
aged man *(m).* dawdi.

aged men *(f).* dawdis.
agree with *v.* eiseida.
agreed - aynich.
agreed with *v.* eikseit.
ahead of - fanna-heah.
aided *v.* gebatt.
air *(f).* luft.
air out *v.* auslufta.
aired out *v.* ausgluft.
airy - luftich.
alcoholic *(m).* siffah.
alive - levendich *(used in Bible)*
alive - levvich *(common use)*
all - allem.
all - alli.
all - awl.
all kinds (sorts, types)
        alli-sadda
all together - mitt-nannah.
allied with - ei *(prefix)*
allow *v.* alawva.
allowance *(f).* alawbnis.
allowances *(f).* alawbnissa.
allowed *v.* alawbt.
allowed *v.* daufa.
almighty - awlmechtich.
almighty - almechtich
        (used in Bible)
almost - baut.
almost - fasht / shiah.
alone - laynich.
alone - selvaht.
already - shund.
alright - awl-recht.
also - aw.
altar *(m).* awldah.
altar (for a false god) *(m).*
        abgott-awldah.
altars *(f).* awldahra.

altars (for false gods) *(f)*.
abgott-awldahs.
altars (used to sacrifice upon) *(f)*.
opfah-awldahra.
alteration *(f)*. fa'ennahring.
alterations *(f)*. fa'ennahringa.
always - immah.
am *v.* binn *(verb conj. of sei)*
"Ich binn"
amazing - vundahboah.
amazingly - vundahboahlich.
ambassador *(m)*. botshaftah.
an - en.
an - ma *(dative case)*
anchor *(m)*. enkah.
anchor hook *(m)*.
enkah-hohka.
anchors *(f)*. enkahs.
and - un.
angel *(m)*. engel.
angels *(f)*. engla.
anger *(m)*. zann.
angle - shrayks.
angry -bays.
animal (wild) *(neu)* diah.
animal herder *(m)*.
fee-heedah.
animals (wild) *(f)*. diahra.
ankle *(m)*. enkel.
ankles *(f)*. enkels.
anklet *(f)*. bay-kedli.
anklets *(f)*. bay-kedlen.
annoy *v.* fa'eiyahra.
annoyed *v.* fa'eiyaht.
anoint *v.* salba.
anointed *v.* ksalbt.
another - noch.
another one (used with *feminine
noun*) anri.

another one *(used with m. noun)*
anrah.
another one *(used with
neu. noun)* anres.
answer *v.* andvadda.
answer *(f)*. andvatt.
answer *v.* fa'andvadda.
answered *v.* fa'andvatt.
answered *v.* gandvat.
answers *(f)*. andvadda.
ant *(f)*. ummens.
antichrist *(m)*. viddah-christ.
antichrists *(f)*.
viddah-chrishta.
ants *(f)*. ummensa.
anvil *(m)*. ambohs.
anvils *(f)*. ambohsa.
anxieties *(f)*. engshta.
anxiety *(m)*. angsht.
anxious engshtlich.
any - ennichah. *(m. form)*
anyhow - ennichah.
anyone - ennich-ebbah.
anything - ennich-ebbes.
apostasy *(m)*. abfall.
apostatize *v.* abfalla.
apostatized *v.* abkfalla.
apostle *(m)*. aposhtel.
apostles *(f)*. aposhtla.
appear *v.* sheina.
appear (to someone) *v.* lauda.
appearance *(m)*. foahshein.
appearance *(m)*. shein.
appeared *v.* ksheind.
appendicitis *(f)*.
deahmenszinda.
appetite *(m)*. abeditt.
appetites *(f)*. abedidda.
apple *(m)*. abbel.

apples *(f)*. ebbel.
appoint *v*. setza.
appointed *v*. ksetzt.
appointed (a date or time) *v*.
    kshteld.
appropriate - shiklich.
approved of - kfellich.
April *(m)*. Abrill.
apron *(m)*. shatz.
aprons *(f)*. shatza.
apt - aebt.
archangel *(m)*. hohch-engel.
archangels *(f)*. hohch-engela.
are *v*. bisht *(verb conj. of sei)*
    ("du bisht")
are *v*. sinn *(verb conj. of sei)*
    ("miah sinn" , "si sinn")
area *(neu)*. gaygend.
areas *(f)*. gaygenda.
argue *v*. zarra / zadda.
argued *v*. gezatt.
argued *v*. gmauld.
arguing *(neu)*. gezahh.
arguing *(m)*. zank.
ark *(f)*. oahrich.
ark of the covenant *(m)*.
    bundes-lawt.
arks *(f)*. oahrichs.
arm *(m)*. oahm.
armor *(neu)*. greeks-ksha.
arms *(f)*. eahm.
army people *(f)*. greeks-leit.
around - rumm.
around front - fanna-rumm
arrive *v*. anna-kumma.
arrogant -grohs-feelich
    (feeling "big" about yourself)
arrogant - grohs-hansich
    (acting like you're "big & tough")

as - vi.
ash pan *(f)*. esh-pann.
ash pans *(f)*. esh-panna.
ashes *(f)*. esh.
ask *v*. frohwa.
ask for *v*. bidda.
asked *v*. kfrohkt.
assemble *v*. fasamla.
assembled - bei-nannah.
assembled *v*. fasammeld.
assistance *(f)*. hilf.
associate with *v*. eigay.
associated with *v*. eiganga.
assuredly - fashuah.
astonish *v*. fashtauna.
astonish *v*. favunnahra.
astonished *v*. fashtaund.
astonished *v*. favunnaht.
astonishing - unbegreiflich.
at - anna.
at home - dihaym.
at last - baddamoll.
at once - amohl
    (always proceeded by "uf")
at one time - als.
at that time - ivvahdemm.
at times - als.
ate *v*. gessa.
attain *v*. alanga.
attained *v*. alangt.
attempt *v*. fasucha.
attempt *v*. unnah-nemma.
attempted *v*. unnah-gnumma.
attend *v*. einemma.
attended *v*. eignumma.
auction (venue) *(f)*. fenyoo
auctions (venues) *(f)*. fenyoos
August *(m)*. Augsht.
authority *(f)*. macht.

autumn *(neu).* shpoht-yoah
avenger of blood *(m).*
    bloot-auseevah.
awake - vakkah.
away - vekk.
away (away from home) fatt.

awful - shlimm.
ax head *(m).* ax-kobb.
ax heads *(f).* ax-kebb.
axes *(f).* ex.
axle *(f).* ax.

B - b

babble *v.* babla.
babbled *v.* gebabbeld.
babied *v.* fabobbeld.
babies (baby dolls) *(f).* bobba
babies *(f).* boblen.
baby (baby doll) *(f).* bobb
baby *(neu).* bobli.
baby *v.* fabobla.
baby horse *(neu).* hutshli.
baby horses *(f).* hutshlen.
back *(m).* bukkel.
back (located to the back) hinna
back (toward a former place or
    state) zrikk
backs *(f).* bukla.
backward - hinnahsich.
bacon (side fat) *(neu)*
    seida-shpekk.
bad (inanimate object) shlecht.
bad (animate object) veesht.
badger skin *(f).* badger-haut.
badger skins *(f)* badger-heidah.
bag *(m).* sakk.
bags *(f).* sekk.
bake *v.* bakka.
bake oven *(m).* bakk-offa.
bake ovens *(f).* bakk-effa.

baked *v.* gebakka.
baker *(m).* bakkah.
bakeries *(f).* bakkahreiya.
bakery *(f).* bakkahrei.
bald - bawld.
bald head *(m).* bawl-kobb.
bald heads *(f).* bawl-kebb.
baldheaded - bawl-kebbich.
ball *(m).* balla.
balsam salve *(f)* balsam-shmiah.
ban *(m).* bawn.
banged up *v.* fabumbt.
banging noise *v.* demmahra.
baptism *(f).* dawf.
baptisms *(f).* dawfa.
baptize *v.* dawfa.
baptized *v.* gedawft.
baptizer *(m).* dawfah.
barefeet *(f).* boah-fees.
barefoot *(m).* boah- foos.
barefooted - boah-feesich.
bareheaded - blutt-kebbich.
bark *v.* gautza.
barked *v.* gegautzt.
barley *(f).* geahsht.
barley bread *(neu)*
    geahsht-broht.

(m) = da   (f) = di   (neu) = es   127

barn *(f)*. sheiyah.
barns *(f)*. sheiyahra.
barrel *(neu)*. fass.
barrels *(f)*. fessah.
basement *(m)*. kellah.
basements *(f)*. kellahs.
bashful - shemmich.
basket *(m)*. koahb.
basket full *(m)*. koahb-foll.
baskets *(f)*. keahb.
baskets full *(f)*. keahb-foll.
bat (animal) *(f)*. fleddah-maus.
batch *(f)*. baetsh.
batches *(f)*. baetshes.
bathroom *(f)*. bawt-shtubb.
bathroom *(f)*. bawt-shtubba.
bats (animal) *(f)*. fleddah-meis.
batter *v*. fademmahra.
battered *v*. fademmaht.
battle *v*. shtreida.
battle field *(neu)*. fechta-feld.
battle fields *(f)*. fechta-feldah.
battled *v*. kshtridda.
bawl out *v*. fagreisha.
bawled out *v*. fagrisha.
be *v*. sei.
be able to (can) *v*. kann.
be careful *v*. acht-gevva.
be of the opinion *v*. glawva.
beak (of a bird) *(m)*. shnavvel
beak / bill (of a bird) *(m)* pikkah
bean *(f)*. bawn.
bean pole *(m)*.
     bawna-shtekka.
beans *(f)*. bawna.
bear *(m)*. beah.
bear (or suffer) *v*. shtenda
bear (with patience) *v*. dulda.
beard *(m)*. boaht.

beards *(f)*. beaht.
beared *v*. kshtend.
bears *(f)*. beahra.
beast that blasphemes *(neu)*.
     leshtah-diah.
beasts that blaspheme *(f)*.
     leshtah-diahra.
beat *v*. globba.
beat out flames *v*.
     auskshlauwa / ausshlauwa.
beat up *v*. abgeglobt.
beat up *v*. abglobba.
beat up *v*. fashlauwa.
beat up *v*. faglobt. *(past)*
beat up *v*. faglobba
     (present, future)
beaten *v*. geglobt.
beautiful - shay.
because - veil.
because of it - dideich.
become *v*. vadda.
become (moldy) *v*. fagrohtzt.
     (past)
become (moldy) *v*. fagrohtza.
     (present, future)
become older *v*. fa'elda.
become rusty *v*. faroshta.
bed *(neu)*. bett.
bed sheet *(neu)*. bett-zeech.
bedding *(neu)*. bett-sach.
bedroom *(f)*. bett-kammah.
bedroom *(f)*. bett-shtubb.
bedroom *(f)*. kammah.
bedrooms *(f)*. bett-kammahra.
bedrooms *(f)*. kemmahra.
beds *(f)*. beddah.
bedsheets *(f)*. bett-zeecha.
bedtime *(f)*. bett-zeit.
bee *(f)*. eem.

beech *(m)*. boocha.
beer *(neu)*. biah.
bees *(f)*. eema.
before - difoah.
before - eb.
before - fa.
before now - foahrich.
beforehand - ebdihand.
beg *v*. bedla.
began *v*. ohkfanga.
beggar *(m)*. bedlah.
begged *v*. gebeddeld.
begin *v*. ohfanga.
beginning *(m)*. ohfang.
beginnings *(f)*. ohfanga.
behave *v*. behayfa.
behave *v*. ohshikka.
behaved *v*. behayft.
behaved *v*. ohkshikt.
behead *v*. kebba.
beheaded *v*. gekebt.
behind - hinna-noch
(example: running behind on time)
behind - hinnich.
behind - nohch.
belief *(m)*. glawva.
believe *v*. glawva.
believed *v*. geglawbt.
believing - glawvich.
belittle *v*. faglennahra.
belittled *v*. faglennaht.
bell *(f)*. bell.
bellies *(f)*. beich.
bells *(f)*. bella.
belly *(m)*. bauch.
belong *v*. heahra.
belong there *v*. anna-heahra.
belonged *v*. keaht.
belonged there *v*. anna-keaht.

beloved - beleebt.
beloved - leeb.
belt *(m)*. belt.
belts *(f)*. beldah.
bemoan *v*. beglawwa.
bemoan *v*. fayammahra.
bemoaned *v*. beglawkt.
bemoaned *v*. fayammaht.
bench *(f)*. bank.
benches *(f)*. benk.
bend *v*. beeya.
bend (out of shape) *v*. fabeeya.
bend over *v*. ivvah-beeya.
benefit *v*. badda.
benefited *v*. gebatt.
bent *v*. gebohwa.
bent (out of shape) *v*. fabohwa.
bent over *v*. ivvah-gebohwa.
berate *v*. fashelda.
berated *v*. fasholda.
berries *(f)*. beahra.
berry *(f)*. beah.
beside - nayvich.
best - besht.
betray *v*. farohda.
betrayed - bedrohwa.
better - bessah.
better thing - bessahs.
between - zvisha.
between - zvishich.
beverage *(neu)*. drinks.
beware of *v*. heeda.
bewildered *v*. fashtatzt.
Bible *(f)*. Bivvel.
Bibles *(f)*. Bivla.
bicker *v*. zaufa.
bickered *v*. gezauft.
bid (peace, greeting etc.) *v*. bidda.
bid *v*. beeda.

big - grohs.
bigger - graysah.
biggest - graysht.
bill (on a bird) *(m)* shnavvel
bin *(m)*. kashta.
bind *v.* fabinna.
bird *(m)* fohl *(common use)*
bird *(m)* fokkel *(used in the Bible)*
bird catcher *(m)*. fekkel-fangah.
bird of prey *(m)*. flaysh-fokkel.
birds *(f)* feyyel *(common use)*
birds *(f)* fekkel *(used in the Bible)*
birds of prey *(f)*. flaysh-fekkel.
birthday *(m)*. yeahs-dawk.
birthdays *(f)*. yeahs-dawwa.
bishop *(m)*. bishof.
bishop office *(m)*
     fellicha-deensht
bishops *(f)*. bishofs.
bite *(m)*. beis.
bite *v.* beisa.
bite off *v.* abbeisa.
bitten *v.* gebissa.
bitten off *v.* abgebissa.
bitter biddah.
bitter herbs (wormwood) *(f)*.
     biddah-greidah.
bitterly - biddahlich.
blab *v.* blaebbahra.
blabbed *v.* geblaebbaht.
blabbermouth *(neu)*.
     blaebbah-maul.
blabbermouths *(f)*
     blaebbah-meilah.
black - shvatz.
blackberries *(f)*. blaekbeahra.
blackberry *(f)*. blaekbeah.
blacksmith *(m)*. blaekshmitt.
blacksmiths *(f)*. blaekshmidda.

blame *(f)*. shuld.
blameless - shuldlohs.
blameless - unshtrayflich
     (lit.- not punishable)
blames *(f)*. shulda.
blameworthy - shuldich.
blanket *(f)*. dekk.
blankets *(f)*. dekka.
blaspheme *v.* faleshtahra.
blaspheme *v.* leshtahra.
blasphemed *v.* faleshtaht.
blasphemed *v.* gleshtaht.
blasphemer *(m)*. leshtahrah.
blaspheming (habitual)
     geleshtah
blaze *v.* flamma.
blazed *v.* kflamd.
bleat *v.* bladda.
bleated *v.* geblatt.
bled *v.* geblooda.
bleed *v.* blooda.
bleeding sickness *(f)*.
     bloots-granket.
bleeding sicknesses *(f)*.
     bloots-grankeda.
bless *v.* saykna.
blessed *v.* ksaykend.
blessed - saylich.
blessing *(m)*. sayya.
blind - blind.
blind (with a bright light) *v.*
     fablenna.
blinded (by a bright light) *v.*
     fablend.
blindness *(f)*. blindheit.
blindnesses *(f)*. blindheida.
blink *v.* blikka.
blink *(m)*. blikk.
blink (wink eye) *(m)*. awwa-blikk

blink (eyes) *v.* blinsla.
blinked *v.* geblikt.
blinked (eyes) *v.* geblinseld.
blister *(m).* blohdah.
blisters *(f).* blohdahra.
block *(m).* blakk.
blocks *(f).* blaks.
blood *(neu).* bloot.
blood guilt - bloot-shuld.
blood guilty - bloot-shuldich.
blood red - bloot-roht.
blood shedder *(m)*
        bloot-fageesah.
blood spot *(m).* bloot-blakka.
blood sucker - bloot-suklah.
blood thirsty - bloot-dashtich.
bloodstream *(m).*
        bloot-shtrayma.
bloody - bloodich.
bloom *v.* bleeya.
bloomed *v.* gebleet.
blow *v.* blohsa.
blow away *v.* fablohsa.
blow off *v.* abblohsa.
blower *(m).* blohsah.
blown *v.* geblohsa.
blown off *v.* abgeblohsa.
blue - bloh.
bluebird *(m).* bloh-fohkel.
bluebirds *(f).* bloh-fayyel.
blues *(f).* bloos.
board *(neu).* boaht.
boards *(f).* beaht.
boat *(neu).* boht.
boats *(f).* bohts.
bodies *(f).* leivah.
body *(m).* leib.
boil *(f).* kshveah.
boiler *(m).* beilah.

boils *(f).* kshveahra.
bold (in a bad sense) - frech
bondage *(neu).* fabindnis.
bondages *(f).* fabindnisa.
bone *(m).* gnocha.
book *(neu).* buch.
book keeper *(m).* buch-haldah.
Book of Life *(neu).* layves-buch.
booklet *(neu).* bichli.
booklets *(f).* bichlen.
books *(f).* bichah.
boot *(m).* shtiffel.
bore (with patience) *v.* geduld.
bored laydich.
born *v.* geboahra.
borrow *v.* layna.
borrowed *v.* glaynd.
bossy - batzich.
bossy - bawsich.
bossy - foahvitzich.
both - awl-zvay *(lit. - "all- two")*
bother *(m).* baddah.
bother *v.* badra.
bother *(m).* blohk.
bother *v.* blohwa.
bothered *v.* gebaddaht.
bothered *v.* geblohkt.
bothers *(f).* baddahra.
bothersome - blohwich.
bottle *(f).* boddel.
bottle (small) *(neu)* bodli.
bottles *(f).* bodla.
bottles (small) *(f).* bodlen.
bought *v.* abgekawft.
bought *v.* gekawft.
bought out *v.* ausgekawft.
boulder *(m).* felsa.
bound *v.* fabunna.
bow *v.* bikka.

bow (made of string or ribbon) *(m)* shlobb

 bowed *v.* gebikt.

bowl *(f)*. bohl.

bowl full *(f)*. bohlfoll.

bowl (large, serving) *(f)*. shissel.

bowls *(f)*. bohla.

bowls full *(f)*. bohlafoll.

bowls (large, serving) *(f)*. shisla.

box *(f)*. box.

box stall *(m)*. box-shtall.

box stalls *(f)*. box-shtell.

boxes *(f)*. boxa.

boy *(m)*. boo.

boy (little) *(neu)*. boovli.

boys *(f)*. boova.

boys (little) *(f)*. boovlen.

brace *v.* shteibahra.

braced *v.* kshteibaht.

brag *v.* braekka.

braggart *(m)*. braekkah.

bragged *v.* gebraekt.

braid *v.* zebba.

braided *v.* gezebt.

branch *(f)*. hekk.

branch *(m)*. nasht.

branches *(f)*. hekka.

branches *(f)*. nesht.

bread *(neu)*. broht.

bread baker *(m)*. broht-bakkah.

bread dough *(m)*. broht-dayk.

bread doughs *(f)*. broht-dayka.

bread pan *(f)*. broht-pann.

bread pans *(f)*. broht-panna.

break *v.* brecha.

break (into crumbs) *v.* fagrimla.

break (into pieces) *v.* fabrecha.

break off *v.* abbrecha.

break out (rash) *v.* usbrecha

breast *(f)*. brusht.

breast piece*(neu)*. brusht-shtikk.

breast plates *(f)*. brusht-playts.

breastplate *(neu)*. brusht-playt.

breasts *(f)*. brisht.

breath *(f)*. ohften.

breathe *v.* shnaufa.

breathe in *v.* eishnaufa.

breathed *v.* kshnauft.

breathed in *v.* eikshnauft.

bred *v.* gebreed.

breed *v.* breeda.

breezy - luftich.

bribe *v.* abkawfa.

bribed *v.* abgekawft.

brick *(m)* bakka-shtay.

      (lit. - baked stone)

bride *(neu)*. hochtzich-maydel.

bridegroom *(m)*. hochtzeidah.

bridegroom *(m)*.

    hochtzich-mann.

bridegrooms *(f)*.

    hochtzich-mennah.

brides *(f)*. hochtzich-mayt.

bridge *(f)*. brikk.

bridges *(f)*. brikka.

bridle *(m)*. zohm.

bridles *(f)*. zaym.

brightness *(m)*. glantz.

bring *v.* bringa.

bring (from somewhere) *v.*

    bei-bringa.

broiler (chicken) *(m)*. brawlah.

broiler house *(m)*.

    brawlah-shtall.

broiler houses *(f)*.

    brawlah-shtell.

broilers (chicken) *(f)*. brawlahs.

broke *v.* gebrocha.

broke (into crumbs)*v*. fagrimmeld
broke out (rash) *v*. ausgebrocha.
broken *v*. fabrocha.
broken off *v*. abgebrocha.
broken pots - fabrochani-heffa.
bronze altar *(m)* bronze-awldah
bronze alters *(f)*
        bronze-awldahra.
brook *(f)*. grikk.
brooks *(f)*. grikka.
broom *(m)*. baysa.
broom tree *(m)*. baysa-bohm.
broom trees *(f)*. baysa-baym.
brother *(m)*. broodah.
brotherhood *(f)*. broodah-shaft.
brotherhoods*(f)* broodah-shafta
brotherly - breedahlich.
brothers *(f)*. breedah.
brought *v*. gebrocht.
brought (from somewhere) *v*.
        bei-gebrocht.
brown - brau.
bruise *v*. fabummba.
bruise *v*. fashunna.
bruised *v*. fabumbt.
brush off *v*. abbashta
(example: to brush dirt or dust off
    your shirt).
brushed off *v*. abgebasht.
bucket *(m)*. aymah.
bucks *(f)*. bekk.
bud (on a plant) *(m)*. blee-gnobb.
buds (on a plant) *(f)*. blee-gnebb.
bug (insect) *(m)*. kaeffah.
bugs (insects) *(f)*. kaeffahra.
build *v*. bauwa.
building *(neu)*. gebei.
buildings *(f)*. gebeiyah.
built *v*. gebaut.

built-in *v*. nei-gmacht.
bull *(m)*. bull.
bull rush *(m)*. bull-rosh.
bull rushes *(f)*. bull-rosha.
bull-headed - bull-kebbich.
bulls *(f)*. bulla.
bumble bee *(m)*. hummel.
bumble bees *(f)*. humla.
bumbling (clumsy) dabbich.
bump *v*. blotza.
bump *(m)*. blotzah.
bump *v*. bumba.
bump *(m)*. bumbah.
bump *v*. fabummba.
bumped *v*. geblotzt.
bumped *v*. gebumpt.
bumpy - blotzich.
bumpy - bumbich.
bundle *(m)*. bundel.
bundles *(f)*. bundla.
bunnies *(f)*. hawslen.
bunny (small rabbit) *(neu)*.
        hawsli.
burden *(f)*. lasht.
burden *v*. nunnah-lawda.
burdened *v*. nunnah-glawda.
burdens *(f)*. lashta.
burial place *(neu)*. begraybnis.
burial place *(m)*. grawb-blatz.
burial places *(f)*.
        begraybnis-bletz.
burn *v*. brenna.
burn blister *(m)*. feiya-blashtah.
burn out *v*. ausbrenna.
burn up *v*. fabrenna.
burned *v*. gebrend.
burned out *v*. ausgebrend.
burned up *v*. fabrend.
burnt offering*(neu)*brand-opfah

burnt offering alters *(f)*.
  brand-opfah-awldahra.
burnt offerings *(f)*.
  brand-opfahra.
burp *v*. ufshtohsa.
burped *v*. ufkshtohsa.
burst *v*. fablohsa.
burst (explode like a firecracker)
  v. fashpritza.
burst (exploded like a firecracker)
  v. fashpritzt.
burst *v*. fabost *(past)*
burst *v*. fabosta *(present, future)*
bury *v*. fagrawva.
bushel *(f)*. bushel.
bushel baskets *(f)*.
  bushel-keahb.
bushel-basket *(m)*
  bushel-koahb
busybody - aus'shnubbahrah.
but - avvah.
butcher *(m)*. butshah.
butcher *v*. butshahra.
butcher house *(neu)*
  butshah-haus

butcher houses *(f)*.
  butshah-heisah.
butchered *v*. gebutshaht.
butchered (an animal) *v*.
  kshlacht
butchers *(f)*. butshahs.
butter *(m)*. buddah.
butter churn *(neu)*
  buddah-fass
butter churns *(f)*
  buddah-fessah
buttermilk *(f)*. buddah-millich.
button *(m)*. gnobb.
buttons *v*. gnebb.
buy *v*. kawfa.
buy off *v*. abkawfa.
buy out *v*. auskawfa.
buzz *v*. brumma.
buzzard *(m)*. flaysh-fokkel.
buzzards *(f)*. flaysh-fekkel.
buzzed *v*. gebrumd.
buzzing - brummich.
by - bei.
by shortcut - grawtzu.

C - c

cabbage *(neu)* graut.
cabinet *(m)*. shank.
cackle *v*. gaksa.
cackled *v*. gegakst.
cake *(m)*. kucha.
calander *(m)*. klennah.
calculate *v*. fikkahra.
calculated *v*. kfikkaht.

calf *(neu)*. hamli.
calf *(neu)* kalb *(used in the Bible)*
call *v*. haysa.
call *(m)*. roof.
call *v*. roofa.
call (an animal) *v*. lokka.
call (on the phone) *v*. kawla.
call (out of) *v*. raus-roofa.

call (upon) *v.* ohroofa.
called *v.* groofa.
called *v.* kaysa.
called (on the phone) *v.* gekawld.
called out *v.* ausgroofa.
called out *v.* groofa.
called (out of) *v.* raus-groofa.
called (upon) *v.* ohgroofa.
calling *(m).* beroof.
calls *(f).* roofa.
calm roowich.
calves *(f).* hamlen.
calves *(f)* kelvah *(used in theBible)*
came *v.* kumma.
camel *(m).* kamayl.
camels *(f).* kamayla.
can *v.* kann.
cancer *(neu)* grebs.
cane *(m).* shtokk.
canes *(f).* shtekk.
cantaloupe *(f).* moshmalawn.
cantaloupes *(f).* moshmalawna.
cap *(f).* kabb.
cape *(neu).* hals-duch
    (lit. - neck cloth).
capes *(f).* hals-dichah
    (lit. - neck cloths).
caps *(f).* kabba.
capsize *v.* umshmeisa.
captain *(m).* hauptmann.
captain *(m).* shiff-meishtah
    (lit. - shipmaster).
captains *(f).* hauptmennah.
captains *(f).* shiff-meishtahra
    (lit. - shipmasters).
car *(f).* keah.
cared *v.* gmeind.
cared for *v.* keet.
cared for *v.* kseikt.

caress (small strokes) *(neu)*
    shtrichli.
caretaker *(m).* heedah.
carnal - nadiahlich.
carnal nature *(m).* naduah.
carpenter *(m)* shreinah /zimmah
carpentery work *v.* shreinra.
carpentry (finish) *v.*
    ausshreinahra
carpentry worker *v.*
    zimmahra
carried *v.* gedrawwa.
carried (in from somewhere) *v.*
    bei-gedrawwa.
carried out *v.* ausgedrawwa.
carried out *v.* auskfiaht.
carry *v.* drawwa.
carry (in from somewhere) *v.*
    bei-drawwa.
carry out *v.* ausdrawwa.
carry out *v.* ausfiahra.
carrying poles - drawk-pohls.
cars *(f).* keahra.
cast *v.* kshtohsa.
cast *v.* shtohsa.
cast a spell *v.* fahext *(past)*
cast a spell *v.* fahexa.
    (present, future)
cast back *v.* zrikk-shtohsa.
cast out *v.* auskshtohsa.
cast out *v.* ausshtohsa.
cat *(f).* katz.
catapiller *(m).* vulli-voahm
    (lit. – wolly worm)
catapillers *(f).* vulli-veahm.
    (lit. – wolly worms)
catch *v.* fanga.
catcher *(m).* fangah.
cats *(f).* katza.

caught *v.* kfanga.
cause (to stumble) *v.* fashtatza.
caused (to stumble) *v.* fashtatzt.
causing offense - eiyahlich.
celler *(m).* kellah.
cellers *(f).* kellahs.
cemetaries *(f).* grawb-hohfa.
cemetary *(m).* grawb-hohf.
cemeteries *(f)* begraybnis-bletz
cemetery *(m)* begraybnis-blatz
cent *(m)* cent.
centurion *(m)* unnah-hauptmann
      (lit.- under captain)
centurions*(f)* unnah-auptmennah
      (lit. - under captains)
ceremonial hut (built of
      branches) *(neu).* lawb-haus.
ceremonial huts (built of
      branches) *(f).* lawb-heisah.
ceremonial showbread -
      (neu). tempel-broht
      (lit.- temple bread).
certainly - voahhaftich.
certainly - voll.
chaff *(neu)* shprau.
chain *(f)* kett.
chains *(f)* kedda.
chair *(m)* shtool.
chairs *(f)* shteel.
chance *(m)* tsheins.
change *v.* tshaynsha.
change (something) *v.*
      fa'ennahra.
changed *v.* fa'ennaht.
changed *v.* getshaynsht.
chapter *(neu)* gabiddel.
chapters *(f).* gabidla.
charge *v.* tsheahtsha.
charged *v.* getsheahtsht.

chase *v.* yawwa.
chase away *v.* fayawwa.
chased *v.* gyawkt.
chased away *v.* fayawkt.
chastity *(f).* keishheit.
cheat *v.* tsheeda.
cheated *v.* getsheet.
checked out *v.* ausgetshekt.
cheek *(m).* bakka.
cheek bone *(m).* bakka-gnocha.
cheese *(m).* kays.
cherries *(f).* kasha.
cherry *(f).* kash.
chest (furniture) *(m).* kashta.
chest (furniture) *(f).* kisht.
chests (furniture) *(f).* kishta.
chew *v.* tshawwa.
chewed *v.* getshawt.
chick *(neu)* beebli.
chicken *(neu)* hinkel.
chicken pox *(f).* vassah-pabla.
chickens *(f)* hinkla.
chicks *(f)* beeblen.
child *(neu)* kind.
childish - kindish.
children *(f).* kinnah.
Children of Thunder -
      Dimmels-Kinnah.
chimney *(m).* shanshtah.
chimneys *(f).* shanshtahs.
chin *(m).* boaht.
chins *(f).* beaht.
chipmunk *(neu).* fensa-meisli
      (lit. – fence mouse)
chipmunks *(f).* fensa-meislen
      (lit. – fence mice)
choice *(f).* avayling.
choices *(f).* avaylinga.
choose *v.* avayla.

choose *v.* pikka.

choose (ahead of time) *v.* foahroofa.

chop off *v.* abhakka.

chopped off *v.* abkakt.

chosen *v.* avayld.

chosen *v.* gepikt.

chosen (called) - groofa.

chosen (called ahead of time) *v.* foahgroofa.

Christ *(m).* Christus.

christian - grishtlich.

Christian people *(f).* Grishta-leit.

Christian person *(m).* Grishta-mensh.

chubby - diksekkich.

chubby person *(m).* diksak.

church (congregation) *(f).* gmay.

church house *(neu).* gmay-haus.

church houses *(f).* gmay-heisah.

church rules *(f).* adning.

churches (congregations) *(f).* gmayna.

cider *(neu).* seidah.

cigar *(f).* sikkeah.

cigars *(f).* sikkeahra.

circumcise *v.* beshneida.

circumcised *v.* beshnidda.

circumcision *(f).* beshneiding.

circumcisions *(f).* beshneidinga.

circumstance *(m).* umshtand.

circumstances *(f).* umshtenda.

clap *v.* bletsha.

clapped *v.* gebletsht.

clarified *v.* fakleaht.

clarify *v.* fakleahra.

classy - baddich.

clean *(adj.)* sauvah.

clean *v.* butza.

clean off *v.* abbutza.

clean out *v.* ausbutza.

clean out *v.* ausrohma.

cleaned *v.* gebutzt.

cleaned off *v.* abgebutzt.

cleaned out *v.* ausgebutzt.

cleaned out *v.* ausgrohmd.

cleanse *v.* reinicha.

cleansed *v.* greinicht.

clear - kliah.

clear *v.* kliahra.

clear off (a surface) *v.* abrohma.

clear off (weather, etc.) *v.* abkliahra.

cleared *v.* gekliaht.

cleared off *v.* abgekliaht.

cleared off (surface) *v.* abgrohmd

clearly - deitlich.

clearness *(f).* gloahheit.

climb *v.* gradla.

climbed *v.* gegraddeld.

clock *(f).* uah.

clocks *(f).* uahra.

closed - zu.

closely (around it) drumm.

closet *(neu).* kemmahli.

closets *(f).* kemmahlen.

cloth *(neu).* duch.

cloth belt *(neu).* duch-belt.

cloth belts *(f).* duch-belts.

clothe *v.* glayda.

clothed *v.* geglayt.

clothes *(f).* glaydah.

clothing *(f).* glaydah.

cloths *(f).* dichah.

cloud *(f)*. volk.
clouds *(f)*. volka.
cloudy - dreeb.
cloudy - volkich.
clover *(m)*. glay.
club *(m)*. globb-shtekka.
clump (of bushes) *(m)*.
      hekka-putsha.
clump (of thorns) *(m)*.
      danna-putsha.
clump *(m)*. glumba.
clumsy (bumbling) dobbich.
clumsy - glumsich.
clutter (confusion) *v*. fahudla.
cluttered(confused) *v*. fahuddeld
coal *(f)*. kohl.
coals *(f)*. kohla.
coat *(m)*. vammes.
coats *(f)*. vemmes.
cob *(m)*. kolva.
coffin *(f)*. lawt.
coffins *(f)*. lawda.
cold - kald.
colder - keldah.
coldest - keldsht.
collar *(m)*. band.
collars *(f)*. banda.
collection *(f)*. samling.
color *(m)*. kollah.
color *(m)*. faub.
color *v*. kollahra.
color (by using dye) *v*. feahva.
colored *v*. gekollaht.
colored (by using dye) *v*.
      kfeahbt.
colorless - ausgvesha.
      (lit. – washed out)
colors *(f)*. kollahs.
colors *(f)*. fauva

colt *(m)*. hutsh.
colts *(f)*. hutsha.
comb *(m)*. kamm.
comb *v*. kemma.
combed *v*. gekemd.
come *v*. kumma.
come (from somewhere) *v*.
      bei-kumma.
come to mind *v*. bei-falla.
comfort *v*. drayshta.
comfort *(m)*. drohsht.
comfort *v*. drohshta.
comforted *v*. fadraysht.
comforted *v*. gedraysht.
comforted *v*. gedrohsht.
comforter *(m)*. drayshtah.
comforting - drayshtlich.
command *(m)*. addah.
command *(neu)*. gebott.
commanding officer *(m)*.
      ivvah-deenah.
commands *(f)*. gebodda.
commit adultery *v*. aybrecha.
committed adultry *v*.
      aygebrocha.
communities *(f)*. gaygenda.
community *(neu)*. gaygend.
comparatively - fellich.
compel *v*. zvinga.
compelled *v*. gezvunga.
complain *v*. glawwa.
complain *v*. gneiksa.
complain about *v*. beglawwa.
complain about *v*. faglawwa.
complain about *v*. fagrumla.
complained *v*. geglawkt.
complained *v*. gegneikst.
complained about *v*.
      beglawkt.

complained about *v.*
  faglawkt.
complained about *v.*
  fagrummeld.
complainer *(adj).* gneiksich.
complaint *(f).* glawk.
complaints *(f).* glawwa.
completely - goah.
completely through
  gans-deich.
comply *v.* eigevva.
comprehend *v.* begreifa.
comprehended *v.* begriffa.
comprehensible begreiflich.
comprehension *(f).*
  fashtendnis.
comrade *(m).* kumrawt.
comrades *(f).* kumrawda.
concede *v.* eigevva.
conceited - grohs-feelich
  (feeling "big" about yourself)
conceited - grohs-hansich
  (acting like you're "big & tough")
concept *(m).* begriff.
concern *(f).* bekimmahnis.
concern about *v.* bekimmahra.
concerned *v.* bekimmaht.
concerning - veyyich / veyya.
concerning it - drumm.
concerns *(f).* bekimmahnisa.
conclusion *(m).* ausgang.
condemn *v.* fadamma.
condemnation *(f).* fadamins.
condemnations *(f).* fadamnisa.
condemned *v.* fadamd.
conduct *(m).* layves-lawf.
confess *v.* bekenna.
confessed *v.* bekend.
confession *(neu).* bekendnis.

confessions *(f).* bekendnissa.
confidence *(m).* fadrauwa.
confidence *(f).* fadrauwung.
confidences *(f).* fadrawunga.
confine *v.* eishpadda.
confined *v.* eikshpatt.
confuse *v.* fahudla.
confuse *v.* fashtatza.
confused *v.* fahuddeld.
confused *v.* fashtatzt.
congregation *(f).* gmay.
congregations *(f).* gmayna.
connected to - fesht.
conscience *(neu).* gvissa.
considered unimportant *v.*
  fa'acht.
consume by fire *v.* fazeahra.
consumed by fire *v.* fazeaht.
consuming - fazeahrich.
contagious - eahblich.
contempt *(f).* fa'achtung.
contempts *(f).* fa'achtunga.
content - zu-fridda.
contentious - fechtich.
continue *v.* oh'halda.
continue *v.* onhalda.
continued *v.* ohkalda.
contracting against - veddah.
convulsions *(f).* gichtahra.
cook *v.* kocha.
cooked *v.* gekocht.
cool - keel.
cool *v.* keela.
cool off *v.* abkeela.
cooled *v.* gekeeld.
cooled off *v.* abgekeeld.
copied *v.* abgekabbit.
copied (by hand) *v.* abkshrivva.
copper *(neu).* kubbah.

coppersmith *(m)* kubbah-shmitt.
coppersmiths *(f)* kubbah-shmidda.
copy *v.* abkabbiya.
copy (by hand) *v.* abshreiva.
core *(m).* grutza.
corn *(neu).* velshkan.
corn cob *(m).* grutza.
corn tassels *(f).* fawna.
corner *(neu).* ekk.
corner post *(m).* ekk-poshta.
corner stone *(m).* ekk-shtay.
corners *(f).* ekkah.
correct - recht.
cost *v.* koshta.
cost *v.* gekosht. *(past)*
costly - koshtboah.
cough *(m).* hooshta.
could *v.* kenda.
counsel *v.* rohda.
counseled *v.* grohda.
count *v.* kaunda.
count *v.* zayla.
count off *v.* abzayla.
counted *v.* gekaund (*English word using PA-German rules*)
counted *v.* gezayld.
counted off *v.* abgezayld.
couple (pair) - poah.
courage *(f).* moot.
court house *(neu).* gericht-haus.
court houses *(f)* gericht-heisah.
courtyard *(m).* haus-hohf.
courtyards *(f).* haus-hohfa.
covenant *(m).* bund.
covenants *(f).* bunda.
cover *v.* dekka.
cover *(m).* dekkel.
cover *v.* zu-dekka.

cover over *v.* ivvah-dekka.
cover (with patches) *v.* faflikka.
covered *v.* gedekt.
covered *v.* zu-gedekt.
covered over *v.* ivvah-gedekt.
covered (with patches) *v.* faflikt.
covered (with stings) *v.* fashtocha
covered (with writing) *v.* fashrivva.
covers *(f).* dekla.
covetous - geitzich.
covetous (of honor) eahgeitzich.
covetousness *(m).* geitz.
covetousness *(f).* lushtahrei.
cow *(f).* koo.
cows *(f).* kee.
crab *(f).* grebs.
crabs *(f).* grebsa.
cradle *(neu).* bedli.
cradles *(f).* bedlen.
craftiness *(f).* shlichtichkeit.
crafty - shlichtich.
cranky *(adj.)* gneiksich.
crawl *v.* gradla.
crawled *v.* gegraddeld.
crayfish *(f).* grebs.
crayfish *(f).* grebsa.
crazy *v.* farukt.
creak *v.* greksa.
creaked *v.* gegrekst.
cream *(m).* rawm.
created *v.* kshaffa.
crevice *(m).* grawva.
crib *(neu).* bedli.
cribs *(f).* bedlen.
cried *v.* gebrild.
cried *v.* gebrutzt.
cried out *v.* gegrisha.

cripple *v.* fagribla.
cripple *(m).* gribbel.
cripple *v.* gribla.
crippled *v.* fagribbeld.
crippled *v.* gegribbeld.
crippled one *(f).* fagribbeldah.
cripples *(f).* gribla.
crock *(m).* haffa.
crooked - grumm.
cross *(neu).* greitz
crosses *(f).* greitza.
crotch *(m).* graddel.
crow *(f).* grabb.
crowd *(f).* drubb.
crowds *(f).* drubba.
crowed (like a rooster) *v.* gegrayt.
crown *(m).* krohn.
crown *v.* krohna.
crown of flowers *(m).* blumma-krohn.
crown of life *(m).* layves-krohn.
crowned *v.* gekrohnd.
crowns of flowers *(f).* blumma-krohna.
crows *(f).* grabba.
crucified *v.* gegreitzicht.
crucify *v.* greitzicha.
crumb *(f).* grimmel.
crumb (can refer to solids within a liquid) *(m).* brokka.
crumble *v.* fagrimla.
crumbled *v.* fagrimmeld.
crumbly - grimlich.
crumbs *(f).* grimla.
crumple *v.* fadobla.
crumpled *v.* fadobbeld.
crust *(f).* grusht.
crust *(f).* shawl.
crusts *(f).* shawla.

crutch *(f).* grikk.
crutches *(f).* grikka.
cry *v.* brilla.
crying *(neu)* brilles.
crying (constantly) *(neu).* gebrill.
cried out *v.* greisha.
cry out *v.* greisha.
crystal glasses *(f).* crystal-glessah.
crystal-glass *(neu)* crystal-glaws
cucumber *(f).* gummah.
cucumbers *(f).* gummahra.
cup *(neu).* kobli.
cups *(f).* koblen.
curious gvunnahrich.
curse *(m).* fluch.
curse *v.* flucha.
curse words *(f).* fluch-vadda.
cursed *v.* faflucht.
cursed *v.* kflucht.
curses *(f).* flucha.
curtain *(m).* curtain.
custard *(m).* koshtaht.
custom *(m).* gebrauch.
customarily - gvaynlich.
customs *(f).* gebraucha.
cut *v.* shneida.
cut off *v.* abkshnidda.
cut off *v.* abshneida.
cut off (with scissors) *v.* absheahra.
cut off (with sissors) *v.* abkshoahra.
cut *v.* kshnidda. *(past)*
cut up *v.* fashnidda. *(past)*
cut up *v.* fashneida. *(present, future)*
cut (with scissors) *v.* sheahra.
cute shnokk.

D - d

dad *(m)*. daett.
dads *(f)*. daedda.
daily - dayklich.
daily - tayklich *(used in the Bible)*
damage *v.* fadauva.
damage *v.* fadeahva.
damage *v.* fasauwa.
damaged *v.* fasaut.
damp - feicht.
dance *(f)*. dans.
dance *v.* dansa.
danced *v.* gedanst.
dances *(f)*. dansa.
danger *(f)*. kfoah.
dangerous - kfeahlich.
dangers *(f)*. kfoahra.
dare *v.* drauwa.
dared *v.* gedraut.
dark - dunkel.
darken *v.* fadunkla.
darkened *v.* fadunkeld.
darkness *(f)*. dunkelheit.
darknesses *(f)*. dunkelhayda.
daughter *(f)*. dochtah.
daughter-in-law *(f)*.
   shviah-dochtah.
daughters *(f)*. dechtah.
daughters-in-law *(f)*.
   shviah-dochtahra.
day *(m)*. dawk.
day-after-tomorrow -
   ivvah-meiya.
daylight *(f)*. dawks-helling.
day of fasting *(m)*. fasht-dawk.
day of feast *(m)*. ess-fesht-dawk.

day of judgement *(m)*.
   richtah-dawk.
day of preparation *(m)*.
   risht-dawk.
days *(f)*. dawwa.
days of fasting *(f)*.
   fasht-dawwa.
days of feast *(f)*.
   ess-fesht-dawwa.
days of judgement *(f)*.
   richtah-dawwa.
days of preparation *(f)*.
   risht-dawwa.
daytime - dawks.
dead - doht.
deaf - dawb.
deal with *v.* handla.
dealt with *v.* kandeld.
dear (love) leeb.
death angel *(m)*. dohdes-engel.
death angels *(f)*. dohdes-engla.
death bed *(neu)*. dohdes-bett.
death beds *(f)*. dohdes-beddah.
death blow *(m)*. dohdes-blohk.
death blow - doht-shlakk.
death blows *(f)*. dohdes-blohwa.
debating *(neu)*. gezah.
debris *(neu)*. kfrays.
debt *(f)*. shuld.
debts *(f)*. shulda.
deceitful - shlitzoahrich.
deceitful - zvay-ksichtich.
   (lit. — two faced)
deceive *v.* fafiahra.
deceiver *(m)*. fafiahrah.

decency *(m)*. fashtand.
decent - tshaett.
deception *(f)*. fafiahrahrei.
deceptive - fafiahrich.
deceptiveness *(f)*. fafiahrichkeit.
decide *v*. ausmacha.
decided *v*. ausgmacht.
decieved *v*. fafiaht.
deck *(m)*. dekk.
decrepit *v*. nunnah-grand.
deed *(neu)*. ksheft.
deeds *(f)*. kshefta.
deep - deef.
deer *(m)*. hash.
defect - fayl.
defense *(m)*. viddah-shtand.
define *v*. ausdrawwa.
defined *v*. ausgedrawwa.
deliberately (on purpose) poahbes.
deliverance *(f)*. frei-shtelling.
deliverer *(m)*. frei-drayyah.
deluge *(f)*. sindfloot (global flood in Noah's day that God used to destroy the wicked inhabitants of the earth.) *(lit.- sin-flood)*.
demand *v*. foddahra / fodra.
demanded *v*. kfoddaht.
demons *(f)*. deivela.
denied *v*. abksawt.
denied *v*. falaykeld.
dent *(m)*. dalla.
dent *v*. fademmahra.
dented *v*. fademmaht.
deny *v*. falaykla.
depart *v*. falossa.
depending on - demnohch.
depending on - dinohch.

depressed - bloosich.
depth *(f)*. deefing.
desert *v*. ablawfa.
deserted *v*. abgloffa.
desire *(m)*. falanga.
desire *(f)*. falanging.
desire *(m)*. glushta.
desire *v*. glushta.
desire *(m)*. villa.
desire (longing) *v*. falanga.
desire (want misfortune for another) *v*. fagunna.
desire (want what is wrong) *(f)*. lusht.
desired *v*. falangt.
desired *v*. geglusht.
desired *v*. glusht.
desires *(f)*. falanginga.
desires (that are wrong) *(f)*. lushta.
desirous - glushtich.
despise *v*. fa'achta.
despised *v*. fa'acht.
destroyer *(m)*. fadeahvah.
destruction *(f)*. fadeahving.
destructive - fadeahblich.
detonate *v*. absheesa.
detonated *v*. abkshossa.
devastate *v*. faveeshta.
devastated *v*. faveesht.
devastation *(f)*. faveeshtung.
devestations *(f)*. faveeshtunga.
devil *(m)*. Deivel.
devilish - deivilish.
devils *(f)*. deivela.
devour *v*. fressa.
devoured *v*. kfressa.
dew *(m)*. dau.
deworm *v*. veahma.

dewormed *v.* gveahmd.
diaper *(f).* vindel.
diaper cloth *(neu).* vindla-duch.
diaper cloths *(f)* vindla-dichah.
diapers *(f).* vindla.
diarrhea *(f).* deich-lawf.
die *v.* shtauva.
die *v.* shteahva.
die (of thirst) *v.* fadashta.
die off *v.* abshtauva.
died *v.* kshtauva.
died (of thirst) *v.* fadasht.
died off *v.* abkshtauva.
difference *(m).* unnahshitt.
differences *(f).* unnahshidda.
dig *v.* grawva.
dig out *v.* ausgrawva.
diligence *(f).* fleisichkeit.
diligent - fleisich.
dilute *v.* fadinnahra.
dilute *v.* fashvecha.
diluted *v.* fadinnaht.
diluted *v.* fashvecht.
dip *v.* dunka.
dipped *v.* gedunkt.
dipper *(m).* shebbah.
directly (straight) grawt.
dirt *(m).* drekk.
dirtied *v.* fadrekt.
dirtied *v.* fasuddeld.
dirty - drekkich.
dirty *v.* fadrekka.
dirty *v.* fasudla.
disappear *v.* fagay.
disappeared *v.* faganga.
disappointed - fadrossa.
disassemble *v.* farobba.
disassembled *v.* farobt.
disburse (money) *v.* ausbezawla

disbursed (money) *v.* ausbezawld
disciple *(m).* yingah.
discourage (from) *v.* abveahra
discouraged (from) *v.* abgveaht.
discouraging - fadreeslich.
discover (by chance) *v.* druff-dabba.
discovered (by chance) *v.* druff-gedabt.
discuss *v.* fashvetza.
discussed *v.* fashvetzt.
disgrace *(f).* shand.
disgrace *(m)* shohm *(used in the Bible)*
disgraceful - shandlich.
disgraces *(f).* shanda.
disgust *v.* abdrayya.
disgusted *v.* abgedrayt.
disgusting - abdrayyish.
disgusting - ayklich.
disgusting - grausich.
dish *(neu)* ksha.
dishes *(f)* ksharra.
dishonest - shlichtich.
dishonest - uneahlich.
disobedient - ungehorsam.
disorder *(f).* unadning.
disorient *v.* fahunsa.
disoriented *v.* fahunst.
disposed - psunna.
disposition *(m).* naduah.
disposition of - naduaht.
disregard (purposely) *v.* ivvah-gukka.
disregarded (purposely) *v.* ivvah-gegukt.
distaste *(m).* aykel.
distasteful *v.* aykla.

distasteful *v.* gaykeld.
distastefully - ayklich.
distemper *(f).* dishtembah.
distinguishable - unnahshidlich
distribute *v.* ausdayla.
distributed *v.* ausgedayld.
disturb *v.* fabaddahra.
disturbance free - blohk-frei.
disturbed *v.* fabaddaht.
disunities *(f).* unaynichkeida.
disunity - unaynich.
disunity *(f).* unaynichkeit.
ditch *(m).* grawva.
division (of priests) *(f).*
　　preeshtah-adning.
divisions (of priests) *(f).*
　　preeshtah-adninga.
divorce writing *(neu).*
　　divorce-shreives.
divorce writings *(f).*
　　divorce-shreivinga.
dizzy - daumlich.
do - du.
doctor *(m).* doktah.
doctor *v.* doktahra.
doctored *v.* gedoktaht.
doctors *(f).* doktahs.
doctrinally correct (sound) -
　　saund.
doctrine *(f).* lanning.
doctrines *(f).* lanninga.
dog *(m).* hund.
dollar *(m).* dawlah.
dominance *(f).* ivvah-hand.
don, pull on (clothing) *v.*
　　ohzeeya
donation *(neu)* kshenkah-geld.
donation box *(f).* geld-box
　　(lit. - money box)

donation boxes *(f).* geld-boxa
　　(lit. - money boxes)
done (finished) - faddich.
done *v.* gedu.
donkey *(m).* aysel.
donkey colt *(m).* aysel-hutsh.
donkey colts *(f).* aysel-hutsha.
donkey head *(m).* aysel-kobb.
donkey heads *(f).* aysel-kebb.
donkey mare *(f).* aysel-mah.
donkey mares *(f).* aysel-mahra.
donkeys *(f).* aysela.
donned, pulled on (clothing)
　　v. ohgezowwa
door *(f).* deah.
door frame *(neu).* deahra-fraym.
door frames *(f).* deahra-frayms.
door knob *(m).* deahra-gnobb.
door knobs *(f).* deahra-gnebb.
door rail *(f).* doah-rikkel.
door rails *(f).* doah-rikla.
door (small) *(neu).* deahli.
doorkeeper *(m).* deah-heedah.
doorpost *(m).* deah-poshta.
doors *(f).* deahra.
doors (small) *(f).* deahlen.
dot *(m).* dubba.
double - dobbeld.
doubt *v.* zveifla.
doubted *v.* gezveifeld.
dough *(m).* dayk.
dough bowl *(f).* dayk-shissel.
dough bowls *(f).* dayk-shisla.
dough trough *(m).* dayk-drohk.
dough troughs *(f).* dayk-drayk.
doughnut *(m).* fett-kucha.
doughs *(f).* dayka.
dove *(f).* daub.
doves *(f).* dauva.

down (toward a lower location)
    nunnah

down (from above)   runnah

down here - hunnah

down payment *(f)*.
    nunnah-bezawling.

down payments *(f)*.
    nunnah-bezawlinga.

down there - drunnah.

dozen - dutzend

drag *v.* shlayfa.

dragged *v.* kshlayft.

dragon *(neu)* dracha-diah.

dragons *(f)*. dracha-diahra.

drank *v.* gedrunka.

drank in *v.* eigedrunka.

draw moisture *v.* ohzeeya.

drawer *(f)*. shublawt.

drawers *(f)*. shublawda.

dream *(m)*. drohm.

dream *v.* drohma.

dreamed *v.* gedrohmd.

dreamer *(m)*. drohmah.

dreams *(f)*. drohma.

dress (put on) *v.* ohdu.

dress *(m)*. rokk.

dressed (put on) *v.* ohgedu.

dresses *(f)*. rekk.

dribble (on oneself) *v.* fakafla.

dribbled (on oneself)
    v. fakaffeld.

dried *v.* gedrikkeld.

dried out *v.* ausgedrikkeld.

dried up *v.* fadrikkeld.

driest - drukkesht.

drill *v.* boahra.

drilled *v.* geboahra.

drink *(m)*. drink.

drink *v.* drinka.

drink (used with animals or with
one drinking to an excess) *v.* saufa

drink in *v.* eidrinka.

drink offering *(neu)*.
    drink-opfah.

drink offerings *(f)*.
    drink-opfahra.

drinking cup *(neu)*.
    drink-kobli.

drinking cups *(f)*.
    drink-koblen.

drinking vessel *(neu)*
    drink-ksha.

drinking vessels *(f)*.
    drink-ksharra.

drinks *(f)*. drinks.

drive *v.* foahra.

drive apart *v.* fadreiva.

drive around *v.* ausfoahra.

drive out *v.* ausdreiva.

driven *v.* gedrivva.

driven apart *v.* fadrivva.

driven around *v.* auskfoahra.

driven out *v.* ausgedrivva.

driver (of a team of horses) *(m)*.
    fuah-dreivah.

drop *(m)*. drobba.

drop *v.* drobsa.

drop *v.* falla-lossa. *(lit. - let fall)*

drop (used with solids,
    not liquids) *v.* fazodla.

drop of blood *(m)*.
    bloots-drobba.

drop off *v.* abdrobsa.

droped *v.* falla-glost.

droped off *v.* abgedrobst.

dropped (used with solids, *not*
    liquids) *v.* fazoddeld

dropped *v.* gedropst.

dropsy *(f)*. vassah-sucht.
drove *v*. kfoahra.
drown *v*. fasaufa.
drowned *v*. fasoffa.
drunk *v*. ksoffa.
drunkenness *(f)*. saufahrei.
dry *v*. drikla.
dry - drukka.
dry out *v*. ausdrikla.
dry up *v*. fadrikla.
dryer (more dry) drukkanah.
dug *v*. gegrawva.
dug out *v*. ausgegrawva.
dull - shtumb.
dumb - dumm.

dump *v*. damba.
dumped *v*. gedambt.
dumped (by accident) *v*. fadambt
dunk *v*. dunka.
dunked *v*. gedunkt.
dusk *(m)*. dushbah.
dust *(m)*. shtawb.
dusty - shtawvich.
dwell *v*. voona.
dwelled *v*. gvoond.
dwelling *(f)*. vohning.
dwelling place *(f)*. voon-blatz.
dwelling places *(f)*. voon-bletz.
dwellings *(f)*. vohninga.
dysfunctional - aylendich.

E - e

each - yaydah.
each one - alli-vann.
each other - nannah.
eager - hitzich.
eagerly - geahn.
eagle *(m)*. awdlah.
eagle wing *(m)*. awdlah-flikkel.
eagle wings *(f)*. awdlah-flikla.
ear *(neu)* oah.
ear of corn *(m)*. kolva.
earlier *v*. foah-heah.
earlier time *(f)*. foahzeit.
earlier times *(f)*. foahzeida.
early - free.
early rain *(m)*. free-reyyah.
earn *v*. fadeena.
earned *v*. fadeend.
earnestly - eahnshtlich.
earnestness *(f)*. eahnshtlichkeit.

ears *(f)*. oahra.
earth *(f)*. eaht.
earthen - eahdich.
earthly - eahtlich.
earthquake *(f)*. eaht-bayben.
earthquakes *(f)*. eaht-baybens
earths *(f)*. eahda.
easily startled - fashpukkich
east - eest.
Easter - Ohshtah
easy - eesi.
eat *v*. essa.
eat (animals) *v*. fressa.
eat or work (sloppily) *v*.
  fakossla.
eat (too fast or impolitely) *v*.
  fressa
eaten (animals) *v*. kfressa.
eaten away *v*. fafressa.

eaten or worked (sloppily) *v.* fakosseld.
eaten (too fast) *v.* kfressa.
eater *(m).* essah.
education *(f).* lanning.
educations *(f).* lanninga.
eerie - kshpukkich.
egg *(neu).* oi.
egg (cooked with soft yolk) *(neu).* dunk-oi.
egg yolk *(m).* doddah.
egg yolks *(f).* dodra.
eggs *(f).* oiyah.
eggs (cooked with soft yolk) *(f).* dunk-oiyah.
eight - acht.
eighteen - achtzay.
eighteenth - achtzayt.
eighth - acht.
eighty - achtzich.
either (a choice between two alternatives) eedah.
elder *(m).* eldishtah.
elders *(f).* eldishti.
eleven - elf.
eleventh - elft.
else - shunsht.
emaciated - dau.
emaciated *(adj.)* mawwa.
embarrassed *v.* kshemd.
embarrassment (to feel shame) *v.* shemma
embitter *v.* fabiddahra.
embittered *v.* fabiddaht.
embroider *v.* ausnayya.
embroidered *v.* ausgnayt.
emptier - leahrah.
emptiest - leahsht.
empty - leah.

enact *v.* ausfiahra.
encourage *v.* ufmundahra.
encouraged *v.* ufgmundaht.
end *(neu)* end.
end *v.* enda.
ended *v.* gend.
ends *(f).* endah.
endure *v.* ausshtikka.
endure *v.* deich-macha.
endure (patiently) *v.* ohnemma.
endured *v.* auskshtokka.
endured *v.* deich-gmacht.
endured (patiently) *v.* ohgnumma.
enemies *(f).* feinda.
enemy *(m).* feind.
enemy hands *(f).* feinda-hend.
energetic - rawsich.
engage (marriage) *v.* ausroofa.
engaged (marriage) *v.* ausgroofa.
enough *v.* genunk.
enrage *v.* fazanna.
enraged *v.* fazand.
ensure *v.* seiya.
entering - fanna-nei *(at the front)*
enthusiasm *(m).* eifah.
enthusiasm *(f).* moot.
enthusiastically - eifahrich.
entire - gans.
entire life span - layves-lang.
entirely - goah.
entrance *(m).* eigang.
entrance room *(f).* eigang-shtubb.
entrance rooms *(f).* eigang-shtubba.
entrances *(f).* eiganga.
entrust *v.* fadrauwa.

envious - fagunnish/fagunshtlich
envious - ohgunnish.
envy *v.* fagunna.
envy *(m).* fagunsht.
envy *(m).* ohgunsht.
equal gleicha.
erode (with water) *v.* ausvesha
    (lit. – to wash out)
eroded (with water) *v.* ausgvesha
    (lit. - washed out)
error - fayla.
escaped - haus.
especially - patiklah.
establish *v.* grunda.
established *v.* gegrund.
esteem *v.* ohsayna.
esteemed *v.* ohksenna.
eternal - ayvich.
eternally - ayvichlich.
eternities *(f).* ayvichkeida.
eternity *(f).* ayvichkeit.
ethnic group *(neu)* kshlecht.
ethnic groups *(f)* kshlechtah
eunuch *(m).* kemmahrah.
evade (a task) *v.* ausvitsha.
evangelist *(m).* effangelisht.
evangelistic - effangaylish.
evangelists *(f).* effangelishta.
evaporate *v.* fagay.
evaporated *v.* faganga.
Eve (first woman in the Bible)
    (f). Ayfaw.
evening *(m).* ohvet.
evening meal *(neu).*
    ohvet-essa.
evening red ohvet-roht.
evenings *(f).* ohveda.
ever - selayva.
every - alli.

every once in a while -
    alli-gebott.
every time - alli-mohl.
everyone - alli-ebbah.
everything - alles.
everywhere - ivvahrawl.
evil - veesht.
evils *(f).* eevila.
exactly - grawt.
examine *v.* austshekka.
examine *v.* unnah-sucha.
examined *v.* ausgetshekt.
examined *v.* unnah-ksucht.
example *(neu).* foahbild.
examples *(f).* foahbildah.
excavate *v.* ausgrawva.
excavated *v.* ausgegrawva.
exceedingly - drivvah-naus.
except - mays.
excommunication (ban) *(m)*
    bawn.
excuse *v.* ausredda.
excuse *(f).* ausret.
excused *v.* ausgret.
excuses *(f).* ausredda.
exert (oneself) *v.* abblohwa.
exerted (oneself) *v.* abgeblohkt.
exhale *v.* ausshnaufa.
exhaled *v.* auskshauft.
expel *v.* ausdreiva.
expelled *v.* ausgedrivva.
expensive - deiyah.
explicitly - deitlich.
express agreement *v.*
    fa'aynicha.
express (oneself) *v.* fa'andvadda
expressed (agreement) *v.*
    fa'aynicht.
expressed (opinion) *v.* fa'andvatt

extinguish (light or fire) *v.* ausmacha.
extinguished (out) - aus.
extinguished (light or fire) *v.* ausgmacht.
extra - extri.
extremely - heslich.
extremely - ivvah-dimaws.
eye *(neu).* awk.
eye salve *(f).* awwa-shmiah.
eye salves *(f).* awwa-shmiahra.

eye socket *(neu).* awwa-loch.
eye sockets *(f).* awwa-lechah.
eyeball *(m).* awks-balla.
eyeglasses *(f).* brill.
eyeglasses *(f).* brilla.
eyelid *(m).* awks-dekkel.
eyelid *(m).* awwa-dekkel.
eyelids *(f).* awks-dekla.
eyelids *(f).* awwa-dekla.
eyes *(f).* awwa.

F - f

fabel *(f).* fawbla-shtoahri.
fable *(f).* fawbel.
fables *(f).* fawbla.
fables *(f).* fawbla-shtoahris.
face *(neu).* ksicht.
faces *(f).* ksichtah.
fade *v.* abblayyicha.
faded *v.* abgeblayyicht.
fail to perform (because of neglect) *v.* falabba.
failed to perform (because of neglect) *v.* falabt.
fair - feah.
fairly - adlich.
faith *(m).* glawva.
faithful - shtandhaftich.
faithfulness *(f).* shtandhaftichkeit.
fall (season) *(neu).* shpoht-yoah
fall *v.* falla.
fall (asleep) *v.* eishlohfa.
fall (away) *v.* abfalla.
fall (down) *v.* anna-falla.

fall (off) *v.* abfalla.
fall (out with) *v.* ausfalla-mitt.
fall (through) *v.* deich-falla.
fallen *v.* kfalla.
fallen (asleep) *v.* eikshlohfa.
fallen (away) *v.* abkfalla.
fallen (off) *v.* abkfalla.
false - falsh.
false - abfiahrich.
false (appearance) *(f).* fashtelling
false (appearances) *(f).* fashtellinga.
false teeth *(f).* blatt.
falsehood *(f).* unvoahret.
falsehood *(f).* falshhayt.
falsehoods *(f).* falshhayda.
falsehoods *(f).* falshheida.
familiar - bekand.
families roots *(f).* family-shtemm.
family roots *(m).* family-shtamm.
famine *(f).* hungahs-noht.

famines *(f)*. hungah-nohda.
fancy - fei.
fancy - fratzich.
fancy (in a bad way) frech
far - veit.
fare *v*. ausmacha.
fared *v*. ausgmacht.
farm *v*. bavvahra.
farm *(f)*. bavvahrei.
farmed *v*. gebavvaht.
farmer *(m)*. bavvah.
farms *(f)*. bavvahreiya.
fast - shteik.
fast *v*. fasht.
fastened - fesht.
fastened (to the front)
       fanna-droh.
fat *(adj.)* fett.
father *(m)*. faddah.
father (master of the house)
       (m). haus-faddah.
fatherland *(neu)*. faddah-land.
fatherlands *(f)*. faddah-lendah.
fathers *(f)*. feddah.
fathers (masters of the house)
       (f). haus-feddah.
fatigued - ausgedrosha.
faucet *(m)*. grohna.
fault - fayl.
fault *(m)*. faylah.
fault *(f)*. shuld.
fault finder *(m)*. faylah-suchah
       (lit.- fault seeker).
faults *(f)*. shulda.
fax *v*. faxa.
fear *v*. feicha.
fear *v*. firchta.
fear *(f)*. furcht.
fear of God *(f)*. Gottes-furcht.

feared *v*. kfeicht.
feared *v*. kfircht
       (used in the Bible)
fearful - feichboah.
fearful - feichbutzich
       ("fraidy cat")
fearless - feichtlohs.
feast of bread *(neu)*.
       broht-fesht.
feast of dedication *(neu)*.
       tempel-fesht *(lit.- temple feast)*
feasts of bread *(f)*.
       broht-feshta.
feasts of dedication *(f)*.
       tempel-feshta *(lit.- temple feasts)*
feather *(m)*. feddah.
feathers *(f)*. feddahra *("fedra" -
       common pronunciation)*
fed *v*. kfeedaht.
fed up - laydich.
feed *v*. feedra.
feed (fodder) *(neu)*. foodah.
feel *v*. feela.
feel *v*. shpiahra.
feeling *(neu)*. kfeel.
feeling (reluctance) falayt.
feelings *(f)*. kfeelah.
feet *(f)*. fees.
fell *v*. kfalla.
fell down *v*. anna-kfalla.
fell through *v*. deich-kfalla.
fellow *(m)*. kall.
fellow elder *(m)*. mitt-eldishtah.
fellow elders *(f)*. mitt-eldishti.
fellow heir *(m)*. mitt-eahvah.
fellow helper *(m)*. mitt-helfah.
fellow servant *(m)*. mitt-deenah.
fellow servant or slave *(m)*.
       mitt-gnecht.

fellow servants or slaves *(f).*
 mitt-gnechta.
fellow soldier *(f).* mitt-shtreidah.
fellows *(f).* kals.
fellowship *(f).* gmeinshaft.
felt *v.* kfeeld.
felt *v.* kshpeiaht.
female donkey*(f).* donkey-mah.
female donkeys *(f).*
 donkey-mahra.
female horse *(f).* mau.
female horses *(f).* madda.
female person *(neu).*
 veibsmensh.
female persons *(f).* veibsleit.
female pig *(f).* lohs.
female pigs *(f).* lohsa.
female prophet *(f).*
 fraw-brofayt.
female prophets *(f).*
 fraw-brofayda.
fence *(f).* fens.
fence in *v.* eifensa.
fenced in *v.* eikfenst.
fences *(f).* fensa.
festival *(neu).* fesht.
festival gathering *(f).*
 fesht-fasmling.
festival time *(f).* fesht-zeit.
festival times *(f).* fesht-zeida.
festivals *(f).* feshta.
fetch *v.* hohla.
fetch (from somewhere) *v.*
 bei-hohla.
fetched *v.* kohld.
fetched (from somewhere) *v.*
 bei-kohld.
fever *(m).* feevah.
feverish - feevahrich.

few - vennich.
field *(neu).* feld.
field of blood *(neu).* bloot-feld.
field overseer / captain *(m).*
 feld-hauptmann.
field overseers / captains *(f).*
 feld-hauptmennah.
field (with a crop) *(neu)*
 frucht-feld.
fields *(f).* feldah.
fields of blood *(f).* bloot-feldah.
fields (of crops) *(f).* frucht-feldah.
fiery - feiyahrich.
fifteen - fuftzay.
fifteenth - fuftzayt.
fifth - fimft.
fiftieth - fuftzichsht.
fifty - fuftzich.
fig cake *(m).* feiya-kucha.
fig tree *(m).* feiya-bohm.
fig trees *(f).* feiya-baym.
fight *(f).* fecht.
fight *v.* fechta.
fighter *(m).* fechtah.
fights *(f).* fechta.
figs *(f).* feiya.
figure out (a solution) *v.*
 ausdenka.
figured out *v.* ausgedenkt.
file *(f).* feil.
file *v.* feila.
filed *v.* kfeild.
files *(f).* feila.
fill *v.* filla.
fill (container) *v.* fassa.
fill in *v.* eifilla.
fill (air with dust) *v.* fussahra.
filled *v.* kfild.
filled (container) *v.* kfast.

filled in *v.* eikfild.
filled (air with dust) *v.* kfussaht.
finally - baddamoll.
finally - endlich.
find *v.* finna.
find out *v.* ausfinna.
fine - fei.
finely ground - fei-gmawla.
finger *(m).* fingah.
finger ring *(m).* fingah-ring.
finger rings *(f).* fingah-rings.
finger (something) *v.* fingahra.
finger (to touch with the fingers) *v.* fafingahra.
fingered *v.* kfingaht.
fingered (touched with the fingers) *v.* fafingaht.
fingernail *(m).* fingah-nakkel.
fingernails *(f).* fingah-nekkel.
finicky *(adj.)* fagnohtsht.
finished - faddich.
fire *(neu).* feiyah.
fire (to lose job). feiyahra
fire (a gun) *v.* absheesa.
fire oven *(m).* feiyah-offa.
fire ovens *(f).* feiyah-effa.
fire pan *(m).* feiyah-pann.
fire pans *(f).* feiyah-panna.
fire pit *(m).* feiyah-pitt.
fire pits *(f).* feiyah-pits.
fired (a gun) *v.* abkshossa.
fired (lost a job) *v.* kfeiyaht.
fireflies *(f).* blitz-keffahra.
(lit. – flash bugs)
firefly *(m).* blitz-keffah.
(lit. – flash bug)
fires *(f).* feiyahra.
firewood *(neu)* feiyah-hols.
first - eahsht.

first - seahsht.
first fruit *(f).* eahsht-frucht.
first fruit day *(m).* eahsht-frucht-dawk.
first fruit offering *(neu).* eahsht-frucht-opfah.
first fruits *(f).* eahshti-frichta.
first fruits offerings *(f).* eahsht-frucht-opfahra.
first gate *(neu).* eahsht-doah.
firstborn - eahsht-geboahra.
fish *v.* fisha.
fish catcher *(m).* fish-fangah.
Fish Gate *(neu).* Fish-Doah.
fish hook *(m).* fish-hohka.
fish line *(f).* fish-lein.
fish scale *(m).* shawb.
fish scales *(f).* shawva.
fished *v.* kfisht.
fisherman *(m).* fishah-mann.
fishermen *(f).* fishah-mennah.
fishing lines *(f).* fish-leina.
fishing pole (rod) *(f).* fishgatt.
fist *(f).* fausht.
fists *(f).* faushta.
five - fimf.
flake *(m).* flokka.
flame *v.* flamma.
flame *(neu).* flamm.
flame of fire *(neu)* feiyah-flamm
flamed *v.* kflamd.
flames *(f).* flamma.
flames of fire *(f).* feiyah-flamma.
flaming - flammich.
flap *(m).* flabbah.
flap (vigorously) *v.* fladra.
flapped (vigorously) *v.* kfladdaht

(m) = da   (f) = di   (neu) = es   153

flaps *(f)*. flabbahs.
flare up *v.* flamma.
flared up *v.* kflamd.
flash *(m)*. blitz.
flash *v.* blitza.
flashed *v.* geblitzt.
flashes *(f)*. blitza.
flashlight *(neu)*. fleishleit.
flashlights *(f)*. fleishleits.
flat - ayva.
flatter *v.* shmaychla.
flavor *(m)*. flayvah.
flavors *(f)*. flayvahs.
flea *(f)*. flay.
flee *v.* fleeya.
flesh *(neu)*. flaysh.
fleshly - flayshlich.
flew *v.* kflohwa.
flexible - lummahrich.
flies *(f)*. mukka.
flint *(m)*. flint-shtay.
flock *(f)*. drubb.
flocks *(f)*. drubba.
flood *(f)*. flott.
floods *(f)*. flots.
floor *(m)*. bodda.
floor *(m)*. floah.
floored *v.* kfloaht.
floors *(f)*. floahra.
flour *(neu)*. mayl.
flow of blood *(m)*. bloot-fluss.
flower *(f)*. blumm.
flower bed *(neu)*. blumma-bett.
flower beds *(f)*. blumma-beddah.
flower beds (small) *(f)*. blumma-lendlen.
flower garden *(m)*. blumma-goahra.

flowerbed *(neu)* blumma-land
flowerbeds *(f)*. blumma-lendah.
flowerbed (small) *(neu)*. blumma-lendli.
flowers *(f)*. blumma.
flown apart *v.* faflohwa.
flute (pipe / musical instrument) *(f)*. peif
flute (musical pipe player) *(m)*. peif-shpeelah.
fly *v.* fleeya.
fly *(f)*. mukk.
fly apart *v.* fafleeya.
foal *(neu)* hutshli.
foals *(f)* hutshlen.
foam *(m)* shaum.
foam *v.* shauma.
foamed *v.* kshaumd.
foamy - shaumich.
fog *(m)*. nevvel.
fogged (steamed up glass) *v.* geduft.
foggy - nevlich.
foliage *(f)*. lawb.
follow *v.* folya *(used in the Bible)*
follow *v.* nohch-folya.
follow *v.* nohch-macha.
follow (an example) *v.* nohch-macha.
followed *v.* kfolkt.
followed *v.* nohch-gmacht.
followed *v.* nohch-kfolkt.
followed (an example) *v.* nohch-gmacht.
follower *(m)*. nohch-folyah.
follower (one who follows an example) *(m)* nohch-machah
following - nohch.
food *(neu)* ess-sach.

food *(f)*. shpeis *(used in the Bible)*
food offering *(neu)*.
  ess-sach-opfah.
food offerings *(f)*.
  ess-sach-opfahra.
food scraps (fed to pigs, slop)
  (neu). shlabb
foods *(f)* shpeisa
  (used in the Bible)
fool *(m)*. nah.
foolhardy - unksheit.
foolish - naddish.
foolishness - dumhayda.
foolishness *(f)*.
  dumhaydichkeit.
foolishnesses *(f)*.
  dumhaydichkeida.
fools *(f)*. narra.
foot *(m)*. foos.
foot hold *(m)*. foos-hohld.
foot holds *(f)*. foos-hohlds.
foot rest *(f)*. foos-bank.
foot rests *(f)*. foos-benk.
foot stools *(f)*. foos-shteel.
foot stools (little) *(f)*.
  foos-shteelen.
footed - feesich.
footer *(m)*. fuddah.
footers *(f)*. fuddahs.
footsteps *(f)*. foos-dredda.
footstool *(neu)*. benkli.
footstool *(m)*. foos-shtool.
footstool (little) *(neu)*.
  foos-shteeli.
footstools *(f)*. benklen.
for - fa.
for sure - fashuah.
for sure - geviss.
for that reason - fasell.

forbid *v.* fabeeda.
forbidden *v.* fabodda.
force *(m)*. foahs.
fore (prefix - "before" / "taking
  the lead") foah.
forefather *(m)*. foahfaddah.
forefathers *(f)*. foaheldra.
forefathers *(f)*. foahfeddah.
forehead *(f)*. shtann.
foreheads *(f)*. shtanna.
foreign - auslendish.
foreigner *(m)*. auslendah.
foreman *(m)*. foahgayyah.
forenoon *(m)*. fammidawk.
foresaw *v.* foahksenna.
foresee *v.* foahsayna.
foreseeing - foahsichtich.
foresight *(f)*. foahsicht
  (lit.- seeing ahead).
foreskin *(f)*. foah-haut.
foreskins *(f)*. foah-heit.
forest *(m)*. bush.
forest fire *(neu)*. bush-feiyah.
forest fires *(f)*. bush-feiyahra.
forests *(f)*. busha.
foretimes *(f)*. foahzeida.
forever - ayvichlich.
forever - fa'immah.
  (lit. – for always)
forewarn *v.* favanna.
forewarned *v.* favand.
forge *(m)*. eisa-offa.
forget *v.* fagessa.
forgetful fagesslich.
forgive *v.* fagevva.
fork *(f)*. gavvel.
forks *(f)*. gavla.
formerly - eahshtah.
forswear *v.* fashveahra.

forsworn *v.* fashveaht.
forth - fiaht.
fortunate - gliklich.
fortune teller *(m).*
      voah-sawwah.
forty - fatzich.
forward - faddi.
forward (direction)
      fassich / feddahsich.
forward most - feddahsht.
fought *v.* kfochta.
found *v.* kfunna.
found out *v.* auskfunna.
foundation (of a wall) *(f).*
      mavvah.
foundations (of walls) *(f).*
      mavvahra.
founded *v.* gegrund.
four - fiah.
four cornered - fiah-ekkich.
four-footed - fiah-feesich.
fourteen - fatzay.
fourteenth - fatzayt.
fox *(m).* fox.
frame *(neu).* fraym.
frames *(f).* frayms.
free - frei.
free will offering *(neu).*
      frei-villich-opfah.
free will offerings *(f).*
      frei-villich-opfahra.
freedom *(f).* freiheit.
freeze *v.* friahra.
frequent - oft.
frequently - eftahs.
fresh - frish.
Friday - Freidawk.
fried *v.* gebrohda.
friend *(m).* freind.

friendliness *(f).* freindlichkeit.
friendly - freindlich.
frighten *v.* fashpukka.
frightened *v.* fashpukt.
fringe *(m).* fransel.
fringes *(f).* fransla.
frog *(m).* frosh.
frogs *(f).* fresh.
from - funn.
from above - ovva-heah.
from here - difunn.
front - fanna.
frost *(m).* frosht.
frosty - froshtich.
froze *v.* fafroahra.
froze *v.* kfroahra.
frugally used *v.* kshpoaht.
fruit *(f).* frucht.
fruit *(neu).* obsht *(not common)*
fruitful fruchtboah.
fruits *(f).* frichta.
frustrating - fazatt.
fry *v.* brohda.
fulfill *v.* folfilla.
fulfilled *v.* folkfild.
full - foll.
full (satisfied with food) satt
full growth *v.* ausvaxa
                  (present, future)
full growth *v.* ausgvaxa *(past)*
full (of holes) falechaht.
fullness *(f).* folheit.
fullness *(f).* folkummaheit.
fully - folshtendich.
funeral *(m).* leicht.
funeral song *(neu).* leicht-leet.
funerals *(f).* leichta.
funeral-songs *(f).* leicht-leedah.
funnel *(m).* drechtah.

funny - fannich.
furious - zannich.
furnace grate *(f)*. feiyah-grate
furnace grates *(f)*.
    feiyah-grates.
furrow *(f)*. feich.

furrow (left by a plow) *(f)*.

    blooks-feich.
furrows *(f)*. feicha.
furrows (left by a plow) *(f)*.
    blooks-feicha.
further - veidah.
furthest - veitsht.
fussy *(adj.)* gneiksich.

G - g

gain favor *v.* ohmacha.
gained favor *v.* ohgmacht.
gallon *(f)*. gall.
gallons *(f)*. galla.
garden *(m)*. goahra.
gardener *(m)*. goahra-haldah.
garment *(neu)*. glayt.
garment bag *(m)*. glaydah-sakk.
garment bags *(f)*. glaydah-sekk.
garment (made of sackcloth)
    (neu). sakk-glayt.
garments *(f)*. glaydah.
garments (made of sackcloth)
    (f). sakk-glaydah.
gate *(neu)*. doah.
gate keeper - doah-heedah.
gates *(f)*. doahra.
gather *v.* fasamla.
gather *v.* geddahra.
gather *v.* samla.
gather in *v.* eisamla.
gathered bei-nannah.
gathered *v.* fasammeld.
gathered *v.* gegeddaht.
gathered *v.* ksammeld.
gathered in *v.* eiksammeld.

gathering *(f)*. samling.
gatherings *(f)*. samlinga.
gaunt *(adj)* mawwa.
gear wheel *(neu)*. kumrawt.
gear wheels *(f)*. kumreddah.
geese *(f)*. gens.
genealogies *(f)*.
    freindshaft-shtemm.
genealogy *(m)*.
    freindshaft-shtamm.
genealogy register *(m)*.
    freindshaft-registah.
genealogy registries *(f)*.
    freindshaft-registahra.
generation *(neu)*. kshlecht.
generations *(f)*. kshlechtah.
Gentile *(m)*. Heid.
Gentiles *(f)*. Heida.
gentle - sanftmeedich.
get *v.* greeya.
get even *v.* ayva kumma.
get from somewhere *v.*
    bei-greeya.
get up *v.* uf-shtay *(lit. – stand up)*
get used to *v.* gvayna.
gift *(neu)*. kshenk.

gifted - begawbt.
gifts *(f)*. kshenka.
gifts (of money) *(neu)*.
     kshenkah-geld.
giggle *v.* fakiddahra.
giggled *v.* fakiddaht.
girl *(neu)*. maydel.
girl (little) *(neu)*. maytli.
girls *(f)*. mayt.
girls (little) *(f)*. maytlen.
give *v.* gevva.
give (a gift) *v.* shenka.
give control (of a matter to
     another) *v.* ivvah-gevva.
give in to *v.* eigevva.
give off *v.* abgevva.
given (a gift) *v.* kshenkt.
given (water to livestock) *v.*
     gedrenkt.
giver *(m)*. gevvah.
giving thanks *(neu)*. danke.
glad - froh.
gladly - geahn.
glass *(neu)*. glaws.
glassy - glawsich.
glittering - glitzahrich.
glories *(f)*. hallichkeida.
glorified *v.* fakleaht.
glorify *v.* fakleahra.
glorious - hallich.
glory *(f)*. gloahheit.
glory *(f)*. hallichkeit.
glove *(m)*. henshing.
glutton *(m)*. fressah.
gluttony *(f)*. fressahrei.
gnat *(neu)*. mikli.
gnats *(f)*. miklen.
go *v.* gay.
go in *v.* eigay.

go off (alarm) *v.* abgay.
go out (fire, light) *v.* ausgay.
go there *v.* anna-gay.
goat *(m)*. gays.
goat skins *(f)*. gaysa-heit.
goatskin *(f)*. gaysa-haut.
God *(m)*. Gott.
God fearing *(f)*. Gott-firchtich.
goddess *(f)*. gettin
Godhead *(f)*. Gottheit.
godliness *(f)*. getlichkeit.
godly - getlich.
God's - Gottes.
gods *(f)*. gettah.
gold peices *(f)*. gold-shtikkah.
gold piece *(neu)*. gold-shtikk.
golden - goldich.
gone out (fire, light) *v.* ausganga.
good - goot.
good fortune *(m)*. glikk.
good looking - goot-gukkich.
good or bad will (in a group)
     (neu) kfeel.
good smell - goot-shmakkich.
good will *(neu)*. vohl-kfalla.
goose *(f)*. gans.
goosebumpy - gensa-heidich.
gospel (good news) *(neu)*.
     effangaylium.
got *v.* grikt.
got up *v.* uf-kshtanna.
     (lit. - stood up)
gotten (from somewhere) *v.*
     bei-grikkt.
gotten (older) *v.* fa'eld.
gotten (used to) *v.* gegvaynd.
gouge *v.* fahakka.
gouged *v.* fahakt.
government *(f)*. ovvahrichkeit.

governments *(f)*.
　ovvahrichkeida.
grab *v.* graebba.
grabbed *v.* gegraebt.
grace (God's grace) *(f)*. gnawt.
grace (grace of God) *(f)*. gnawdi.
graft *v.* zveicha.
grafted *v.* gezveicht.
grain bin *(m)*. frucht-kashta.
grandchild *(f)*. kins-kind.
grandchildren *(f)*. kins-kinnah.
grandfather *(m)*. dawdi.
grandfathers *(f)*. dawdis.
grandmother *(f)*. mammi.
grandmothers *(f)*. mammis.
grape *(f)*. draub.
grapes *(f)*. drauva.
grapevine *(f)* drauva-rank.
grapevine *(m)* drauva-shtokk
　　　(lit.- grape plant)
grapevine *(m)* vei-shtokk
　　　(lit. - wine plant)
grapevines *(f)* drauva-ranka.
grapevines *(f)* drauva-rankla.
grapevines *(f)* drauva-shtekk
　　　(lit.- grape plants)
grapevines *(f)* vei-shtekk
　　　(lit.- wine plants)
grass *(neu)*. graws.
grasses *(f)*. grawsa.
grasshopper *(m)*. hoi-shrekk.
grasshoppers *(f)*. hoi-shrekka.
grave *(neu)*. begraybnis.
grave *(neu)* grawb
　　　(common use)
graves *(f)*. begraybnissa.
graves *(f)*. fagrawbnissa.
graves *(f)*. grayvah.
graveyard *(m)*. grawb-hohf.

graveyards *(f)*. grawb-hohfa.
gray - groh.
grease *(m)*. shmutz.
grease *v.* shmutza.
greased *v.* kshmutzt.
greasy - shmutzich.
great-grandfather *(m)*.
　grohs-dawdi.
great-grandfathers *(f)*.
　grohs-dawdis.
great-grandmother *(f)*.
　grohs-mammi.
great-grandmothers *(f)*.
　grohs-mammis.
greedy - greedich.
Greek *(adj.)* Greeyish.
green - gree.
greet *v.* greesa.
greeted *v.* gegreest.
greeting *(m)* groos.
grieve *v.* bedreeva.
grieved *v.* bedreebt.
grind *v.* mawla.
grind (completely) *v.* famawla.
grinding mill *(f)*. meel.
grinding mills *(f)*. meela.
grinding stone *(m)*.
　meel-shtay
ground *(m)*. bodda.
ground *(m)*. grund.
ground *v.* grunda.
ground (such as meat or coffee)
　v. gmawla.
ground up - famawla.
grounded *v.* gegrund.
groundhog *(f)*. grundsau.
groundhogs *(f)*. grundsei.
group *(f)*. drubb.
group of believers *(f)*. gmay.

group of families *(f)*
    family-drubb.
groups *(f).* drubba.
groups of families *(f).*
    family-drubba.
grow *v.* vaxa.
grow over *v.* favaxa.
grown *v.* gvaxa.
gruesome - grausich.
grumble *v.* grumla.
grumbled *v.* gegrummeld.

grumbled *v.* gegnuddaht.
grumbler *(m).* grumlah.
guest *(f).* psuch.
guests *(f).* psuch-leit.
guide *v.* geida.
guided *v.* gegiet.
gully *(m).* grawva.
gun *(f).* bix.
guns *(f).* bixa.
gutted *v.* ausgnumma.

H - h

habit *(m).* gebrauch.
habits *(f).* gebraucha.
habitual fighting *(neu).*
    gefecht
had *v.* katt.
hail *v.* shlohsa.
hailed *v.* kshlohsa.
hailstones *(f).* shlohsa.
hair *(f).* hoah.
hairy - hoahrich.
half - halb.
half (used with time) halvah
    (example: " halvah zvay " -
    half-til-two or 1:30)
half (pronoun) *(f).* helft
    (example: "di annah helft")
    (the other half)
halter *(m).* halftah.
halters *(f).* halftahs.
halves *(f).* helfta.
hammer *(m).* hammah.
hammer *v.* hammahra.
hammer out *v.* aushemmahra.

hammered *v.* kammaht.
hammered out *v.* auskemmaht.
hammers *(f).* hammahs.
hand *(f).* hand.
hand towel *(m).* hand-lumba.
handkerchief *(n).* shnubb-duch.
handkerchiefs *(f).*
    shnubb-dichah.
handle *v.* haendla.
handle (unnecessarily) *v.*
    fagnohtsha.
handled *v.* kaendeld.
handled (unnecessarily) *v.*
    fagnohtsht.
hands *(f).* hend.
handwriting *(neu).*
    hand-shreives.
hang *v.* henka.
hang onto *v.* oh'henka.
happen *v.* blatz-nemma.
happen *v.* gevva.
happen *v.* ohgay.
happened *v.* ohganga.

happening *(f)*. kshicht.
happenings *(f)*. kshichta.
hard - hatt.
hard (of hearing) hatt-heahrich.
harden (one's heart) *v.*
   fashtokka.
harden (the heart) *v.* fahadda.
hardened (the heart) *v.* fahatt.
hardworking - hatt-shaffich.
harlot *(f)*. huah.
harlots *(f)*. huahra.
harm *(m)*. shawda.
harm *v.* shadda.
harmed *v.* kshatt.
harness *(neu)*. ksha.
harnesses *(f)*. ksharra.
harp *(f)*. harf.
harp player *(m)*. harf-shpeelah
harps *(f)*. harfa.
harrow *(f)*. ayk.
harrow *v.* ayka.
harrowed *v.* gaykt.
harrows *(f)*. ayka.
harvest *(f)*. eahnd.
harvest *v.* eisamla.
Harvest Feast *(neu)*.
   Eisamling-Fesht.
Harvest Feasts *(f)*.
   Eisamling-Feshta.
harvest timber *v.* aushakka.
harvested *v.* eiksammeld.
harvested timber *v.* auskakt.
harvests *(f)*. eahnda.
has *v.* hott.
hat *(m)*. hoot.
hate *v.* hassa.
hated *v.* kast.
hateful - fahast.
hats *(f)*. heet.

haughty - hohchmeedich.
haul *v.* foahra.
hauled *v.* kfoahra.
have *v.* habb
   (used with pronoun, "Ich")
have *v.* havva.
have an opinion *v.* mayna.
having an opinion *v.*
   geglawbt.
having an opinion *v.*
   gmaynd.
having faith *v.* geglawbt.
having faith glawvich.
hay *(neu)*. hoi.
he - eah.
head *(m)*. kobb.
head on - fanna-bei.
headcovering (worn by women)
   (f). kabb.
headcoverings (worn by
   women) *(f)*. kabba.
headfirst - kobb-feddahsht.
heads *(f)*. kebb.
heal *v.* hayla.
healed *v.* kayld.
health *(f)*. ksundhayt.
healthy - ksund.
heap *(m)*. haufa.
hear *v.* heahra.
heard *v.* keaht.
hearing ability - heahrich
   (example: "hatt-heahrich")
heart *(neu)*. hatz.
heartfelt - hatzlich.
heartily - greftichlich.
hearts *(f)*. hatza.
hearty - greftich.
heat *(f)*. hitz.
heat *v.* hitza.

heated *v.* kitzt.
heaven *(m).* Himmel.
heavenly - himlish.
heavenly establishment *(f).*
    Himmelshaft.
heavenly establishments *(f).*
    Himmelshafda.
heavens *(f).* himla.
heavy - shveah.
heavy outer coats *(f).*
    ivvah-rekk. *(lit. – overcoat)*
heavy-set - ksetzt.
heed *v.* achta.
heeded *v.* gacht.
hefty - haftich.
heifer *(neu).* rind.
heifers *(f).* rinnah.
height *(f).* haych.
heights *(f).* haycha.
heir *(m).* eahvah.
held *v.* kohva.
held off *v.* abkohva.
helmets *(f).* greeks-heet.
            (lit. – war hats)
help *v.* helfa.
help *(f).* hilf.
helped *v.* kolfa.
helper *(m).* helfah.
helpful - behilflich.
her - iahra.
her (she) see.
her (referring to unmarried girls)
    es / 's.
herb plant *(m).* rauda-shtokk.
herb plants *(f).* rauda-shtekk.
herbal oil *(neu).* greidah-ayl.
herbs *(f).* greidah.
here - do.
here (toward) heah.

hers - iahra.
hers - sei *(possessive pronoun,*
    *used **with** a noun).*
hers - sein *(possessive pronoun,*
    *used **without** a noun).*
herself - sich-selvaht.
hidden *v.* fashlubt.
hidden *v.* fashtekkeld.
hide *v.* fashlubba.
hide *v.* fashtekla.
hiding place *(m).*
    fashtekkel-blatz.
hiding places *(f).*
    fashtekkel-bletz.
high - hohch.
higher - haychah.
highest - haychsht.
Highest (God) *(m).*
    Alli-Haychsht.
highest of all - alli-haychsht.
highly esteemed - hohch-gacht
highly praised - hohch-gelohbt
hill *(m).* hivvel.
hills *(f).* hivvela.
hilly - hivlich.
him - een.
him - eem. *(dative case)*
himself - sich-selvaht.
hinder *v.* fahinnahra.
hindered *v.* fahinnaht.
hindrance *(neu).* hinnahnis.
hindrance *(f).* hinnahnissa.
hip *(f).* hift.
hips *(f).* hifda.
hire *v.* dinga.
hired *v.* gedunga.
hired hand *(m).* gnecht.
hired hands *(f).* gnechta.
hired maid *(f).* mawt.

hired maids *(f)*. mawda.
hired out (oneself or another)
   v. fadunga.
his - sei *(possessive pronoun,*
   used with a noun).
his - sein *(possessive pronoun,*
   used without a noun).
hit *v.* dreffa.
hit *v.* gedroffa.
hit *v.* kshlauwa.
hit *v.* shlauwa.
hitch (animal to a carriage or
   implement) *v.* eishpanna.
hitched (animal to a carriage or
   implement) *v.* eikshpand
hoe *(f)*. hakk.
hoe *v.* hakka.
hoed *v.* kakt.
hoes *(f)*. hakka.
hog *(f)*. sau.
hogs *(f)*. sei.
hold *v.* hayva.
hold off *v.* abhayva.
hole *(neu)*. loch.
holes *(f)*. lechah.
holiday *(m)*. feiyah-dawk.
holidays *(f)* feiyah-dawwa.
Holiest (God) *(m)*.
   Alli-Haychsht.
holiest of all - alli-heilichsht.
hollow *(neu)*. deich.
hollow out *v.* aushohla.
hollowed out *v.* auskohld.
holy - heilich.
Holy Spirit *(m)*. Heilich Geisht
home *(f)*. haymet.
home (toward) haym.
homes *(f)* haymedah.
homesick - zeitlang.

honest - eahlich.
honest - ufrichtich.
honesty *(f)*. ufrichtichkeit.
honey *(m)*. hunnich.
honor *(f)*. eah.
honor *v.* eahra.
honored *v.* geaht.
honored (highly) *v.* ohgnaymd.
hook *(m)*. hohka.
hop *v.* hupsa.
hope *v.* hoffa.
hope *(f)*. hofning.
hoped *v.* koft.
hopes *(f)*. hofninga.
hopped *v.* kupst.
horn *(f)*. hann.
hornet *(m)*. hannaysel.
hornets *(f)*. hannaysla.
horns *(f)*. hanna.
horse *(m)*. gaul.
horseman *(m)*. geils-mann.
horsemen *(f)*. geils-mennah.
horses *(f)*. geil.
hot - hays.
hot (enough to melt iron)
   eisa-shmelsich.
hotel *(neu)*. shlohf-haus.
   (lit. - sleep house)
hotels *(f)*. shlohf-heisah.
   (lit. - sleep houses)
hour *(f)*. shtund.
hours *(f)*. shtunda.
house *(neu)*. haus.
house of prayer *(neu)*.
   bayt-haus.
house of worship *(neu)*.
   deensht-haus.
house of worship *(neu)*.
   gmay-haus.

house roof *(neu)* haus-dach.
house roofs *(f)*. haus-dechah.
household *(neu)* haus-halding.
household *(neu)* haus-hohld.
householder *(m)*. haus-haldah.
households *(f)*. haus-haldinga.
households *(f)*. haus-hohlda.
houses *(f)*. heisah.
houses of prayer *(f)*.
        bayt-heisah.
houses of worship *(f)*.
        deensht-heisah.
houses of worship *(f)*.
        gmay-heisah.
how - vi.
huge - grohs.
human *(m)*. mensh.
humans *(f)*. mensha.
humble - daymeedich.
humbled *v.* gedaymeedicht.
humid - dunshtich.
humility *(f)*. daymeedichkeit.

humility *(f)*. daymoot.
hundred - hunnaht.
hung *v.* kanka.
hung onto *v.* ohkanka.
hunger *(m)*. hungah.
hungry - hungahrich.
hunt *v.* hunda.
hunted *v.* kunt.
hurried *v.* gedummeld.
hurry *v.* dumla.
hurt *v.* shmatza.
hurt *v.* vay-du *(present, future)*
hurt *v.* vay-gedu *(past)*
hurt *v.* kshmatzt *(past)*
husband *(m)*. mann.
husbands *(f)*. mennah.
husk *(f)*. basht.
husk *v.* bashta.
husked *v.* gebasht.
husks *(f)*. bashta.
hypocrite *(m)*. heichlah.

I - i

I - ich.
idea *(f)*. eidi.
ideas *(f)*. eidis.
identical (alike) - gleicha.
idol *(m)*. abgott.
idol maker *(m)*
        abgeddah-machah.
idol priest *(m)*.
        abgott-preeshtah.
idol (like a calf) *(neu)* abgott-kalb
idol worship *(m)*.
        abgeddah-deensht.

idol worshiper *(m)*
        abgott-deenah.
idolatries *(f)*. abgeddahreiya.
idolatrous - abgeddish.
idolatrous offering *(neu)*.
        abgott-opfah.
idolatrous offerings *(f)*.
        abgott-opfahra.
idolatry *(neu)* abgeddahrei.
idols *(f)*. abgeddah.
if - vann.
ignite *v.* ohgay.

ignited *v.* ohganga.
ignorant people *(f).*
   dumm-kebb.
ignorant person -
   (m). dumm-kobb.
ill (deathly sick) doht-grank.
ill will *(m).* fagunsht.
illuminated (with daylight)
   dawk.
illumination (very bright).
   (adj.) hell
image *(neu).* bild.
image (used for false worship)
   (neu). abbild.
images *(f).* bildah.
images (used for false worship)
   (f). abbildah.
imitate *v.* nohch-macha.
imitated *v.* nohch-gmacht.
immediately - bletzlich.
immediately - grawt.
immodest - frech.
immorality *(f).* lushtahrei.
imperishable - unfagenglich.
important - vichtich.
impossible - ummeeklich.
impression *(m).* eidruk.
impressions *(f).* eidrukka.
imprison *v.* eishtekka.
improper - unkshikt.
improper - unshiklich.
improve *v.* fabessahra.
improved *v.* fabessaht.
impure - unrein.
impurity *(f).* unreinichkeit.
in - in.
in (as a prefix) - ei
in (toward inner location) - nei
in (from outside) - rei

in a - innen.
in advance - fanna-naus.
in disagreement - unaynich.
in excess (too much) - zu.
in front of - fanna-droh.
in front of - fannich.
in good condition - saund.
in great detail - pinklich.
in place of - imblatz.
in the - im.
in the forenoon - fammidawks.
in the front part -fanna-drinn.
in the general vicinity
   rumm-heah.
in the lead - fanna-heah.
in there - drinn.
in this manner - deahravayk.
incarcerate *v.* eishtekka.
incense altar *(m)* insens-awldah
incense altars *(f).*
   insens-awldahra.
incense cup *(neu).*
   insens-kobli.
incense cups *(f).*
   insens-koblen.
inch *(f).* zoll.
incite *v.* hetza.
incited *v.* ketzt.
include *v.* einemma.
included - ditzu.
included *v.* eignumma.
included with - dibei *(present)*
incomprehensible -
   unbegreiflich.
increase *v.* fameahra.
increased *v.* fameaht.
incur *v.* ohbringa.
incurred *v.* ohgebrocht.
indebted to - shuldich.

indifferent - aldvannish.
indulged (debauchery) *v.* kuaht
industrious - shaffich.
infect another
   (with a contagious sickness) *v.*
   ohshtekka
infected another -
   (with a contagious sickness) *v.*
   ohkshtokka
inherit *v.* eahva.
inheritance *(f).* eahbshaft.
inheritance (given to children)
   (f) kinnah-eahbshaft
inheritances *(f).* eahbshafta.
inheritances (given to children)
   (f). kinnah-eahbshafta.
inherited *v.* geahbt.
ink *(f).* dinda.
inn *(neu).* shlohf-haus.
innocence *(f).* unshuldichkeit.
innocent - unshuldich.
inns *(f).* shlohf-heisah.
inoperable *v.* fasauwa.
   (present, future)
inoperable *v.* fasaut *(past)*
inquire about *v.* ausfrohwa.
inquired about *v.* auskfrohkt.
insect (bug) *(m).* kaeffah.
insects (bugs) *(f).* kaeffahra.
insensible - unksheit.
insert *v.* shtekka.
inserted *v.* kshtokka.
inside - inseit.
insight *(f).* eisicht.
insights *(f).* eisichta.
instead - imblatz.
instrument of war *(m).*
   greeks-tavvah.
interest (financial) *(f).* indressa

interrogate *v.* ausfrohwa.
interrogated *v.* auskfrohkt.
intestines *(f).* deahm.
intimidate *v.* fashaycha.
intimidated *v.* fashaycht.
intoxicated *v.* ksoffa.
invite *v.* eilawda.
invite *v.* haysa.
invited *v.* eiglawda.
invited *v.* kaysa.
invoice *(neu).* bill.
invoices *(f).* bills.
inward - innahlich.
irk *v.* fa'eiyahra.
irked *v.* fa'eiyaht.
irked *v.* geboaht.
iron *(neu).* eisa.
iron *v.* bikla.
iron furnace *(m).* eisa-offa.
iron smelter *(m)* eisa-shmelsah
iron smith *(m).* eisa-shmitt.
iron smiths *(f).* eisa-shmidda.
iron (used for fabric) *(neu).*
   bikkel-eisa.
ironed *v.* gebikkeld.
irritate *v.* abdrayya.
irritate *v.* fa'eiyahra.
irritated *v.* abgedrayt.
irritated *v.* fa'eiyaht.
irritating - abdrayyish.
irritation *(neu).* eiyahnis.
irritations *(f).* eiyahnisa.
is - is.
it - es / 's.
itchy - beisich.
its - sei *(possessive pronoun,*
   *used **with** a noun).*
itself - sich-selvaht.

J - j

jail *(neu).* kfengnis.
jailed *v.* eikshtekt.
jails *(f).* kfengnissa.
jar *(m).* tsheah.
jars *(f).* tsheahs.
Jew *(m).* Yutt.
Jewish - Yiddish.
Jewish church *(f)* Yudda-gmay
Jewish churches *(f).*
   Yudda-gmayna.
Jewish council *(f).*
   Yudda-council.
Jews *(f).* Yudda.
job (work) *(f).* eahvet.
job *(m).* tshaub.
joints *(f).* gveahva.
joy *(f).* frayt.
joy *(f).* freyyaheit.
joyful - fraylich.
joyfulness *(f).* fraylichkeit.
Jubilee year*(neu)* frei-setz-yoah
judge *v.* richta.
judge *(m).* richtah.
judged *v.* gricht.

judgement *(neu).* gericht.
judgement *(f).* richtichkeit.
judgement *(f).* gerichtichkeit.
judgement day *(m).*
   gerichts-dawk.
judgement days *(f).*
   gerichts-dawwa.
judgement hall *(neu).*
   richt-haus.
judgement halls *(f).*
   richt-heisah.
judgement seat *(m).*
   richtah-shtool.
judgement seats *(f).*
   richtah-shteel.
judgements *(f).* gerichta.
juice *(f).* saft.
juices *(f).* safta.
juicy - breeyich.
jump *v.* tshumba.
jumped *v.* getshumbt.
jumpy - tshumbich.
just - yusht.
just now - foahrich.

K - k

keep *v.* halda.
keep (in remembrance) *v.* eidenka.
kept *v.* kalda.
kernel (grain) *(f).* kann.

kerosine *(neu).* licht-ayl.
kettle *(m).* kessel.
kettles *(f).* kesla.
key *(m).* shlissel.

(m) = da   (f) = di   (neu) = es   167

keys *(f)*. shlisla.
kick *v*. kikka.
kicked *v*. gekikt.
kid (baby goat) *(neu)*. gaysli.
kids (baby goats) *(f)*. gayslen.
kill *v*. doht-macha.
    (lit. – make dead)
kill *v*. umbringa.
killed *v*. doht-gmacht.
killed *v*. umgebrocht.
kind - goot-maynich.
kind - satt.
kinda - sadda.
kindness *(f)*. goot-maynichkeit.
kindnesses *(f)*.
    goot-maynichkeida.
kinds - sadda.
king *(m)*. kaynich.
kingdom *(neu)*. kaynich-reich.
kingdom *(neu)*. reich.
Kingdom of Heaven *(neu)*.
    Himmel-Reich.
kingdoms *(f)*. reicha.
kings *(f)*. kaynicha.
kiss *v*. kissa.
kiss *(m)*. kuss.
kissed *v*. gekist.
kitchen *(f)*. kich.
kitchens *(f)*. kicha.
kitten *(neu)*. busli.
kittens *(f)*. buslen.
knee *(neu)*. gnee.
kneel *v*. gneeya.

kneeled *v*. gegneet.
knew *v*. gvist.
knife *(neu)* messah.
knives *(f)*. mesra.
knobby - gnovlich.
knock off *v*. abshlauwa.
knock on a door *v*. globba.
knock on a door *v*. ohglobba.
knock out *v*. ausshlauwa.
knocked *v*. geglobt.
knocked *v*. ohgeglobt.
knocked off *v*. abkshlauwa.
knocked out *v*. auskshlauwa.
knot *(m)*. gnibb.
knot *v*. gnibba.
knot (in wood) *(m)*. gnatt.
knots *(f)*. gnibba.
knots (in wood) *(f)*. gnadda.
knotted *v*. gegnibt.
knotty (wood) gnaddich.
know (information or facts).
    v. vissa
know (ahead of time, foreknow)
    v. foahvissa
know (someone or something) *v*.
    kenna.
knowledge *(f)*. vissaheit.
known *v*. gvist.
known(ahead of time, foreknown)
    v. foahgvist.
known (someone or something)
    v. gekend.

L - l

lackadaisical - aldvannish.
lacking (ambition) aldvannish.
lacking (social graces) ungland
ladder *(f)*. laydah.
ladders *(f)*. laydra.
lagging - hinna-noch
(example: running behind on time)
laid *v*. glaykt.
laid *v*. gleyya.
laid down *v*. anna-glaykt.
laid off *v*. abglaykt.
laid on (hands or clothes) *v*.
     ohglaykt
lamb *(neu)* lamm *(used in Bible)*
lamb *(n)*. shibli.
lambs *(f)* lemmah *(used in Bible)*
lambs *(f)*. shiblen.
lame - lohm.
lament *v*. yammahra.
lamentable - yammahlich.
lamented *v*. gyammaht.
land *(neu)*. land.
lands *(f)*. lendah.
landscape *(neu)*. landshaft.
landscapes *(f)*. landshafta.
language *(f)*. shprohch.
languages *(f)*. shprohcha.
lantern *(f)*. ladann.
lanterns *(f)*. ladanna.
lap *(f)*. shohs.
laps *(f)*. shohsa.
lard *(neu)*. fett.
large - grohs.
large container (used for
     canning) *(m)*. beilah.

larger - graysah.
largest - graysht.
lash *v*. fagayshla.
lashed *v*. fagaysheld.
last - letsht.
late - shpoht.
later - shpaydah.
lathe *(f)*. dray-bank.
lathes *(f)*. dray-benk.
laugh *v*. lacha.
laugh at *v*. auslacha.
laugh at *v*. falacha.
laughed *v*. glacht.
laughed at *v*. ausglacht.
laughed at *v*. falacht.
laundry *(f)*. vesh.
law *(neu)* ksetz.
law breaker *(m)* ksetz-brechah
law giver *(m)*. ksetz-gevvah.
lawless - unadlich.
lawn *(m)*. hohf.
lawnmower *(m)*. hohf-mayah.
lawnmowers *(f)*. hohf-mayahs.
laws *(f)*. ksetza.
lawyer *(m)*. lawyah.
lay *v*. layya.
lay down *v*. anna-layya.
lay off *v*. ablayya.
lazy - faul.
lazy person *(m)*. faulensah.
lead *v*. fiahra.
lead astray *v*. abfiahra.
lead (be in charge) *v*. foahgay.
lead singer *(m)*. foahsingah.
leader *(m)*. foahgayyah.

leaf *(f)*. blatt.
leaf *(f)*. lawb.
leafy - bleddahrich.
leak *v.* rinna.
leaked *v.* grind.
leaky - rinnich.
learn *v.* lanna.
learned *v.* gland.
least - vennichsht.
leather *(neu)*. leddah.
leave *v.* falossa.
leave control (of a matter to another) *v.* ivvah-lossa.
leave on (a light, clothes, etc.) *v.* ohlossa
leave quickly *v.* fabutza.
leaves *(f)*. bleddah.
leaves *(f)*. lawva.
led *v.* kfiaht.
led astray *v.* abkfiaht.
led (having been in charge) *v.* foahganga.
left (direction) lings
left control (of a matter to another) *v.* ivvah-glost.
left early *v.* abkshprunga.
left on (light, clothes, etc.) *v.* ohglost
left over - ivvahrich.
left quickly *v.* fabutzt.
leg *(neu)*. bay.
lend *v.* layna.
length *(f)*. leng.
lengthen *v.* falengahra.
lengthened *v.* falengaht.
lent *v.* glaynd.
leprosy *(m)*. aussatz.
leprous - aussetzich.
less - vennichah.

let *v.* lossa.
let fall *v.* falla-lossa.
let loose *v.* frei-lossa. *(present, future)*
let loose *v.* frei-glost *(past)*
let on *v.* ohglost.
let out *v.* ausglost.
let *v.* glost. *(past)*
letter of alphabet*(m)* bushtawb
letter of praise *(m)*. lohb-breef
letter (postal) *(m)*. breef.
letters of praise *(f)* lohb-breefa
letters of alphabet *(f)*. bushtawva
letters (postal) *(f)*. breefa.
lettuce *(neu)*. salawt.
level - ayva.
lever *(m)*. leevah.
levers *(f)*. leevahra.
liar *(m)*. leeyah.
liar *(m)*. liknah.
liars *(f)*. liknah.
lick (with the tongue) *v.* shlekka
licked (with the tongue) *v.* kshlekt
lid *(m)*. dekkel.
lid (small) *(neu)*. dekli.
lids *(f)*. dekla.
lids (small) *(f)*. deklen.
lie *(m)*. leek.
lie down *v.* anna-leiya.
lie (position) *v.* leiya.
lie (untruth) *v.* leeya.
lied *v.* gleekt.
lies *(f)*. leeya.
life *(neu)*. layva.
lifetime *(f)*. layves-zeit.
lift off *v.* abhayva.
lifted off *v.* abkohva.
light *(adj.)* hell.

light *v.* ohgay.
light *(neu).* licht.
light (to make *a fire* / turn on
    a lamp) *v.* ohmacha
light (*a fire or lamp* with a
    matchstick) *v.* ohshtekka
light (and /or its properties)
    (f). helling.
light colored - leicht.
light up *v.* uflichta.
light weight - leicht.
lighthearted - leicht-hatzich.
lightning *(m).* veddah-laych.
lightning flash *v.*
    veddah-laycha.
lightning flashed *v.*
    veddah-glaycht.
lightning flashes *(f).*
    veddah-laycha.
lights *(f).* lichtah.
lightstand *(m).* licht-shtaend.
lightstands *(f).* licht-shtaenda.
like *v.* gleicha.
like - vi.
liked *v.* geglicha.
likely - aebt.
liken to *v.* fagleicha.
likened to *v.* faglicha.
likeness *(f).* fagleichnis.
likeness *(neu).* gleichnis.
likenesses *(f).* fagleichnissa.
likenesses *(f).* gleichnissa.
likewise - gleichaveis.
lilies *(f).* lilya-blumma.
lily *(f).* lilya-blumm.
limber - lummahrich.
lime (mineral, as in limestone)
    kallich
limp - lummahrich.

line *(f).* lein.
linen fabric *(neu).* linnen-duch.
lines *(f).* leina.
lint *(m).* flauma.
lint *(m).* fussah.
lint covered - fussahrich.
lints *(f).* fussahra.
lion *(m).* layb.
lions *(f).* layva.
lip *(f).* leftz.
lips *(f).* leftza.
liquid *(f).* bree.
listen *v.* heicha.
listen to *v.* abheicha.
listen to (obediently) *v.*
    oh'heicha.
listened *v.* keicht.
listened to *v.* abkeicht.
listened to (obediently) *v.*
    ohkeicht.
lit a fire or lamp *v.*
    ohkshtokka.
lit a fire or lamp *v.*
    ohgmacht.
lit up *v.* ohganga.
lit up *v.* ufglicht.
litter *(neu).* kfrays.
little (tiny bit) bisli.
little (bit) bissel.
little - vennich.
little while - veil.
live *v.* layva.
live out *v.* auslayva.
lived *v.* glaybt.
lived out *v.* ausglaybt.
lived (where a person used to live)
    v. gvoond.
liver *(f).* levvah.
livestock (animal) *(neu)* fee.

load *v.* lawda.
load *(f).* loht.
load down *v.* nunnah-lawda.
loaded *v.* glawda.
loaded down *v.* nunnah-glawda.
loaf *(m).* layb.
loathsome - ayklich.
locate *v.* favisha.
located *v.* favisht.
located to the side - nayva.
lock *v.* shleesa.
lock *(f).* shloss.
lock in *v.* eishleesa.
lock out *v.* ausshleesa.
lock up (completely) *v.* fashleesa
locked *v.* kshlossa.
locked in *v.* eikshlossa.
locked out *v.* auskshlossa.
locked up (completely)
     v. fashlossa.
locks *(f).* shlossa.
log *(m).* blokk.
log barn *(f).* blokk-sheiyah.
log barns *(f).* blokk-sheiyahra.
log cabin *(neu).* blokk-haus.
log cabins *(f).* blokk-heisah.
logs *(f).* blekk.
long - lang.
longer - lengah.
longest - lengsht.
look *v.* gukka.
look at *v.* ohgukka.
look forward to *v.* foahgukka.
look over *v.* ivvah-gukka.
looked *v.* gegukt.
looked *v.* ksheind.
looked at *v.* ohgegukt.
looked forward to *v.*
     foahgegukt.

looked over *v.* ivvah-gegukt.
loom (to make cloth) *(f).*
     duch-loom.
loose - lohs.
LORD *(m).* HAH / Hah *(In the Bible whenever the word "LORD" occurs in all capital letters, the name in the orignal Hebrew is "YHWH" / "Jehovah").*
lords *(f).* hahra.
lose *v.* faliahra.
lost *v.* faloahra.
lot - latt.
loud - laut.
loud call *(m).* grish.
loud calls *(f).* grisha.
love - leeb.
love *v.* leeva.
loved *v.* gleebt.
loveliest - alli-shensht.
loving - leeblich.
loving - leevich.
low - niddah.
lower - niddahrah (nidrah -
    common pronunciation)
lowest - niddahsht.
lowly esteemed - fadechtich.
lubricate *v.* ayla.
lubricated *v.* gayld.
luck *(m).* glikk.
lukewarm - lebbish.
lumber *(neu).* lambah.
lump (in batter) *(m).* gnoddel
lumps (in batter) *(f).* gnodla
lumpy (in batter) gnodlich
lunch (mid-day meal) *(neu)*
    middawk.
lust *(m).* falusht.

lust *(f)*. lusht.
lust *v*. lushta.
lusted *v*. glusht.
lustful - lushtboah.

lustfulness *(f)*. lushtboahkeit.
lusts *(f)*. falushta.
lusts *(f)*. lushta.

M - m

made *v*. gmacht.
made (banging noise) *v*.
    gedemmaht.
made (thundering niose) *v*.
    gedunnaht.
made again *v*. ivvah-gmacht.
made (oath) *v*. kshvoahra.
made better *v*. fabessaht.
made (holy) *v*. keilicht.
made known *v*. fakindicht.
made new *v*. nei-gmacht
    (*pronounced*: neiy-gmacht).
made of bricks -
    bakka-shtaynich.
made of glass - glawsich.
made of iron - eisich.
made sick to stomach *v*.
    gegraust.
magic *v*. fahexa (*present, future*)
magic *v*. fahext (*past*)
magical healing (powwow) *v*.
    braucha.
magistrate *(m)*. shtatt-richtah.
majesty *(f)*. kaynich-eah.
make *v*. macha.
make again *v*. ivvah-macha.
make better *v*. fabessahra.
make contact with *v*. dreffa.
make holy *v*. heilicha.
make known *v*. fakindicha.

male person *(m)*. manskal.
male persons *(f)*. manskals.
malicious -
    fagunnish/fagunshtlich.
man *(m)*. mann.
man *(m)*. manskal.
mane *(f)*. mawna.
manger *(m)*. foodah-drohk.
mangers *(f)*. foodah-drayk.
manner of talking *(neu)*.
    kshvetz.
manure *(f)*. misht.
many - feel.
many - latt.
many - mannich.
mar *v*. fagratza.
mare *(f)*. mau.
mares *(f)*. madda.
mark *(m)*. meik.
mark *v*. meika.
mark off *v*. abmeika.
mark up *v*. fameika.
mark with stakes *v*. abshtikla.
marked *v*. gmeikt.
marked off *v*. abgmeikt.
marked up *v*. fameikt.
marked with stakes *v*.
    abkshtikkeld.
market building *(neu)*.
    kawf-haus.

market buildings *(f)*.
 kawf-heisah.
market place *(m)*.
 fakawfa-blatz.
market place *(neu)*. kawf-haus.
market places *(f)*. kawf-heisah
marks *(f)*. meiks.
marred *v.* fagratzt.
married *v.* keiyaht.
marry *v.* heiyahra.
marvel *(m)*. vunnah.
marvels *(f)*. vunnahs.
master *(f)*. meishtah.
masters *(f)*. meishtahra.
matrimony *(m)*. ayshtand.
matter *v.* ausmacha.
matter *(f)*. sach.
matter *v.* shadda.
mattered *v.* ausgmacht.
mattered *v.* kshatt.
maybe *v.* fleeya.
me - mich.
me - miah *(dative case)*.
meal *(neu)*. essa. *(common use)*
meal *(m)*. eems. *(not common)*
mean *v.* mayna.
meaning *(f)*. mayning.
meanings *(f)*. mayninga.
meant *v.* gmaynd.
measles *(f)*. raydla.
measure *v.* messa.
measure (by stepping off) *v.*
 abshridda.
measure off *v.* abmessa.
measure out *v.* ausmessa.
measured *v.* gmessa.
measured off *v.* abgmessa.
measured out *v.* ausgmessa.
meat *(neu)*. flaysh.

meat fork *(f)*. flaysh-gavvel.
meat forks *(f)*. flaysh-gavla.
meat market *(m)* flaysh-market
meat markets *(f)*.
 flaysh-markets.
meek - daymeedich.
meek - sanftmeedich.
meekness *(f)*. sanftmeedichkeit.
meekness *(f)*. sanftmoot.
meet *v.* ohdreffa.
meeting *(f)*. fasamling.
meeting house *(neu)*.
 fasamling-haus.
meeting houses *(f)*.
 fasamling-heisah.
meeting place *(m)*.
 fasamling-blatz.
meeting places *(f)*.
 fasamling-bletz.
melon *(f)*. malawn.
melons *(f)*. malawna.
melt *v.* fashmelsa.
melt off *v.* abshmelsa.
melted *v.* fashmolsa.
melted off *v.* abkshmolsa.
member *(neu)*. gleet.
members *(f)*. gleedah.
memorized - ausvennich.
memory *(f)*. meind.
men *(f)*. manskals.
men *(f)*. mennah.
men folk *(f)*. mansleit.
mend *v.* flikka.
mended *v.* kflikt.
merchant *(m)*. kayfah.
merchants *(f)*. kawf-leit.
merciful - bamhatzich.
mercifulness *(f)*.
 bamhatzichkeit.

mercifulnesses *(f)*.
   bamhatzichkeida.
merciless - unbamhatzich.
Messiah *(m)*. Heiland.
met *v.* gedroffa.
met *v.* ohgedroffa.
mice *(f)*. meislen.
mid-day *(f)*. middawk.
middle - middelsht.
midnight *(f)*. halb-nacht.
midnight *(f)*. mitt-nacht.
might *(f)*. macht.
might *v.* mechta.
mighty - mechtich.
mildew *(neu)*. grohtz.
mile *(f)*. meil.
miles *(f)*. meila.
military captain *(m)*.
   greeks-hauptman.
military captians *(f)*.
   greeks-hauptmennah.
military clothing *(m)*.
   greeks-vammes
   (lit. - war coat).
military clothing *(f)*.
   greeks-vemmes
   (lit. - war coats).
military employee *(m)*.
   greeks-deenah.
military helmet *(m)*.
   greeks-hoot.
milk *v.* melka.
milk *(f)*. millich.
milked *v.* gmolka.
mind *(f)*. meind.
mind *v.* meinda.
minded *v.* gmeind.
minded - psunna.
mindful of *v.* eigedenkt.

mine - mein.
minister *(m)*. deenah.
ministers *(f)*. deensht-leit.
ministry *(m)*. deensht.
mint plant *(f)*. mint-blansa.
minute *(f)*. manutt.
minutes *(f)*. manudda.
miracle *(m)*. zaycha.
miracle worker *(m)*.
   zaycha-shaffah.
miracle workers *(f)*.
   zaycha-sheffah.
mirror *(m)*. shpikkel.
mirrors *(f)*. shpikla.
miscellaneous - allah- hand.
mischievous - raulich.
miserable - aylendich.
misery - aylend.
misfortune *(neu)*. unglikk.
misleading abfiahrich.
misplace *v.* falayya.
misplace (by someone else)
   v. fashlayfa.
misplaced *v.* falaykt.
misplaced (by someone else)
   v. fashlayft.
miss out *v.* fafayla.
miss out on *v.* ausfafayla-uf.
missed out *v.* fafayld.
missed out on *v.* ausfafayld-uf
mixed together - deich-nannah
mock *v.* auslacha.
mock *v.* ausshenda.
mock *v.* aus'shpodda.
mock *v.* fashpodda.
mock *v.* shpodda.
mock (laugh at) *v.* falacha.
mocked *v.* ausglacht.
mocked *v.* auskshend.

mocked *v.* auskshpott.
mocked *v.* fashpott.
mocked *v.* kshpott.
mocked (laughed at) *v.* falacht.
mocker *(m).* shpoddah.
mockers *(f).* shpeddah.
moderate - ksheit.
moderation *(m).* fashtand.
moist - feicht.
mold *(neu).* grohtz.
moldy - grohtzich.
mom *(f).* maemm.
moms *(f).* maemma.
Monday *(m).* Moondawk.
Mondays *(f).* Moondawks / Moondawwa.
monetary exchange *(m)* vexel
money *(neu).* geld.
money bag *(m).* geld-sakk.
money bags *(f).* geld-sekk.
money box *(f).* geld-box.
money boxes *(f).* geld-boxa.
money changer*(m)* geld-vexlah
money lenders *(f).* layns-leit.
month *(m).* moonet.
months *(f).* moonada.
mood *(f).* moot.
more - may.
more flat (level) ayvenah.
more level - ayvenah.
morning *(m).* meiyet.
mornings *(f).* meiyets.
mortal - shteahblich.
Mosaic Law *(neu).* ksetz.
mosquito *(f).* shnohk.
mosquitos *(f).* shnohka.
most - mensht.
most centered - middelsht.
most flat - ayvesht.

most holy place *(m).* alli-heilichsht-blatz.
most level - ayvesht.
moth *(m).* shawb.
mother *(f).* muddah.
mother-in-law *(f).* shviah-muddah.
mothers *(f).* muddahra.
mothers-in-law *(f).* shviah-muddahra.
moths *(f).* shawva.
motivate *v.* dreiva.
motivated *v.* gedrivva.
Mount of Olives *(m).* ayl-berg.
mountain *(m).* berg.
mountins *(f).* berga.
mournful - davvahlich.
mouse *(neu).* meisli.
mouth *(neu).* maul.
mouthful *(neu).* maul-foll.
mouthpiece of a bridle *(neu).* gebiss.
mouthpieces of bridles *(f).* gebissah.
mouths *(f).* meilah.
move (energetically) *v.* rawsa.
move (move to another residence) *v.* zeeya
moved - bevaykt.
moved (energetically) *v.* grawst.
moved (stealthily) *v.* kshlicha.
moved (to another residence) *v.* gezohwa.
mow *v.* mayya.
mow off *v.* abmayya.
mowed *v.* gmayt.
mowed off *v.* abgmayt.
much - feel.
mud puddle *(neu).* drekk-loch.

mulberry *(f)*. maulbeahra.
murder *v.* shlawdra.
murderer *(m)*. doht-shlayyah.
murderer *(m)*. maddah
   (not common).
murderous actions *(f)*.
   maddahrei.
must *v.* missa *("miah missa")*.
must *v.* muss *("Ich muss")*.
must *v.* misht ("du misht")
   (future tense)

must (would have to) *v.* mista
   (future tense)
mustache *(m)*. shnautzah.
mustard *(m)*. moshtaht.
musty - grohtzich.
mutter *v.* gnudra.
muttered *v.* gegnuddaht.
my - mei.
my - meim *(dative case)*.
my - meina. *(plural)*
myself - mich-selvaht.

N - n

nagger *(adj)*. gneiksich.
nail *(m)*. nakkel (nawwel -
   common pronunciation).
nail *v.* nakla.
nail hole *(neu)*. nakkel-loch.
nail holes *(f)*. nekkel-lechah.
nailed *v.* gnakeld.
nails *(f)*. nekkel (nayyel -
   common pronunciation).
naked - blutt.
naked - nakkich.
name *v.* haysa.
name *v.* nayma.
name *(m)*. nohma.
name of blasphemy *(m)*.
   leshtah-nohma.
named *v.* kaysa.
named *v.* gnaymd.
namely - naymlich.
names *(f)*. nayma.
names of blasphemy *(f)*.
   leshtah-nayma.
narrate *v.* fazayla.

narrated *v.* fazayld.
narrow - shmawl *(common use)*.
narrow - eng. *(not common)*
nation *(neu)*. folk.
native inhabitants *(f)*.
   lands-leit.
natural - nadiahlich.
natured - naduaht.
naughty - labbich.
near - nayksht.
nearer - naychah.
nearest - naykshtisht.
nearly - ball.
nearly - baut.
nearly - fasht / shiah.
necessary - nohdvendich.
necessities *(f)*. nohda.
necessity *(f)*. noht.
neck *(m)*. hals.
necks *(f)*. hels.
need *v.* braucha.
needed *v.* gebraucht.
needle *(f)*. nohdel.

needles *(f)*. nohdla.
neighbor *(m)*. nochbah.
neighborhood *(f)*. nochbahshaft.
neighborhoods *(f)*. nochbahshafta.
neighbors *(f)*. nochbra.
nest *(neu)*. nesht.
nests *(f)*. neshtah.
net *(neu)*. nett.
net (for catching) *(neu)*. fang-net.
nets *(f)*. netts.
nets (for catching) *(f)*. fang-nets.
never - nee *(not used alone)*.
never - neemols.
never - nee-naett (used alone).
never - selayva-naett.
new - nei *(pronounced neiy)*.
new - neiya.
next - neksht.
nice - shay.
nicer - shennah.
nicest - alli-shensht.
nicest - shensht.
night *(f)*. nacht.
night (during the night) nachts
nights *(f)*. necht.
nine - nein.
ninety - neintzich.
ninety-nine - neina-neintzich.
ninteen - nientzay.
ninth - neind.
nippers *(f)*. beis zang.
nippers *(f)*. beis-zanga.
no - nay.
no longer - nimmi.
no more - nimmi.
no one - nimmand.
noble birth - hohch-geboahra.

noise *(f)*. raekket *(common use)*.
noise *(m)*. saund.
noise *(f)*. yacht.
noises *(f)*. raekkeda *(common use)*
noises *(f)*. yatchta.
noisy - rablich *(common use)*.
noisy - yachtich.
non-Greek nationality - Ungreeyish.
non-Amish - hohch.
none - kenn *(used with a noun)*.
none - kens.
nonsense - dumhayda.
noodle *(m)*. noodel.
noodles *(f)*. noodla.
noon meal *(neu)*. middawk.
noon period *(f)*. middawk.
north *(f)*. natt.
northeast natt-eest.
northward (going in the northern direction) nadda
northwest - natt-vest.
nose *(f)*. naws.
noses *(f)*. nays.
nosey - gvunnah-naws.
nostril *(neu)*. naws-loch.
nostrils *(f)*. naws-lechah.
not - naett.
not eager - falayt.
not even once - neemols.
not heavy - leicht.
not hidden - fanna-rumm.
not taken care of - unfaseikt.
nothing - nix.
notice *v*. acht-havva.
notice *v*. fameika.
noticed *v*. acht-katt.
noticed *v*. fameikt.
notion *(m)*. begriff.

nourishment *(neu)* layves-mawl
now - nau.
nowhere - neiyetz.

number *(m)*. nambah.
numbers *(f)*. nambahs.

O - o

oak tree *(m)*. aycha-bohm.
oak trees *(f)*. aycha-baym.
oak wood *(neu)*. aycha-hols.
oath *(f)*. fashteiking.
oath *v*. shveahra.
oaths *(f)*. fashteikinga.
oats *(m)*. havvah.
obedient - brawf.
obey *v*. heicha.
obeyed *v*. keicht.
obligation *(f)*. shuldichkeit.
obligations *(f)*. shulkichkeida.
obtain *v*. bei-greeya.
obtained *v*. bei-grikkt.
occupation *(f)*. eahvet.
occupation *(m)*. tshaub.
occupations *(f)*. eahveda.
occur *v*. foahkumma.
occur *v*. ohgay.
occur to *v*. bei-falla.
occurred *v*. ohganga.
of - funn.
of a - fumma *(used with a masculine or neuter noun, dative case)*.
of course - voll.
of the - fumm *(used with a masculine or neuter noun, dative case)*.
off - ab.
off set *(m)*. absatz.

offer *v*. beeda.
offer *v*. ohbeeda.
offered *v*. gebodda.
offered *v*. ohgebodda.
offering (made to an idol) *(neu)*. getza-opfah.
offering of blood *(neu)*. bloot-opfah.
offerings of blood *(f)*. bloot-opfahra.
often - oft.
oftentimes - als.
oil *(neu)*. ayl.
oil bottle *(f)*. ayl-boddel *(olive oil)*.
oil bottles *(f)*. ayl-bodla.
oil cloth *(neu)*. ayl-duch.
oil cloths *(f)*. ayl-dichah.
oil (used for anointing) *(neu)*. salba-ayl.
oiled *v*. gayld.
oils *(f)*. ayla.
oily - aylich.
ointment *(f)*. shmiah.
ointments *(f)*. shmiahra.
old - ald.
older - eldah.
older ladies *(f)*. mammis.
older lady *(f)*. mammi.
oldest - eldsht.
olive berries *(f)*. ayl-frichta.

olive berry *(neu)*. ayl-frucht.
olive garden (orchard) *(m)*.
     ayl-goahra.
olive oil mixer *(m)*.
     ayl-mixah.
olive oil mixers *(f)*.
     ayl-mixahs.
olive tree *(m)*. ayl-bohm.
olive trees *(f)*. ayl-baym.
on - uf.
on purpose - poahbes.
on the front - fanna-druff.
on the inside - invendich.
on there - druff.
on top - ovva-druff.
once - moll.
once upon a time - moll.
one - ayn.
one - ay.
one - aym.
one - aynra.
one - ma *(personal pronoun,
     nominative case)*.
one - vann *(pronoun)*.
one given to much chatter
     fagakst.
one of - ayns.
one of several - aynd.
one of them - aynd.
one person - ay-ebbah.
one repetition *(neu)*. mohl.
one tenth *(neu)*. zeyydel.
one time *(neu)*. mohl.
one who (commits adultery)
     (m). aybrechah.
one who (fishes) *(m)*. fishah.
one who(indulges in debauchery)
     (m). huahrah.

one who (pays back) *(m)*.
     zrikk-bezawlah.
one who (releases) *(m)*.
     frei-shtellah.
one who (sets free) *(m)*.
     frei-setzah.
one who (shares the same fate)
     (m). mitt-daylah.
one who (takes care of) *(m)*.
     heedah.
ones - vans *(pronoun)*.
one's own - aykna / ayya.
one's own (understanding) *(m)*.
     ayya-fashtand.
oneself - em. *(personal pronoun,
     accusative case)*
one-sided - ayseidich.
onion *(f)*. zvivvel.
onions *(f)*. zvivla.
only - aynsisht.
only - yusht.
open - uf.
open *v*. ufmacha.
opened *v*. ufgmacht.
openly exposed –
     fanna-rumm.
opinion (thoughts) denkes.
opinion *(f)*. mayning.
opinions *(f)*. mayninga.
opportunities *(f)*.
     gleyyaheida.
opportunity *(f)*. gleyyaheit.
opportunity *(m)*. tsheins.
opposed - digeyya / digayya.
opposed to - geyya / gayya.
opposed to - geyyich / gayyich.
opposition *(m)*. viddah-shtand.
opposition *(m)*. viddah-shteit.
or - adda.

orchard *(m)*. bamgoahra.
   (lit. - tree garden) (common use)
orchard *(m)*. bohm-goahra
     (lit. - tree garden)
orders *(f)*. addahs.
orneriness - aysel-shtraych.
ornery - ausgedrivva.
osprey *(m)*. fish-awdlah.
other - annah.
other worldly - annah-veldlich.
others - anri.
otherwise - annahshtah.
otherwise - shunsht.
ottoman *(m)*. foos-shtool.
ottomans *(f)*. foos-shteel.
our - unsah.
out(toward an outer location) naus
out around - aus a rumm.
out do *v*. ausdu.
out here - haus.
out live *v*. auslayva.
out lived *v*. ausglaybt.
out of - aus.
out of - raus.
out of fix - ausfix.
out perform *v*. ausdu.
out performed *v*. ausgedu.
out (prefix) aus.
out there draus.
outdone *v*. ausgedu.
outer - ausahri.
outer covering *(f)*. shawl.
outer coverings *(f)*. shawla.
outer robe *(m)*. ausah-rokk.
outer robes *(f)*. ausah-rekk.
outermost - ausahsht.
outgrow *v*. ausvaxa.
outgrown *v*. ausgvaxa.
outside - autseit.

outside of - ausa.
outside one - ausah.
outside ones (non-native)
    ausahri.
outsider *(m)*. autseidah.
outsiders *(f)*. autseidahs.
outward - ausvendich.
outward appearance -
    ausahlich.
oven *(m)*. bekkah.
oven *(m)*. offa.
ovens *(f)*. effa.
over - ivvah.
over (toward a location over there)
    nivvah
over (toward here) rivvah
over coat *(m)*. ivvah-rokk.
over coat *(neu)*. ivvah-hemm.
over (past, concluded) fa'ivvah.
over run by animals *v*.
    fashprunga.
over shirt *(neu)*. ivvah-hemm.
over there - drivva.
overcast - dreeb.
overcome *v*. ivvah-kumma.
overcomer *(m)*. ivvah-kummah.
overeat *v*. fressa.
overeaten *v*. kfressa.
overflow *v*. ivvah-lawfa.
overflowed *v*. ivvah-gloffa.
overlay *v*. ivvah-layya.
overlayed *v*. ivvah-glaykt.
overlook *v*. ivvah-gukka.
overlooked *v*. ivvah-gegukt.
overnight - ivvah-nacht.
oversee *v*. ivvah-sayna.
overseen *v*. ivvah-ksenna.
overseer *(m)*. ivvah-saynah.
overshirts *(f)*. ivvah-hemmah.

oversleep *v.* fashlohfa.
overtake *v.* ivvah-nemma.
overtaken *v.* ivvah-gnumma.
overthrow *v.* umshmeisa.
own *v.* aykna.

owned *v.* gaykend.
owner *(m).* ayknah.
ox *(m).* ox.
oxen *(f).* oxa.

P - p

page *(neu).* paytsh.
pages *(f).* paytshes.
paid *v.* betzawld.
paid off *v.* abbezawld.
paid off a debt (by working)
    v. auskshaft.
paid out *v.* ausbezawld.
pail *(m).* aymah.
pain *(m).* shmatz.
pained *v.* kshmatzt.
painful - vay.
pains *(f).* shmatza.
paint *(f).* paynd.
painter *(m).* payndah.
pair - poah.
pair off *v.* abpoahra.
paired off *v.* abgepoaht.
pale color - blayyich.
pale color *(adj)* . hell.
palm tree *(f).* palma.
pamphlet *(neu).* bichli.
pamphlets *(f).* bichlen.
pan *(f).* pann.
pancake *(f).* pannakuch.
pancakes *(f).* pannakucha.
pans *(f).* panna.
pantries *(f).* botrin.
pantry *(f).* botri.
pants *(f).* hossa.

paper *(neu).* babiah.
papers *(f).* babiahra.
parable *(f).* fagleichnis.
parable *(neu).* gleichnis.
parables *(f).* fagleichnissa.
parables *(f).* gleichnissa.
paradise *(f).* paradees.
parents *(f).* eldra.
parsley *(neu).* paydahli.
particular - patiklah.
pass the time *v.* faveila.
passing - fagenglich.
Passover - Ohshtah.
Passover feast *(neu).*
    Ohshtah-fesht.
Passover lamb *(neu).*
    Ohshtah-lamm.
past - fabei.
past - ivvah.
pasture *(f).* vayt.
pastures *(f).* vayda.
path *(f).* pawt.
paths *(f).* pawda.
patience *(f).* geduldheit.
patience - geduld.
patiently - duldich.
patiently - geduldich.
pattern *(neu).* mushtah.
patterns *(f).* mushtahra.

pay *v.* betzawla.
pay off *v.* abbezawla.
pay off a debt (by working) *v.* ausshaffa.
pay out *v.* ausbezawla.
payment *(f).* betzawling.
pea *(f).* eahps.
peace *(m).* fridda.
peace maker *(m).* fridda-machah.
peace offering *(neu).* fridda-opfah.
peace offerings *(f).* fridda-opfahra.
peaceful - fridlich.
peacefully - fridlich.
peach *(m).* pashing.
pear *(f).* biah.
pear tree *(m).* biahra-bohm.
pear trees *(f).* biahra-baym.
pears *(f).* biahra.
peas *(f).* eahpsa.
pebble *(neu).* shtaynli.
pebbles *(f).* shtaynlen.
peddle *v.* pedla.
peddled *v.* gepeddeld.
peel *(f).* shawl.
peel *v.* shayla.
peel off *v.* abshayla.
peeled *v.* kshayld.
peeled off *v.* abkshayld.
peelings *(f).* shawla.
peep *v.* peepsa.
peeped *v.* gepeepst.
pendulum *(m).* bauma-dekkel.
pendulums *(f).* bauma-dekla.
people *(neu).* folk.
people *(m).* leit.
people (in a wedding party) *(f).* hohtzich-leit.
people (visiting) *(f).* psuch-leit.
people (who plow) *(f).* blooks-leit.
pepper *(f).* peffah.
peppers *(f).* peffahra.
perceive *v.* fanemma.
perceived *v.* fanumma.
perfect *v.* folkumma.
perfection *(f).* folkummaheit.
perfection *(f).* folkummashaft.
performed (magical healing arts - powwowed) *v.* gebraucht.
persecute *v.* fafolka.
persecute *v.* fafolya.
persecuted *v.* fafolkt.
persevere *v.* shtikka.
persevered *v.* kshtokka.
perspire *v.* fashvitza.
perspired *v.* fashvitzt.
perspired *v.* kshvitzt.
persuade (by talking) *v.* fashvetza.
persuaded (by talking) *v.* fashvetzt.
phrase *(m).* frays.
phrases *(f).* frayses.
pick *v.* pikka.
pick (fruit from a tree) *v.* robba
pick off *v.* ablaysa.
picked *v.* gepikt.
picked (fruit from a tree) *v.* grobt
picked off *v.* abglaysa.
picture *(neu).* piktah.
pictures *(f).* piktahs.
pie *(m).* boi.
piece *(neu).* shtikk.
pieces *(f).* shtikkah.

pieces (of armor) *(f)*.
  greeks-ksharra.
pierce *v.* shtecha.
pierced *v.* kshtocha.
pig *(f)*. pikk.
pig *(f)*. sau.
piglet *(neu)*. pikli.
piglets *(f)*. piklen.
pigs *(f)*. piks.
pigs *(f)*. sei.
pile *(m)*. peil / haufa.
pile *v.* peila.
pile (little) *(neu)*. heifli.
pile (of ashes) *(m)*. esh-haufa.
pile together *v.* heifla.
piled *v.* gepeild.
piled together *v.* keifeld.
piles *(f)*. heifa.
piles (little) *(f)*. heiflen.
piles (of ashes) *(f)*. esh-heifa.
pillar *(m)*. poshta.
pillow *(neu)*. kissi.
pillows *(f)*. kissis.
pilot *(m)*. shtiah-mann.
pilots *(f)*. shtiah-mennah.
pimple *(f)*. pokk.
pimples *(f)*. pokka.
pimply - pokkich.
pin *(f)*. shpell.
pin *v.* shpella.
pinch *v.* petza.
pinch off *v.* abpetza.
pinched *v.* gepetzt.
pinched off *v.* abgepetzt.
pinned *v.* kshpeld.
pins *(f)*. shpella.
pious - fromm.
pipe (used to smoke tobacco)
  (f). peif

pitcher *(m)*. pitshah.
pitied *v.* gedavvaht.
pitiful - aylendich.
pitiful - bedavvahlich.
pitiful - davvahlich.
pitiful condition *(f)*. oahmoot.
pitiful situation aylend.
pity *v.* davvahra.
place *(m)*. blatz.
place a curse on *v.* faflucha.
place (an object) *v.* shtella.
place of judgement *(m)*.
  richts-blatz.
place of torment *(m)*.
  gvayl-blatz.
place of worship *(neu)*.
  gmay-haus.
places *(f)*. bletz.
places of judgement *(f)*.
  richts-bletz.
places of torment *(f)*.
  gvayl-bletz.
plague *(m)*. blohk.
plan ahead *v.* foahzayla.
plan on *v.* fikkahra.
plank *(f)*. blank.
planks *(f)*. blanka.
planned ahead *v.* foahgezayld.
planned on *v.* kfikkaht.
plant *v.* blansa.
plant *(m)*. shtokk.
plant (little) *(neu)*. shtekli.
planted *v.* geblanst.
plants *(f)*. blansa.
plants *(f)*. shtekk.
plants (little) *(f)*. shteklen.
plaques *(f)*. blohwa.
plaster *(neu)*. bleshtah.
plaster *v.* bleshtahra.

plastered *v.* gebleshtaht.
plasters *(f)*. bleshtahra.
plate *(m)*. dellah.
plate (small) *(neu)*. dellahli.
plates *(f)*. dellahra.
plates (small) *(f)*. dellahlen.
platform *(m)*. shtaend.
platforms *(f)*. shtaends.
play *v.* shpeela.
play hooky *v.* abshpeela.
play lead (such as musical
     instrument) *v.* foahshpeela.
played *v.* kshpeeld.
played lead (such as a musical
     instrument) *v.* foahkshpeeld
playful - fashpeeld.
pleasantly - blesiahlich.
pleased *v.* ksoot.
pleasure *(m)*. blasiah.
pleasure *(m)*. blesiah.
pleasures *(f)*. blasiahra.
pleasures *(f)*. blesiahra.
pleat *(f)*. fald.
pleats *(f)*. falda.
plenty - blendi.
pliers *(f)*. zang.
pliers(little)*(neu)* zengli (singular)
pliers (little) *(f)*. zenglen.
plow *v.* bloowa.
plow *(m)*. blook.
plow out (potatoes, etc.) *v.*
     ausbloowa.
plow share *(f)*. blook-sheah.
plow shears *(f)*. blook-sheahra.
plowed *v.* geblookt.
plowed out (potatoes) *v.*
     ausgeblookt.
plows *(f)*. bloowa.
pluck *v.* abrobba.

pluck (fruit from a tree) *v.* robba
plucked *v.* abgrobt.
plucked (fruit from a tree)
     v. grobt
plum *(f)*. blaum.
plums *(f)*. blauma.
pocket *(m)*. sakk.
pocketknife *(neu)* sakk-messah.
pockets *(f)*. sekk.
pod *(f)*. sheffa.
point *(m)*. punka.
point *(m)*. shpitza.
pointer (on a clock or meter)
     (m). zaycha.
pointy - shpitzich.
poison *v.* fagifta.
poison *(neu)*. gift.
poisoned *v.* fagift.
poisonous - giftich.
poked *v.* grend.
pond *(m)*. damm.
ponds *(f)*. damma.
poor - oahm.
poplar tree *(m)*. bablah-bohm.
poplar (tree) babla.
poplar trees *(f)*. bablah-baym.
porch *(f)*. poahtsh.
porches *(f)*. poahtsha.
pork *(neu)*. sei-flaysh.
portion *(neu)*. dayl.
portion *(f)*. shiah.
portion out *v.* ausdayla.
portion out *v.* dayla.
portioned *v.* gedayld.
portioned out *v.* ausgedayld.
portions *(f)*. daylah.
portions *(f)*. shiahra.
possible - meeklich / mayklich.
post *(m)*. poshta.

post (holding large door or gate)
   (m). doah-poshta.
postpone *v*. abdu.
postpone *v*. abhayva.
postponed *v*. abgedu.
postponed *v*. abkohva.
pot *(m)*. haffa.
pot (large) *(m)*. kessel.
pot (small) *(neu)*. kesli.
potato *(f)*. grumbeah.
potatos *(f)*. grumbeahra.
pots *(f)*. kesla.
pots (small) *(f)*. keslen.
pound *(f)*. pund.
pour *v*. leahra.
pour out *v*. fageesa.
poured *v*. gleaht.
poured out *v*. fagossa.
pout *v*. brutza.
pouted *v*. gebrutzt.
pouting brutzich.
poverty *(f)*. oahmoot.
powder *(neu)*. paddah.
power *(f)*. famayya.
power *(f)*. gvald.
power *(f)*. macht.
powerful - gvaldich.
powers of heaven *(f)*.
   Himmels-grefta.
praise *(neu)*. lohb.
praise *v*. lohva.
praised *v*. geprissa.
praised *v*. glohbt.
pray *v*. bayda.
prayed *v*. gebayda.
prayer *(neu)*. gebayt.
prayers *(f)*. gebaydah.
preach *v*. breddicha.
preached *v*. gebreddicht.

preacher *(m)*. breddichah.
preaching *(neu)*. breddiches.
preaching *(neu)*. gebreddich.
precious - keshtlich.
predetermine *v*. foahrichta.
predetermined *v*. foahgricht.
predict *v*. foahsawwa.
predicted *v*. foahksawt.
preeminence *(m)*. foahgang.
preeminent *v*. foahnaymsht.
preferably - leevah.
pregnant - drawwich.
prepare *v*. rishta.
prepare ahead *v*. foahrishta.
prepared *v*. grisht.
prepared ahead *v*. foahgrisht.
present (included with) dibei.
presently allaveil.
press *v*. drikka.
press out *v*. auspressa.
pressed *v*. gedrikt.
pressed out *v*. ausgeprest.
presumptuous - foahvitzich.
pretend *v*. ohlossa.
pretended *v*. ohglost.
prettier - shennah.
prettiest - shensht.
prettiness *(f)*. shayheit.
pretty - shay.
pretty much - adlich.
prevent *v*. fahalda.
previously - difoah.
prick *v*. giksa.
prick *v*. shtecha.
pricked *v*. gegikst.
pricked *v*. kshtocha.
pricker *(m)*. giksah.
prickly - giksich.
prickly plant *(m)*. giksah-shtokk.

prickly plants *(f)*.
  giksah-shtekk.
pride *(m)*. hohchmoot.
priesthood *(f)*. preeshtahshaft.
priesthoods *(f)* preeshtahshafta
prince *(m)*. kaynichs-sohn.
princes *(f)*. kaynichs-sayna.
print (books or magizines) *v.*
  drukka.
printed *v.* gedrukt.
privilege *(f)*. gleyyaheit.
probably andem.
proclaim *v.* ausshprecha.
proclaim *v.* fakindicha.
proclaimed *v.* auskshprocha.
proclaimed *v.* fakindicht.
procrastinate *v.* (to put off)
  absheeva.
procrastinated *v.* (put off)
  abkshohva.
promise *v.* fashprecha.
promise *(f)*. fashpreching.
promise *(f)*. fashprechnis.
promised *v.* fashprocha.
promises *(f)*. fashprechinga.
promises *(f)*. fashprechnissa.
propel physically *v.* dreiva.
propelled physically *v.*
  gedrivva.
proper - shiklich.
proper - tshaett.
prophecies *(f)*. broffetzeiyinga.
prophecy *(f)*. broffetzeiying.
prophesied *v.* gebroffetzeit.
prophesy *v.* broffetzeiya.
prophet *(m)*. brofayt.
prophetess *(neu)*.
  brofayda-veib.
prophetess *(f)*. brofayda-fraw.

prophetesses *(f.)*
  brofayda-frawwa
prophetesses *(f)*.
  brofayda-veivah.
prophets *(f)*. brofayda.
prophets words *(f)*.
  brofayda-vadda.
prostitute *(f)*. huah.
prostitutes *(f)*. huahra.
prostitution *(neu)*.
  huahrarei.
proud - hohchmeedich.
proud (in a bad sense) shtols
proverb *(neu)*. shprich-vatt.
proverbs *(f)*. shprich-vadda.
Psalm of Thanks *(m)*.
  Dank-Psalm.
Psalms of Thanks *(f)*.
  Dank-Psaltah.
puddle *(m)*. poddel.
puddles *(f)*. podla.
puff *v.* poffa.
puffed *v.* gepoft.
puffy - poffich.
pull *v.* zeeya.
pull apart *v.* farobba.
pull off *v.* abzeeya.
pulled *v.* gezohwa.
pulled off *v.* abgezohwa.
pump *(f)*. bumb.
pump *v.* bumba.
pump dry *v.* ausbumba.
pumped *v.* gebumpt.
pumped dry *v.* ausgebumbt.
pumped out *v.* ausgebumbt.
pumps *(f)*. bumba.
punish *v.* shtrohfa.
punished *v.* kshtrohft.
punishment *(m)*. shtrohf.

punishment day *(m)*.
  shtrohf-dawk.
punishment days *(f)*.
  shtrohf-dawwa.
punishments *(f)*. shtrohfa.
puppies *(f)*. pobbis.
puppy *(m)*. pobbi.
pure - rein.
purefied *v*. greinicht.
purification *(f)*. reiniching.
purify *v*. reinicha.
purity *(f)*. reinichkeit.
push *v*. pusha.
push *v*. sheeva.
push off of *v*. absheeva.

pushed *v*. gepusht.
pushed *v*. kshohva.
pushed off *v*. abkshohva.
put - du.
put down *v*. anna-du.
put down - anna-gedu.
put in charge *v*. ivvah-setza.
put in jail *v*. eishtekka.
put off *v*. abdu.
put on *v*. ohdu.
put on *v*. ohgedu.
put on *v*. ohzeeya.
put *v*. gedu *(past)*
put there *v*. anna-du.
put there *v*. anna-gedu.

Q - q

quail *(neu)*. badreesli.
quails *(f)*. badreeslen.
quart *(f)*. goaht.
quarter - faddel.
question *(m)*. frohk.
question closely *v*. ausfrohwa.
questioned closely *v*.
  auskfrohkt.
questions *(f)*. frohwa.

quickly - dabbah.
quickly - kshvind.
quickly - shnell.
quiet - ruich.
quiet - shtill.
quilt *(m)*. gvild.
quilted *v*. gegvild.
quilts *(f)*. gvilds.
quite a few - edlichi.

R - r

rabbit *(m)*. haws.
rabbits *(f)*. hawsa.
racoon *(m)*. koon.
radish *(f)*. reddich.
rafter *(m)*. shpadda.

rag *(m)*. zoddel.
rage *v*. eifahra.
raged *v*. geifaht.
raged *v*. grawst.
ragged - zodlich.

ragged piece of thread *(m).* fransel.
raging - rawsich.
rags *(f).* zodla.
rain *(m).* reyyah / reyya.
rain *v.* reyyahra.
rain gutter on roof *(f).* kandel.
rain out *v.* ausreyyahra.
rainbow *(m).* reyyah-boh.
rained *v.* greyyaht.
rained on - fareyyaht.
rained out *v.* ausgreyyaht.
rainy - reyyahrich.
raised location *(f).* hay
  (always proceeded by "in di")
rake *v.* recha.
raked *v.* grecht.
rambunctious - deich-gedrivva.
ran *v.* kshprunga.
ran off *v.* abkshprunga.
rant or rage *v.* rawsa.
ranted *v.* grawst.
rarin' to go hitzich.
rat *(f).* ratt.
rather leevah.
rats *(f).* radda.
rattle *v.* rabla.
rattle (used by baby) *(neu)* rabli
rattled *v.* grabbelt.
rattles (used by baby) *(f).* rablen
rattly - rablich
rave *v.* rawsa.
raved *v.* grawst.
raw - roh.
reach *v.* langa.
reached *v.* glangt.
read *v.* glaysa.
read *v.* laysa.

read through *v.* deich-glaysa.
read through *v.* deich-laysa.
reader *(m).* laysah.
reap *v.* eahnda.
reaped *v.* geahnd.
rear (farthest to the back)
  hinnahsht
reason *(f).* uahsach.
reasonable - fashtendich.
reasonable - ksheit.
reasonableness *(f).* fashtendlichkeit.
reasons *(f).* uahsacha.
rebuke *v.* abshtrohfa.
rebuked *v.* abkshtrohft.
receiver *(m).* einemmah.
recently - katzlich.
reception *(m).* auf-nawm.
receptions *(f).* auf-nawma.
recipe *(f).* resayt.
recipes *(f).* resayda.
recognize *v.* kenna.
recognized *v.* gekend.
recompense *(m).* lohn.
reconcile *v.* fasayna.
reconciled *v.* fasaynd.
red roht.
red sky in the morning -
  meiya-roht *(lit. - morning-red)*
redbeet *(f).* roht-reeb.
redbeets *(f).* roht-reeva.
region *(neu).* landshaft.
regret *v.* shpeida.
regretted *v.* kshpeit.
rein in *v.* eirayna.
reined in *v.* eigraynd.
reject *v.* zrikk-shtohsa.
rejected *v.* zrikk-kshtohsa.
rejoice *v.* froiya.

rejoiced *v.* kfroit.
relative *(m).* freind.
relatively - fellich.
relatives *(f).* freindshaft.
religion *(m).* glawva.
religious communion meal - *(neu).* nachtmawl.
religious holiday *(neu).* fesht.
religious holiday feast - *(neu).* feiyah-dawk-fesht
religious holidays *(f).* feshta.
religious holidays feasts *(f).* feiyah-dawk-feshta.
religious love feast *(neu).* leebensmawl.
reluctance *v.* gveaht *(past)*
reluctance (to perform a task) *(f).* lasht.
reluctant - unvillich.
remade *v.* ivvah-gmacht.
remain *v.* bleiva.
remained *v.* geblivva.
remake *v.* ivvah-macha.
remember *v.* meinda.
remembered *v.* gmeind.
remembrance *(neu)* ohdenkes
remind *v.* gmohna.
remind *v.* ohgmohna.
reminded *v.* gegmohnd.
reminded *v.* ohgegmohnd.
remove *v.* abnemma.
remove (clothes) *v.* ausnemma.
remove (from the surface) *v.* abmacha.
remove (the entrails, gut) *v.* ausnemma.
remove(with a pointy instrument) *v.* ausshtecha.
removed *v.* abgmacht.

removed *v.* abgnumma.
removed(clothes) *v.* ausgnumma
removed (with a pointy instrument) *v.* auskshtocha.
renewed *v.* nei-gmacht. *(pronounced: neiy-gmacht).*
renounce *v.* absawwa.
renounced *v.* abksawt.
repent *v.* bekeahra.
repentance *(f).* boos.
repented *v.* bekeaht.
repulse *v.* grausa.
repulsed *v.* gegraust.
repulsive - grauslich.
request *v.* bidda.
require *v.* foddahra / fodra.
required *v.* kfoddaht.
resist *v.* shteibahra.
resisted *v.* kshteibaht.
resolve a matter *v.* ausshaffa.
resolved a matter *v.* auskshaft.
respond (very expressively) *v.* fakaekka.
responded (very expressively) *v.* fakaekt.
rest *(f).* roo.
rest *v.* roowa.
rest (completely) *v.* ausroowa.
rested *v.* groot.
rested (completely) *v.* ausgroot.
restful - ruich.
restless - unruich.
restrain *v.* eirayna.
restrained *v.* eigraynd.
resurrection *(f).* uffashtayung.
resurrections *(f).* uffashtayunga.
return (toward a former place or state). zrikk

revelation *(f)*. offenboahring.
revelation *(f)*. veising.
revelations *(f)*. offenboahringa.
revelations *(f)*. veisinga.
revenge taking *(neu)*. auseeves.
revengeful - auseevish.
revolting - grauslich.
rhubarb *(m)*. shtengel.
rich - reich.
riches *(f)*. reichheit.
richly - reichlich.
ridden *v*. gridda.
ride *v*. foahra.
ride *(m)*. reid.
ride *v*. reida.
rider *(m)*. reidah.
riders *(f)*. reidahs.
rides *(f)*. reids.
right (correct) recht
right (direction) rechts
right away - grawt-nau.
right now - grawt-nau.
righteous - gerecht.
righteousness *(f)*.
     gerechtichkeit.
ring in *v*. eiringa.
ringed in *v*. eigringd.
rinse *v*. shvenga.
rinse off *v*. abshvenka.
rinse out *v*. ausshvenka.
rinsed *v*. kshvengd.
rinsed off *v*. abkshvenkt.
rinsed out *v*. auskshvenkt.
ripe - zeidich.
risky - unksheit.
river *(f)*. revvah.
rivers *(f)*. revvahra.
road *(m)*. vayk.
roads *(f)*. vayya.

rob *v*. rawva.
robbed *v*. grawbt.
robber *(m)*. rawvah.
robe *(m)*. mandel.
robes *(f)*. mandela.
robin *(m)*. amshel.
robins *(f)*. amshela.
rock *v*. shokla.
rock badger *(m)*. felsa-badger.
rock badger *(f)*. felsa-badgers.
rock to sleep *v*. beiya.
rock wall *(f)*. flelsa-vand.
rock walls *(neu)*. felsa-vanda.
rocked *v*. kshokkeld.
rocked to sleep *v*. gebeiyt.
rocking chair *(m)*.
     shokkel-shtool.
rocking chairs *(f)*.
     shokkel-shteel.
rocky - shtaynich.
rod *(f)*. root.
rode *v*. gridda.
rode *v*. kfoahra.
rods *(f)*. rooda.
roll *v*. rolla.
roll off *v*. abrolla.
roll out dough (with a rolling
     pin) *v*. ausdrayla.
rolled *v*. grold.
rolled off *v*. abgrold.
rolled out dough (with a
     rolling pin) *v*. ausgedrayld.
roller *(m)*. rollah.
rollers *(f)*. rollahs.
rolling pin *(neu)*. drayl-hols.
rolling pins *(f)*. dray-hels.
roof *(neu)*. dach.
roofs *(f)*. dechah.
room *(f)*. shtubb.

rooms *(f)*. shtubba.
roost *v*. rooshta.
roosted *v*. groosht.
rooster *(m)*. hohna.
root *(f)*. vatzel.
root in *v*. eivatzla.
rooted in *v*. eigvatzeld.
roots *(f)*. vatzla.
rope *(m)*. shtrikk.
ropes *(f)*. shtrikka.
rot *v*. fadauva.
rot *v*. fadeahva.
rot *v*. fafaula.
rotted *v*. fafauld.
rotten - faul.
rough - roff.
round - rund.
row *(f)*. roi.
rub *v*. reiva.
rub off *v*. abreiva.
rub out *v*. ausreiva.
rubbed *v*. grivva.
rubbed off *v*. abgrivva.
rubbed out *v*. ausgrivva.
rubber - robbah.
rubbish *(neu)*. kfrays.
rudder *(neu)*. shtiah-boaht
     (lit. - steering board).
rudders *(f)*. shtiah-beaht
     (lit.- steering boards).
ruin *(neu)*. fadeahbnis.
ruins *(f)*. fadeahbisa.
ruler (king) *(m)*. roolah.
ruler (tape measure) *(m)*. roolah.
rulers (kings) *(f)*. roolahs.

rulers (tape measures) *(f)*.
     roolahs.
ruling authority *(f)*.
     evvahsht-hand.
rumble (stomach) *v*. bollahra.
rumbled (stomach) *v*. gebollaht.
rummage through *v*.
     deich-veela.
rummaged through *v*.
     deich-gveeld.
rumor *(neu)*. kshvetz.
rumors *(f)*. kshvetzah.
run *v*. shpringa.
run down *v*. nunnah-grand.
run down *v*. nunnah-ranna.
run off *v*. abshpringa.
run off (liquid) *v*. abgloffa.
run off (liquid) *v*. ablawfa.
rushing sound *v*. rausha.
rust *v*. faroshta.
rust *(m)*. rosht.
rust off *v*. abroshta.
rust out *v*. ausroshta.
rusted *v*. farosht.
rusted off *v*. abgrosht.
rusted out *v*. ausgrosht.
rusty roshtich.
rye *(f)*. rokka.

S - s

sack *(m)*. sakk.
sack cloths *(f)*. sakkdichah.
sackcloth *(neu)*. sakkduch.
sacks *(f)*. sekk.
sacrifice *(neu)*. opfah.
sacrifice *v*. opfahra.
sacrifice of praise *(neu)*.
   lohb-opfah.
sacrificed *v*. gopfaht.
sacrifices *(f)*. opfahra.
sacrifices of praise *(f)*.
   lohb-opfahra.
sacrificial fire *(neu)*.
   feiyah-opfah.
sacrificial fires *(f)*.
   feiyah-opfahra.
sacrificial lamb *(neu)*.
   opfah-lamm.
sacrificial lambs *(f)*.
   opfah-lemmah.
sad - bedrohwa.
saddle *(m)*. saddel.
saddle *v*. sadla.
saddled *v*. ksaddeld.
saddles *(f)*. sadla.
safe *(f)*. sayf.
safe - sayf.
safes *(f)*. sayfa.
safty pin *(f)*. vindel-shpell.
said *v*. ksawt.
sailor *(m)*. shiff-gnecht.
sailors *(f)*. shiff-gnechta.
sake *(f)*. sayk.
sakes *(f)*. sayks.
salt *(m)*. sals.

salted (too much) fasalsa.
salty - salsich.
salvation *(f)*. saylichkeit.
salve *(f)*. shmiah.
salves *(f)*. shmiahra.
same - gleicha.
same - saym.
sanctified - heilich.
sanctified *v*. keilicht.
sanctify *v*. heilicha.
sand *(m)*. sand.
sands *(f)*. sanda.
sandy - sandich.
sang lead *v*. foahksunga.
sap *(f)*. saft.
sat *v*. kokt.
sat down *v*. anna-kokt.
Satan *(m)*. Satan.
satiated - satt.
Saturday *(m)*. Samshdawk.
saucer *(neu)*. bletli.
saucers *(f)*. bletlen.
sausage *(f)*. vasht.
saved - saylich.
Savior *(m)*. Heiland.
saw *v*. ksenna.
saw *(f)*. sayk.
saw *v*. sayya.
saw off *v*. absayya.
sawed off *v*. abksaykt.
sawn *v*. ksaykt.
saws *(f)*. sayya.
say *v*. sawwa.
scab *(neu)*. grind.
scald *v*. breeya.

scalded *v*. gebreed.
scale (used to weigh). *(f)*. vohk
scale a fish *v*. shawva.
scaled a fish *v*. kshawbt.
scales (used to weigh) *(f)*. vohwa
scare *v*. fashrekka.
scared *v*. fashrokka.
scarf *(neu)*. kobb-duch
    (lit. - head cloth).
scarves *(f)*. kobb-dichah
    (lit. - head cloth).
scary - kshpukkich.
scary - shreklich.
scatter *v*. fadreiva.
scatter *v*. fashtroiya.
scatter *v*. shkaedra.
scatter *v*. shtroiya.
scatter abroad *v*. ausshtroiya.
scattered *v*. fadrivva.
scattered *v*. fashtroit.
scattered *v*. kshkaeddaht.
scattered *v*. kshtroit.
scattered about *v*. auskshtroit.
scent *(m)*. kshmakk.
scents *(f)*. kshmakka.
schatched up *v*. fagratzt.
schism *(f)*. shpaldinga.
schism *(f)*. shpalding.
school *(f)*. shool.
school teacher *(m)*.
    shool-teetshah.
schoolmaster *(m)*.
    shool-meishtah.
schools *(f)*. shoola.
scissors *(f)*. sheah.
scold *v*. absawwa.
scold *v*. faglawwa.
scold *v*. fashelda.
scold *v*. fashimfa.

scold *v*. zanka.
scolded *v*. abksawt.
scolded *v*. faglawkt.
scolded *v*. fashimft.
scolded *v*. fasholda.
scolded *v*. gezankt.
scoop *v*. shebba.
scoop *(m)*. shebbah.
scooped *v*. kshebt.
scorn *v*. fa'achta.
scorned *v*. fa'acht.
scourge *(f)*. gayshel.
scourge *v*. gayshla.
scourged *v*. gegaysheld.
scourges *(f)*. gayshla.
scourging *(f)*. gayshtling.
scourgings *(f)*. gayshtlinga.
scrap *(neu)*. shkraebb.
scrape *v*. fashunna.
scrape off *v*. abgratza.
scrape off (with a scraper)
    v. shawva.
scraped *v*. kshatt.
scraped off *v*. abgegratzt.
scraped with a scraper *v*.
    kshawbt.
scratch *v*. gratza.
scratch *(m)*. gratzah.
scratch off *v*. abgratza.
scratch over the surface
(scrape or rake dirt on the ground).
    v. shadda
scratch up *v*. fagratza.
scratched *v*. gegratzt.
scratched off *v*. abgegratzt.
scratched over the surface
    v. kshatt.
scratches *(f)*. gratzahs.
scrawny *v*. fabutzt.

scream _v._ greisha.
scream at _v._ fagreisha.
screamed _v._ gegrisha.
screamed at _v._ fagrisha.
screw _(f)._ shraub.
screw _v._ shrauva.
screwed _v._ kshraubt.
screws _(f)._ shrauva.
scribble _v._ shkribla.
scribbled _v._ kshkribbeld.
scribe _(m)._ shrift-geleahrah.
Scripture _(f)._ Shrift.
Scriptures _(f)._ Shrifta.
scrub _v._ shkrobba.
scrubbed _v._ kshkrobt.
sea _(m)._ say.
seal _(m)._ seel.
seals _(f)._ seels.
search out _v._ aussucha.
search out _v._ unnah-sucha.
searched out _v._ ausksucht.
searched out _v._ unnah-ksucht.
seas _(f)._ sayya.
seat _(m)._ sitz.
seat _v._ sitza.
seated _v._ ksitzt.
seats _(f)._ sitza.
second - zvett.
secretly - shlichtich.
see _v._ sayna.
seed _(m)._ sohma.
seek _v._ sucha.
seek favor _v._ shmaychla.
seem _v._ dinka.
seem _v._ gmohna.
seemed _v._ gedinkt.
seemed _v._ gegmohnd.
seemed _v._ ksheind.
seen _v._ ksenna.

seizures _(f)._ gichtahra.
self - selvaht.
self - sich _(reflexive)._
selfish - batzich.
selfish desire (for honor) _(m)._ eahgeitz.
sell _v._ fakawfa.
sell out _v._ ausfakawfa.
seller _(m)._ fakawfah.
send _v._ shikka.
send there _v._ anna-shikka.
sensation _(neu)._ kfeel.
sensations _(f)._ kfeelah.
sent _v._ kshikt.
sent there _v._ anna-kshikt.
separate _v._ deich-macha.
separate _v._ fadayla.
separate (by passing through a sieve) _v._ seena.
separate (from each other) funn-nannah.
separated _v._ fadayld.
separated (by passing through a sieve) _v._ kseend.
seperated _v._ deich-gmacht.
sermon _(f)._ breddich.
sermons _(f)._ breddicha.
servant _(m)._ deenah.
servant _(m)._ gnecht.
servant hood _(f)._ gnechtshaft.
servant maid _(f)._ deensht-mawt.
servant maid _(f)._ mawt.
servant maids _(f)._ deensht-mawda.
servant maids _(f)._ mawda.
servant of God _(m)._ deensht-gnecht.
servants _(f)._ deensht-leit.

servants *(f)*. gnechta.
serve *v*. deena.
serve (as in a store or restaurant)
     v. abvoahra.
served *v*. gedeend.
served (as in a store or restaurant)
     v. abgvoaht.
set *v*. ksetzt.
set *v*. setza.
set an example (or pattern)
     v. foahbilda.
set (an object) *v*. shtella.
set down *v*. anna-kshteld.
set down *v*. anna-shtella.
set forth *v*. foahkshteld.
set forth *v*. foahshtella.
set free *v*. frei-lossa.
     (present, future)
set free *v*. frei-shtella.
     (present, future)
set free *v*. frei-glost. *(past)*
set free *v*. frei-kshteld. *(past)*
set in a position of eminence
     v. foahksetzt.
set in a position of eminence
     v. foahsetza.
set one's confidence upon
     v. setza.
set one's mind upon *v*. setza.
set or placed (an object)
     v. kshteld.
setting hen *(f)*. glukk.
setting hens *(f)*. glukka.
settle *v*. sedla.
settled *v*. kseddeld.
seven - sivva.
seventeen - sivvetzay.
seventh - sivvet.
seventy - sivvetzich.

sew *v*. nayya.
sew on a binding *v*. eibendla.
sewn *v*. gnayt.
shade *(m)*. shadda.
shadow *(m)*. shadda.
shake *v*. shidla.
shake off *v*. abshidla.
shake off *v*. abshlenkahra.
shake out *v*. ausshidla.
shake up *v*. fashidla.
shaken *v*. kshiddeld.
shaken off *v*. abkshiddeld.
shaken off *v*. abkshlenkaht.
shaken out *v*. auskshiddeld.
shaken up *v*. fashiddeld.
shaky - shidlich.
shall *v*. soll.
shall *v*. zayl.
shame *v*. fashohma.
shame *(f)*. shand.
shame (to feel shame) *v*. shemma
shame *(m)*. shohm
     (used in the Bible).
shamed *v*. fashohmd.
shamed *v*. kshemd.
shameful - greilich.
shames *(f)*. shanda.
share *v*. mitt-dayla.
share (willingly) mitt-daylich.
shared *v*. mitt-gedayld.
sharer *(m)*. mitt-daylah.
sharp - shauf.
sharpen *v*. shaufa.
sharpened *v*. kshauft.
shatter *v*. fabrecha.
shattered *v*. fabrocha.
shave *v*. shayfa.
shave off *v*. abshayfa.
shaved *v*. kshayft.

shaved off *v.* abkshayft.
she - see / es / 's.
shed hair *v.* abheahra.
sheep *(m).* shohf.
sheepfold *(m).* shohf-shtall.
sheepfolds *(f).* shohf-shtell.
sheepskin *(f).* shohf-haut.
sheepskins *(f).* shohf-heidah.
shelf *(m).* lawda.
shell *(f).* shawl.
shell (peas) *v.* blikka.
shelled (peas) *v.* geblikt.
shells *(f).* shawla.
shepherd *(m).* shohf-heedah.
shine *v.* sheina.
shined *v.* ksheind.
shiny - sheinich.
ship *(neu).* shiff.
ship crew *(f).* shiff-leit.
ships *(f).* shiffah.
shirk duty *v.* abshpeela.
shirt *(neu).* hemm.
shirts *(f).* hemmah.
shiver *v.* ziddahra.
shivered *v.* geziddaht.
shock *v.* fagelshtahra.
shocked *v.* fagelshtaht.
shoe *(m).* shoo.
shoe lace *(m).* bendel.
shoe laces *(f).* bendla.
shoestring *(m).* shoo-bendel.
shoestrings *(f).* shoo-bendela.
shoot *v.* sheesa.
shorn *v.* kshoahra.
short - katz.
short time ago - katzlich.
shorten *v.* fakatza.
shortened *v.* fakatzt.
shot *v.* kshossa.

should - sedda.
should *v.* soll.
should be - sella.
shoulder *(m).* shuldah.
shoulders *(f).* shuldra.
shout *(m).* grish.
shouted *v.* gegrisha.
shouted *v.* greisha.
shouts *(f).* grisha.
shove *v.* sheeva.
shove or poke *v.* renna.
shoved *v.* grend.
shoved *v.* kshohva.
shovel *(f).* shaufel.
shovel *v.* shaufla.
shovel off *v.* abshebba.
shoveled *v.* kshaufeld.
shoveled *v.* kshebt.
shoveled off *v.* abkshebt.
shovels *(f).* shaufla.
show *v.* veisa.
show mercy *v.* aboahma.
show off *v.* absheesa.
show reluctance *v.* veaht.
showbread *(neu)*
　　　Himmels-broht.
showing *(f).* veising.
showings *(f).* veisinga.
shown *v.* gvissa.
shriked duty (played hooky)
　　　v. abkshpeeld.
shrink *v.* eigay.
shrunk *v.* eiganga.
shun *(m).* bawn.
shut off *v.* abdrayya.
shut off (alarm, radio, etc)
　　　v. abdu.
shut off *v.* abgedrayt.
shut off *v.* abgedu.

shy *v.* kshemd. *(past)*
shy (to feel). *v.* shemma
shy - shemmich.
sick - grank.
sick to stomach *v.* grausa.
sickle *(f).* sens.
sickle *(f).* sichel.
sickles *(f).* sichla.
sickly - eahmlich.
sickness(f) granket *(common use)*
sickness *(f).* grankheit
  (used in the Bible).
sicknesses *(f).* grankada
  (common use).
sicknesses *(f).* grankheida
  (used in the Bible).
side *(f).* seit.
side up with *v.* eiseida.
sided with *v.* eikseit.
sieve *(m).* draynah.
sift *v.* sifta.
sifted *v.* ksift.
signified *v.* bedeit.
signify *v.* bedeida.
silk (made of). seida
silly - kindish.
silver - silvah.
silversmith *(m).* silvah-smitt.
silvery - silvahrich.
similar fate *(neu).* mitt-dayl.
sin *v.* fasindicha.
sin *(f).* sind.
sin *v.* sindicha.
sin offering *(neu).* sind-opfah.
sin offerings *(f).* sind-opfahra.
since - siddah.
sinews *(f).* flexa.
sinful - sindfol.
sinful - sindlich.

sing *v.* singa.
sing lead *v.* foahsinga.
singe *v.* fasenka.
singed *v.* fasenkt.
singer *(m).* singah.
singleness of heart -
  (f). ayfeldichkeit.
sinned *v.* fasindicht.
sinned *v.* ksindicht.
sinner *(m).* sindah.
sins *(f).* sinda.
sister *(f).* shveshtah.
sisters *(f).* shveshtra.
sit *v.* hokka.
sit down *v.* anna-hokka.
six - sex.
sixteen - sechtzay.
sixth - sext.
sixty - sechtzich.
skate *v.* shkayda.
skated *v.* kshkayt.
skedaddle *v.* fabutza.
skillet *(f).* pann.
skillets *(f).* panna.
skim off *v.* abshebba.
skimmed off *v.* abkshebt.
skin *v.* abzeeya.
skin *(neu).* haut.
skinned *v.* abgezohwa.
skins *(f).* heidah.
skip *v.* shkibba.
skipped *v.* kshkibt.
skittish tshumbich.
skull *(m).* shkoll.
skull place *(m).* shkoll-blatz.
skulls *(f).* shkols.
skunk *(f).* biskatz.
skunks *(f).* biskatza.
slander *v.* faleimda.

slander *v.* nunnah-ranna.
slandered *v.* nunnah-grand.
slant - shrayks.
slap *v.* shlaebba.
slap (on the behind) *(m).* flaetsh
slapped *v.* kshlaebt.
slaps (on the behind) *(f).* flaetshah.
slaughter *(f).* shlacht.
slaughter (butcher an animal) *v.* shlachta
slaughter day *(m)* shlacht-dawk
slaughter days *(f).* shlacht-dawwa.
slaughtered (butcher an animal) *v.* kshlacht.
slaughters *(f).* shlachta.
slaugther *v.* shlawdra.
slaugthered *v.* kshlawdaht.
slave *(m).* gnecht.
slave of God *(m.)* deensht-gnecht.
slaves *(f).* gnechta.
sled *(m).* shlidda.
sleep *v.* shlohfa.
sleep *(m).* shlohf.
sleep off *v.* absholhfa.
sleeper *(m).* shlayfah.
sleepy - shlayfahrich.
sleeve *(m).* eahmel.
sleigh *(f).* shlay.
slept *v.* kshlohfa.
slept off *v.* abkshlohfa.
slid off *v.* abgrutsht.
slide off *v.* abrutsha.
slightly more than - fellich.
slimy - shleimich.
slip *v.* shlibba.
slip away *v.* abvitsha.

slip through *v.* deich-vitsha.
slipped *v.* kshlibt.
slipped away *v.* abgvitsht.
slipped through *v.* deich-gvitsht.
slipper *(m).* shlibbah.
slippery - shlibbich.
slit *(m).* shlitz.
slobber *v.* fashlavvahra.
slobbered *v.* fashlavvaht.
slop *(neu).* shlabb.
sloppy - shlabbich.
sloppy person *(f).* shlabb.
slow - shloh.
small - glay.
small amount - bissel.
small bench *(neu).* benkli.
small benches *(f).* benklen.
small bird *(neu).* birdi.
small birds *(f).* birdis.
small book *(neu).* bichli.
small books *(f).* bichlen.
small chicken coop *(neu).* beebli-heisli.
small chicken coops *(f).* beebli-heislen.
small fire *(neu).* feiyahli.
small fires *(f).* feiyahlen.
small oil can *(neu).* ayl-kenli.
small oil cans *(f).* ayl-kenlen.
small towel *(m).* hand-lumba.
smaller - glennah.
smallest - glensht.
smart - shmeaht.
smash *v.* fashmaesha.
smashed *v.* fashmaesht.
smear *v.* fashmiahra.
smeared *v.* fashmiaht.
smell *(m).* kshmakk.

smell *v.* shmakka.
smelled *v.* kshmakt.
smells *(f).* kshmakka.
smelly - shmakkich.
smile *(m).* shmeil.
smile *v.* shmeila.
smiled *v.* kshmeild.
smiley - shmeilich.
smith *(m).* shmitt.
smiths *(f).* shmidda.
smoke *(m).* shmohk.
smoke *v.* shmohka.
smoke stack *(m).*
          shmohk-shtaekk.
smoked *v.* kshmohkt.
smoky - shmohkich.
smooth - glatt.
smother *v.* fashtikka.
smothered *v.* fashtikt.
snake *(f).* shlang.
snakes *(f).* shlanga.
snap *v.* shnaebba.
snap off *v.* abshnaebba.
snapped *v.* kshnaebt.
snapped off *v.* abkshnaebt.
snare *(m).* fang-shtrikk.
snares *(f).* fang-shtrikka.
sneak *v.* shneeka.
sneak away *v.* abshtayla.
sneaked *v.* kshneekt.
snore *v.* shneiksa.
snored *v.* kshneikst.
snout *(f).* shnoot.
snow *(m).* shnay.
snow *v.* shnayya.
snowed *v.* kshnayt.
snowy - shnayyich.
snuck away *v.* abkshtohla.
so - so.

soak (or bathed an injured body
       part)
       v. bawda.
soak in (as paint into wood)
       v. fashlubba.
soaked in (as in paint into wood)
       v. fashlubt.
soaked (or bathed an injured
       body part) *v.* gebawda.
soaking wet - blaetsh-nass.
soap *(f).* sayf.
soaps *(f).* sayfa.
sober - sohbah.
sock *(m).* shtrumb.
socks *(f).* shtrimb.
soft - vayyich.
softer - vayyichah.
softhearted - vayyich-hatzich.
soiled *v.* fadrekt.
soiled *v.* fasuddeld.
sold *v.* fakawft.
sold out *v.* ausfakawft.
soldier *(m).* greeks-gnecht.
soldier *(m).* greeks-mann.
soldiers *(f).* greeks-gnechta.
soldiers *(f).* greeks-mennah.
sole of the foot *(m).* foos-sohl.
soles of the feet *(f).* fees-sohla.
solidly grounded *(m).*
          feshtah-blatz
          (lit.- fastened in place).
some - dayl.
some - samm.
somehow - samm-vayk.
someone - ebbah.
something - ebbes.
sometime - samm-zeit.
sometimes - alsamohl.
sometimes - dayl-zeit.

sometimes - etmohls.
someway - samm-vayk.
somewhere - eiyetzvo.
somewhere - eiyetz.
          (shortened form)
son of the king (prince) *(m)*.
          kaynichs-sohn.
song *(neu)*. leet.
song of praise *(neu)*. lohb-leet.
songs *(f)*. leedah.
songs of praise *(f)*. lohb-leedah.
son-in-law *(m)*. dochtah-mann.
sons of the king *(f)*.
          kaynichs-sayna.
sons-in-law *(f)*.
          dochtah-mennah.
soon - ball.
soon - glei.
soothsayer *(m)*. foahsawwah.
sorcerer *(m)*. hexah.
sorcerer *(m)*. zabbahrah.
sorcery *(neu)*. hexahrei.
sorcery *v.* fahexa.
          (present, future)
sorcery *v.* fahext. *(past)*
sore *(f)*. kshveah.
sore - soah.
sore - vay.
sores *(f)*. kshveahra.
sorrow *(neu)*. bedreebnis.
sorrow *(f)*. dreebsawl.
sorrows *(f)*. bedreebnisa.
sort *v.* falaysa.
sort of - sadda.
sort through *v.* deich-laysa.
sorted through *v.* deich-glaysa.
sortest - vayyichsht.
sought *v.* ksucht.
soul *(f)*. sayl.

souls *(f)*. sayla.
sound *(m)*. saund.
sound *v.* lauda.
sounded *v.* glaut.
sounded *v.* gmacht.
sounds - laut.
sounds *(f)*. saunds.
soup *(f)*. subb.
soups *(f)*. subba.
sour *v.* fasavvahra.
sour - savvah.
sourdough *(m)*. savvah-dayk.
sourdoughs *(f)*. savvah-dayka.
soured *v.* fasavvaht.
south - sauda.
south *(f)*. saut.
southeast - saut-eest.
southwest - saut-vest.
souvenir *(neu)*. ohdenkes.
sow *(f)*. lohs.
sow seed *v.* sayya.
sow seeds *v.* eisayya.
sowed seeds *v.* eiksayt.
sower *(m)*. sayyah.
sown seeds *v.* ksayt.
sows *(f)*. lohsa.
spank *v.* bletsha.
spanked *v.* gebletsht.
spare (from death, pain, distress,
          expense, etc.) *v.* shpeahra
spare (to have excess)
          v. shpeahra
spared *v.* kshpeaht.
sparingly *v.* shpoahra.
sparingly used *v.* kshpoaht.
spark *(f)*. feiyah-funk.
spark *(m)*. funka.
sparks *(f)*. feiyah-funka.
sparrow *(f)*. shpatz.

sparrows *(f)*. shpatza.
speak argumentatively *v.*
   eiyahra.
speak evil of *v.* fashimfa.
speak offensively *v.* eiyahra.
speaker of the language Pennsylvania-German "Deitsh") *(m)*. deitshah.
spear *v.* shpeesa.
spear *(m)*. shpees.
spear *(m)*. shpiah.
speared *v.* kshpeest.
spears *(f)*. shpeesa.
spears *(f)*. shpiahs.
spell *v.* shpella.
spelled *v.* kshpeld.
spend *v.* shpenda.
spent *v.* kshpend.
spicy - shpeisich.
spicy (hot) brennich.
spider *(m)*. shpinn.
spiders *(f)*. shpinna.
spigot *(m)*. grohna.
spill *v.* faleahra.
spill (something on oneself) *v.* fakafla.
spill *v.* fazodla.
*(only used with solids, **not** liquids)*
spill *v.* fashlabba.
   (only used with liquids)
spilled *v.* faleaht.
spilled (something on oneself) *v.* fakaffeld.
spilled *v.* fazoddeld.
*(only used with solids, **not** liquids)*
spilled *v.* fashlabt.
   (only used with liquids)
spin *v.* shpinna.
spirit *(m)*. geisht.

spirit of servant hood *(m)*.
   gnechta-geisht.
spirits *(f)*. geishtah.
spirituality *(f)*. geishtlichkeit.
spit *v.* kshpautzt.
spit *(m)*. shpautz.
spit *v.* shpautza.
spit on *v.* fashpautza.
   (present, future)
spit on *v.* fashpautzt. *(past)*
splinter *(m)*. shliffah.
splinters *(f)*. shliffahra.
split *v.* kshpalda.
split *v.* shpalda.
split apart *v.* fashpalda.
spoil *v.* fadotza.
spoil *v.* fafaula.
spoiled *v.* fadotzt.
spoiled *v.* fafauld.
spoken evil of *v.* fashimft.
spook *v.* fashpukka.
spook *(m)*. kshpukk.
spooked *v.* fashpukt.
spooks *(f)*. kshpukka.
spooky - kshpukkich.
spool *(m)*. shpoola.
spoon *(m)*. leffel.
spoons *(f)*. lefla.
spot *(m)*. blakka.
spot *(m)*. flekka.
spots *(f)*. blekka.
spotted blakkich.
sprained *v.* farenkt.
spray *v.* shpritza.
spray (or splash with liquid) *v.* fashpritza.
sprayed (with liquid) *v.* fashpritzt.
spread apart *(adj.)* ausnannah.

spread out *v.* auskshtroit.
spread out *v.* ausshtroiya.
spring (season) *(neu).* free-yoah
spring like - free-yoahrich.
sprinkle *v.* shpritza.
sprinkle(or spray an object with liquid) *v.* ohshpritza.
sprinkled (or sprayed an object with liquid) *v.* ohkshpritzt.
sprung (door, window) *v.* fashprunga.
spun *v.* kshpunna.
squabbling *v.* fafochta.
squander *v.* deich-blohsa.
squander *v.* fablohsa.
squandered *v.* deich-geblohsa.
square - ekkich.
squeeze *v.* drikka.
squeeze *v.* fadrikka.
squeeze out *v.* ausdrikka.
squeezed *v.* fadrikt.
squeezed *v.* gedrikt.
squeezed out *v.* ausgedrikt.
squirm *v.* gveahva.
squirmed *v.* gegveahvt.
squirrel *(m).* shkvall.
staff *(f).* root.
staffs *(f).* rooda.
stain *(m).* flekka.
stair tread *(f).* drebb.
stair treads *(f).* drebba.
stairway *(f).* shtayk.
stairways *(f).* shtayya.
stall *(m).* shtall.
stalls *(f).* shtell.
stamp *v.* shtamba.
stamp out (fire, etc.) *v.* ausshtamba.
stamped *v.* kshtambt.

stamped out (fire, etc.) *v.* auskshtambt.
stand *v.* shtaya.
stand there *v.* anna-shtay.
stand up *v.* uf-shtay.
star *(f).* shtann.
stars *(f).* shtanna.
start *v.* shteahra.
start off *v.* abshteahra.
start out *v.* ausshteahra.
started *v.* kshteaht.
started off *v.* abkshteaht.
started out *v.* auskshteaht.
startle *v.* fashpukka.
startle *v.* fashrekka.
startled *v.* fashpukt.
startled *v.* fashrokka.
startling fagelshtahlich.
starve *v.* fahungahra.
starved *v.* fahungaht.
stay *v.* bleiva.
stayed *v.* geblivva.
steadfast - shtandhaftich.
steadfastness *(f).* shtandhaftichkeit.
steal *v.* shtayla.
stealing (habitual) *(neu).* geshtayl.
stealthily *v.* shleicha.
steam *(m).* damf.
steam *(m).* shteem.
steamed dumpling *(m).* damf-gnobb.
steamed dumplings *(f).* damf-gnebb.
steamer *(m).* shteemah.
steel *(neu).* shtawl.
steel (made of) shtawlich
steep - shteeb.

steer *v.* geida.
steered *v.* gegiet.
stems *(f).* shtemm.
step *(m).* shtebb.
step *v.* shtebba.
step aside *v.* ausdredda.
stepmother *(f).* shteef-maemm.
stepmothers *(f)* shteef-maemma
stepped *v.* kshtebt.
stepped aside *v.* ausgedrodda.
stepped(into or onto accidentally)
        v. gedabt.
steps *(f).* shtebs.
stick *v.* babba.
stick *v.* shtekka.
stick *(m).* shtekka.
stick *v.* shtikka.
stick (little) *(neu).* shtekli.
stick to it *v.* ausshtikka.
sticks (little) *(f).* shteklen.
sticky - babbich.
stiff - shteif.
still - alsnoch.
still - doch.
still - shtill.
stillborn - doht-geboahra.
sting *v.* shtecha.
sting *(m).* shteech
      (example: a bee sting).
stinger *(m).* shtechah.
stinging - brennich.
stinging nettle *(m).* brenn-aysel.
stinging nettles *(f).* brenn-aysla.
stink *v.* shtinka.
stir *v.* riahra.
stir *v.* shtarra / shtadda.
stir up *v.* ufriahra.
stirred *v.* griaht.
stirred *v.* kshtatt.

stirred up *v.* ufgriaht.
stolen *v.* kshtohla.
stomach *(f).* mawwa.
stomach ache *(neu)* bauchvay.
stomp on *v.* fashtamba.
stomped on *v.* fashtambt.
stone *(m).* shtay.
stone (made of) shtaynich
stone *v.* shtaynicha.
stone (little) *(neu).* shtaynli.
stone tablet *(neu).* shtay-tablet.
stone tablets *(f).* shtay-tablets.
stoned *v.* kshtaynicht.
stones (little) *(f).* shtaynlen.
stood *v.* kshtanna.
stood there *v.* anna-kshtanna.
stood up *v.* uf-kshtanna.
stool *(neu).* shteeli.
stools *(f).* shteelen.
stoop *v.* bikka.
stooped *v.* gebikt.
stop *v.* shtobba.
stopped *v.* kshtobt.
store *(m).* shtoah.
storehouse *(neu).* shtoah-haus.
storehouses *(f).* shtoah-heisah.
stores *(f).* shtoahra.
stories *(f).* shtoahris.
storm *(m).* shtoahm.
storms *(f).* shteahm.
stormy shteahmich.
story *(f).* shtoahri.
stove *(m).* offa.
stovepipe *(neu)* offa-rau.
stoves *(f).* effa.
straight - grawt.
straight away - grawt-nau.
straighten out *v.* ausrohma.
straightened out *v.* ausgrohmd

strainer *(m)*. draynah.
strange - fremd.
strange - kshpassich.
strap *(m)*. shtraebb.
straps *(f)*. shtraebs.
straw *(neu)*. shtroh.
strawberries *(f)*. aebbeahra.
strawberry *(f)*. aebbeah.
stray piece (of thread or fabric) *(m)*. fransel.
streak *(m)*. shtraych.
street *(f)*. shtrohs.
street corner *(neu)* shtrohsa-ekk.
street corners *(f)*. shtrohsa-ekkah.
streets *(f)*. shtrohsa.
strength *(f)*. graft.
strength - grefta.
strength *(f)*. gvald.
strengthen *v*. fagrefticha.
strengthen *v*. fashteika.
strengthened *v*. fagrefticht.
strengthened *v*. fashteikt.
strengths *(f)*. grefta.
stretch *v*. shtrekka.
stretch out *v*. ausshtrekka.
stretch out of shape *v*. fashtrekka.
stretch (over a frame) *v*. ohzeeya.
stretched *v*. kshtrekt.
stretched out *v*. ausshtrekt.
stretched out of shape *v*. fashtrekt.
stretched (over a frame) *v*. ohgezowwa.
strict - shtreng.
stride *(m)*. shritt.

strife *(m)*. zank.
strike *(m)*. shtraych.
striking blow *(f)*. hakk.
striking blows *(f)*. hakka.
string *(m)*. bendel.
string *(m)*. shnuah.
strings *(f)*. bendla.
strip *v*. shtribba.
strip *(m)*. shtribb.
stripe *(m)*. shtrayma.
strips *(f)*. shtribs.
stripped *v*. kshtribt.
stroke *(m)*. shtraych.
stroke *v*. shtreicha.
stroke (small) *(neu)*. shtrichli.
stroked *v*. kshtreecha.
strokes (small) *(f)*. shtrichlen.
strong - greftich.
strong - mechtich.
strong - shtaut.
strong - shteik.
strongly - greftichlich.
stubble *(m)*. shtubbel.
stubbles *(f)*. shtubla.
stubborn - dikk-kebbich.
stubborn *v*. fashtokka.
stubborn - shteibahrich.
stubborn streak - aysel-shtraych.
stuck *v*. kshtikt.
stuck *v*. kshtokka.
stuck it out *v*. auskshtokka.
stuck on *v*. gebabt.
structured (delicately) fei-shtenglich.
stud (horse) *(m)*. hengsht.
student in school *(m)*. shoolah.
studied *v*. kshtoddit.

study *v.* shtodya.
stuff *v.* shtoffa.
stuffed *v.* kshtoft.
stuffy - shtoffich.
stumble *v.* shtatza.
stumble *v.* shtolbahra.
stumbled *v.* kshtatzt.
stumbled *v.* kshtolbaht.
stumbling block *(m).*
      shtolbah-blakk.
stumbling blocks *(f).*
      shtolbah-blaks.
stumbling stone *(m).*
      shtolbah-shtay.
stump *(m).* shtumba.
stung *v.* kshtocha.
stunk *v.* kshtunka.
sturdy - shtaut.
style *(m).* shteil.
suchlike - sohwich.
suck *v.* sukla.
sucked *v.* ksukkeld.
suffer *v.* deich-macha.
suffer *v.* leida.
suffer (or bear) *v.* shtenda.
suffer *v.* soffahra.
suffer (patiently) *v.* ausleida.
suffered *v.* deich-gmacht.
suffered *v.* glidda.
suffered *v.* ksoffaht.
suffered (patiently) *v.* ausglidda.
suffocate *v.* fashmoddahra.
suffocate *v.* fashtikka.
suffocated *v.* fashmoddaht.
suffocated *v.* fashtikt.
sugar *(m).* zukkah.
suit *v.* sooda.
suitable - shiklich.
suited *v.* ksoot.

sulphur *(neu).* shvevvel.
summer *(m).* summah.
summers *(f).* summahra.
sun *(f).* sunn.
Sunday *(m).* Sundawk.
Sundays *(f.)* Sundawks /
      Sundawwa.
sundown - sunn-unnah.
sung *v.* ksunga.
sunny - sinnich.
suns *(f).* sunna.
sunshine - sunn-shein.
sunshiny - sunn-sheinich.
sun-up - sunn-uf.
supper *(neu).* sobbah.
suppers *(f).* sobbahs.
supporter - bei-shtendah.
supposed to - sella.
supreme power *(f).*
      ivvah-macht.
supreme powers *(f).*
      ivvah-machta.
supremely powerful *v.*
      ivvah-mechtich.
suprisingly - fashtaundlich.
surcingle *(m).* bauch-gatt.
surcingles *(f).* bauch-gadda.
sure - shuah.
surely - gevislich.
surprise *v.* fagelshtahra.
surprise *v.* floahra.
surprised *v.* fagelshtaht.
surrender *v.* eigevva.
swallow *v.* shlukka.
swallow(kind of bird)*(f).* shvalma
swallow in *v.* eishlukka.
swallowed *v.* kshlukt.
swallowed in *v.* eikshlukt.
swam *v.* kshvumma.

swarm *(m)*. shwoahm.
swarm *v*. shwoahma.
swarmed *v*. kshwoahmd.
swear *v*. flucha.
swear *v*. shveahra.
swear at *v*. faflucha.
swear off *v*. abshveahra.
swear words *(f)*. fluch-vadda.
swearword *(neu)*. fluch-vatt.
sweat *(m)*. shvitz.
sweat *v*. shvitza.
sweaty - shvitzich.
sweep *v*. keahra.
sweep off *v*. abkeahra.
sweep out *v*. auskeahra.
sweet - sees.
swell *v*. kshvilla.
swept *v*. abgekeaht.
swept *v*. gekeaht.
swept out *v*. ausgekeaht.
swim *v*. shvimma.
swine *(f)*. sau.
swine *(f)*. sei.

swineherder *(m)*. sei-heedah.
swing *(f)*. gaunsh.
swing *v*. gaunsha.
swings *(f)*. gaunsha.
switch on a light *v*. ohmacha.
switched on a light *v*. ohgmacht.
swollen *v*. kshvulla.
sword *(neu)*. shvatt.
sword cut *(m)*. shvadda-shnitt.
swords *(f)*. shvadda.
swore *v*. kflucht.
swore *v*. kshvoahra.
sworn at *v*. faflucht.
sworn off *v*. abkshvoahra.
swum *v*. kshvumma.
swung (on a swing) *v*. gegaunsht.
sympathize *v*. mitt-leida.
sympathized *v*. mitt-glidda.
sythe *(f)*. sens.

T - t

tabernacle *(m)*. tent-tempel
    (lit. - tent temple).
tabernacles *(f)*. tent-tempels.
table *(m)*. dish.
tables *(f)*. disha.
tail *(m)*. shvans.
tails *(f)*. shvens.
take *v*. nemma.
take care of *v*. acht-gevva.
take care of *v*. faseiya.
take care of *v*. heeda.

take care of *v*. seiya.
take in *v*. einemma.
take off (clothing) *v*. ausdu.
take over *v*. ivvah-nemma.
take place *v*. blatz-nemma.
take place *v*. foahkumma.
take revenge *v*. auseeva.
take revenge *v*. ausnemma.
taken *v*. gnumma.
taken care of *v*. faseikt.
taken care of *v*. keet.

taken care of *v.* kseikt.
taken heed *v.* keet.
taken in *v.* eignumma.
taken off (clothing) *v.* ausgedu.
taken over *v.* ivvah-gnumma.
taken revenge *v.* ausgeebt.
taken revenge *v.* ausgnumma.
talk *v.* shvetza.
talkative shvetzich.
talked *v.* kshvetzt.
talker *(m).* shvetzah.
tame - zohm.
tame *v.* zohma.
tamed *v.* gezaymd.
tan (animal hide, leather).
    v. taena
tangle up *v.* favikla.
tangled up *v.* favikkeld.
tanned *v.* getaend.
tanner *(m).* taenah.
tape *(neu).* tayb.
tape *v.* tayba.
taped *v.* getaybt.
taste *v.* fasucha.
taste *v.* taysta.
tasted *v.* fasucht.
tasted *v.* getayst.
tattered - franslich.
taught *v.* geteetsht.
taught *v.* gland.
taught *v.* gleaht
    (used in the Bible).
tax collector *(m).*
    tax-einemmah.
tax collector's desk *(m).*
    tax-dish *(lit.- tax table).*
tax collector's desks *(f).*
    tax-disha *(lit.- tax tables).*
tea *(m).* tay.

teach *v.* lanna.
teach *v.* teetsha.
teacher *(m).* teetshah.
teachers *(f).* teetshahs.
teaching *(neu).* gebreddich.
teaching *(f).* lanning.
teachings *(f).* lanninga.
team (of horses or oxen) *(f).* fuah.
teams *(f).* fuahra.
tear *v.* fareisa.
tear *v.* farobba.
tear *v.* reisa.
tear off *v.* abreisa.
tear out *v.* ausreisa.
tears *(neu).* awwa-vassah.
tease *v.* zarra / zadda.
teased *v.* gezatt.
teaspoon *(neu).* lefli.
teaspoons *(f).* leflen.
teeth *(f).* zay.
tell *v.* fazayla.
tell off *v.* absawwa.
temperament *(m).* naduah.
temple *(m).* tempel.
temples *(f).* tempels.
tempt *v.* ausbroviahra.
tempt *v.* tempta (informal).
tempt *v.* fasucha.
    (used in the Bible)
temptation *(f).* fasuchung.
tempted *v.* ausbroviaht.
tempted *v.* fasucht.
    (used in the Bible)
tempted *v.* getempt. *(informal)*
tempter *(m).* fasuchah.
ten - zeyya.
tendons *(f).* flexa.
tent (used for assembling) *(m).*
    fasamling-tent.

tents (used for assembling) *(f)*.
　　fasamling-tents.
tenth -zeyyet.
terminal illness *(f)*.
　　dohdes-grankheida.
　　(used in the Bible)
terminal illness *(f)*.
　　dohdes-grankheit.
　　(used in the Bible)
terminal illness *(f)*.
　　dohdes-grankeda.
　　(common use)
terminal illness *(f)*.
　　dohdes-granket.
　　(common use)
terrible - shlimm.
terrifying - shreklich.
test *v.* broviahra / boviahra.
test out *v.* ausbroviahra.
Testament *(neu)*. Teshtament.
Testaments *(f)*. Teshtamentah.
tested *v.* ausbroviaht.
tested *v.* broviaht / boviaht.
testified *v.* gezeigt.
testifier (one who testifies).
　　(m). zeiyah
testify *v.* zeiya.
testimony *(neu)*. zeiknis.
tether *v.* ohbinna.
tethered *v.* ohgebunna.
than - vi.
thank *v.* bedanka.
thank *v.* danka.
thank you - denki *(common use)*
thank you - danki.
thank you very much -
　　denki-shay *(common use)*
thank you very much
　　danki-shay.

thanked *v.* gedankt.
thankful - dankboah.
thankfulness *(f)*. dankboahkeit.
thankfulnesses *(f)*.
　　dankboahkeida.
thanks *(m)*. dank.
thanksgiving offering *(neu)*.
　　dank-opfah.
thanksgiving offerings *(f)*.
　　dank-opfahra.
that - vass *(relative pronoun)*.
that - sell *(demonstrative)*.
that - sell *(used with neuter noun)*
that - sellah
　　(used with masculine noun)
that - selli
　　(used with feminine noun).
that - vo *(relative pronoun)*.
that one - sellah.
that - es / 's. *(relative pronoun)*.
thaw *v.* dauwa.
thaw out *v.* ausdauwa.
thawed *v.* gedaut.
thawed out *v.* ausgedaut.
the best - beshta.
the - em. *(dative case)*
the deep *(neu)*. deefa.
the (feminine gender and plural
　　nouns) di.
the half - dihelft.
the (masculine gender) da.
the (neuter form) es / 's.
the one - aynd.
the practice of baptizing
　　(neu). gedawf.
the whole *(adj)*. digans.
theif *(m)*. shtaylah.
their - iahra.
theirs - iahra.

them - si.
them - eena. *(dative case)*
then - ivvahdemm.
then - no.
then (as a consequence) - dann.
then (for that reason) - dann.
then (in that case) - dann.
there - anna.
there - datt.
there (pronoun used to start a
     sentence or clause)   es / 's.
there (toward) hee.
thereby - dideich.
therefore - fasell.
therefore - so.
these - dee.
they - si.
thick - dikk.
thief *(m)*. deeb.
thievery *(f)*. rawvahrei.
thievery *(f)*. shtaylahrei.
thimble *(m)*. fingah-hoot.
thimbles *(f)*. fingah-heet.
thin - dinn.
thin out *v*. fadinnahra.
thing *(neu)*. ding.
thing *(f)*. sach.
things *(f)*. dingah.
things *(f)*. sacha.
think *v*. denka.
think evil of *v*. fadenka.
think out *v*. ausdenka.
think over *v*. ivvah-denka.
thinking ahead *(neu)*.
     foahdenkes.
thinned out *v*. fadinnaht.
third - dridda.
third - dritt.
third part *(neu)*. driddel.

thirst *(m)*. dasht.
thirsty - dashtich.
thirteen - dreitzay.
thirty - dreisich.
this - deahra.
this afternoon - dinochmidawk.
this - demm. *(dative case)*
this forenoon - difammidawk.
this morning - dimeiya.
this noon - dimiddawk.
this one *(m)*. deah.
this (used with feminine nouns)
     (f). dee.
this (used with masculine nouns)
     (m). deah.
this (used with neuter nouns)
     dess.
this time - dessamohl.
this way - deahravayk.
thistle *(m)*. dishtel.
thistles *(f)*. dishtla.
thorn *(f)*. dann.
thorn bush *(m)*. danna-shtokk.
thorn bushes *(f)*. danna-hekka.
thorn bushes *(f)*. danna-shtekk.
thorn fire *(neu)*. danna-feiyah.
thorn fires *(f)*. danna-feiyahra.
thorns *(f)*. danna.
thorny - dannich.
those - deena.
those - selli.
thought *v*. gedenkt.
thought evil of *v*. fadenkt.
thought out *v*. ausgedenkt.
thought over *v*. ivvah-gedenkt.
thought provoking -
     bedenklich.
thoughts *(f)*. gedanka.
thousand *(f)*. dausend.

thousands *(f)*. dausends.
thread *v*. eifaydla.
thread *(m)*. fawda.
thread *v*. faydla.
thread *(m)*. naytz.
threaded *v*. eikfaydeld.
threaded *v*. kfaydeld.
threads *(f)*. naytza.
threaten *v*. droiya.
threatened *v*. gedroit.
three - drei.
three cornered - drei-eikkich.
three pronged - drei-zinkichi.
three-fifths - drei-fimfdel.
three-quarters - drei-faddel.
thresh *v*. dresha.
threshed *v*. gedrosha.
threshing floor *(m)*.
    dresha-floah.
threshing floors *(f)*.
    dresha-floahra.
threshing fork *(f)*.
    dresha-gavvel.
threshing forks *(f)*.
    dresha-gavla.
threshing utensils *(neu)*.
    dresha-ksha.
threshing wheel *(neu)*.
    dresha-rawt.
threshing wheels *(f)*.
    dresha-reddah.
threshold *(f)*. deahra-shvell.
thresholds *(f)*. deahra-shvella.
throat *(m)*. hals.
throats *(f)*. hels.
throne *(m)*. kaynich-shtool.
throne *(m)*. shtool.
thrones *(f)*. kaynich-shteel.
thrones *(f)*. shteel.

through - deich.
through it - dideich.
throughout - gans-deich.
throw *v*. shmeisa.
throw off *v*. abshmeisa.
thrown *v*. kshmissa.
thrown off *v*. abkshmissa.
thrust *v*. kshtohsa.
thumb *(m)*. dauma.
thunder *v*. dimla.
thunder *(m)*. dimmel.
thunder storm *(m)*. gviddah.
thundered *v*. gedimmeld.
thundering noise *v*. dunnahra.
thunders *(f)*. dimla.
thunderstorm *(m)*.
    gviddah-stoahm
    (lit. - lightning storm).
thunderstorms *(f)*.
    gviddah-stoahms
    (lit. - lightning storms).
Thursday - Dunnahshdawk.
ticked off *v*. abgedu.
tickle *v*. kitzla.
tickled *v*. gekitzeld.
ticklish - kitzlich.
tidied up *v*. ufgrohmd.
tidy - zvayk.
tidy up *v*. ufrohma.
tie *v*. binna.
tie in knots *v*. fagnibba.
tie to a fixed object
    v. ohbinna.
tied *v*. gebunna.
tied in knots *v*. fagnibt.
tied to a fixed object *v*.
    ohgebunna.
tight - teit.
tighten *v*. teidna.

tightened   *v.* geteidend.
tile   *(m).* teil.
tiles   *(f).* teils.
time   *(f).* zeit.
time of punishment   *(f).* shtrohf-zeit.
timely - zeitlich.
timepiece   *(f).* vatsh.
times   *(f).* zeida.
times of punishment   *(f).* shtrohf-zeida.
tin   *(neu).* blech.
tin can   *(f).* kann.
tin cup   *(neu).* blech.
tin cups   *(f).* blecha.
tin snips   *(f).* blech-sheah.
tin snips   *(f).* blech-sheahra.
tinkling - klinglich.
tinny - blechich.
tiny - glay.
tiny bit - bisli.
tire   *(m).* teiyah.
tired - meet.
tired of - laydich.
tires   *(f).* tieyahs.
to - zu.
to a – zumma *(use with masculine or neuter noun, dative case)*
to a greater degree - eiyah.
to add to   *v.* ditzudu.
to argue   *v.* maula.
to call out   *v.* ausroofa.
to crow (as a rooster)   *v.* grayya.
to fog over glass   *v.* dufta.
to freeze   *v.* fafriahra.
to have faith   *v.* glawva.
to it - ditzu.
to lay on (hands or clothes).   *v.* ohlayya

to let out   *v.* auslossa.
to quilt   *v.* gvilda.
to the - zumm *(used with masculine or neuter noun, dative case).*
to whom - ditzu.
toad   *(f).* grott.
toads   *(f).* grodda.
tobacco   *(m).* doovakk.
tobacco   *(m).* duahk.
today - heit.
today at noon - dimiddawk.
today before noon - difammidawk.
together - bei-nannah.
together - zammah.
told   *v.* fazayld.
told off   *v.* abksawt.
told untruth   *v.* gleekt.
tolerated   *v.* geduld.
tomato   *(f).* tamaeddes.
tomorrow - meiya.
tongue   *(f).* zung.
tongues   *(f).* zunga.
tonight - dinohvet.
too - zu.
took   *v.* gnumma.
tooth   *(m).* zoh.
topography   *(neu).* landshaft.
torch   *(m).* feiyah-shtekka. *(lit. - fire stick).*
torment   *v.* gvayla.
tormented   *v.* gegvayld.
torn   *v.* farissa.
torn   *v.* grissa.
torn apart   *v.* farobt.
torn off   *v.* abgrissa.
torn out   *v.* ausgrissa.
touch   *v.* ohrayya *(**not** common).*

touch *v.* totsha *(common use).*
touch (with the fingers) *v.*
  fingahra.
touched *v.* getotsht.
touched *v.* ohgraykt
      (not common).
touched (with the fingers)   *v.*
  kfingaht.
touchy - totshich.
tough - toff.
toward - geyya / gayya.
toward - geyyich / gayyich.
towel *(m).* lumba.
towel (drying off)   *(m).*
  abbutz-lumba.
tower *(m).* tavvah.
town *(f).* shtatt.
town (little) *(neu).* shtetli.
towns *(f).* shtett.
towns (little) *(f).* shtetlen.
tractor *(m).* traektah.
tractors *(f).* traektahs.
trade *v.* fahandla.
trade *v.* handla.
trade *v.* trayda *(common use).*
traded *v.* fahandeld.
traded *v.* getrayt.
traded *v.* kandeld.
train *v.* trayna.
trained *v.* getraynd.
trample *v.* fashtamba.
trample *v.* shtamba.
trample underfoot *v.*
  fadredda.
trampled *v.* fashtambt.
trampled *v.* kshtambt.
transgress *v.* fasindicha.
transgress against *v.*
  fashuldicha.

transgressed *v.* fasindicht.
transgressed against *v.*
  fashuldicht.
transgression *(f).* sind.
transgressions *(f).* sinda.
transient - fagenglich.
translate *v.* ivvah-setza.
transplant *v.* ausblansa.
transplanted *v.* ausgeblanst.
trap *(f).* fall.
traps *(f).* falla.
trash *v.* traesha.
trashed *v.* getraesht.
trashy - traeshich.
tread *v.* dredda.
tread out *v.* ausdredda.
tread out *v.* ausgedrodda.
treaded *v.* gedrodda.
treasuries *(f).* tempel-boxa
      (lit. - temple boxes).
treasury *(f).* tempel-box
      (lit. - temple box).
tree *(m).* bohm.
tree branches *(f).* baym-nesht.
trees *(f).* baym.
tremble *v.* ziddahra.
trembled *v.* geziddaht.
trespass *v.* ivvah-dredda.
trespass *(f).* ivvah-dredding.
trespassed *v.* ivvah-gedredda.
trespasser *(m).* ivvah-dreddah.
trespasses *(f).* ivvah-dreddinga.
triangle *(neu).* drei-ekk.
triangle shaped - drei-eikkich.
trick *v.* trikka.
tricked *v.* getrikt.
tricky trikkich.
tried *v.* broviaht / boviaht.
tried out *v.* ausbroviaht.

trigger *(m)*. trikkah.
trouble *v*. druvla.
trouble *(m)*. druvvel.
troubled *v*. gedruvveld.
troublemaker *(m)*.
   druvvel-machah.
troubles *(f)*. druvla.
troublesome - fadreeslich.
trough *(m)*. drohk.
troughs *(f)*. drayk.
true - voah.
truly - veiklich.
truly - voahhaftich.
truly - voahlich.
trumpet *(f)*. blohs-hann.
trumpets *(f)*. blohs-hanna.
trust *v*. drauwa.
trust *(f)*. fadrauwung.
trusted *v*. gedraut.
trusts *(f)*. fadrawunga.
truth *(f)*. voahheit.
truth *(f)*. voahret.
try *v*. broviahra / boviahra.
try out *v*. ausbroviahra.
Tuesday - Dinshdawk.
tumult *(m)*. ufruah.
tumults *(f)*. ufruahra.
tune *(f)*. veis.
tunes *(f)*. veisa.
turn *(f)*. dray.
turn *v*. drayya.
turn aside *v*. abdrayya.
turn aside *v*. ausfoahra.
turn off *v*. abdrayya.
turn out *v*. ausdrayya.

turn over *v*. ivvah-drayya.
turn (usually a negative sense)
   v. fadrayya.
turned *v*. gedrayt.
turned aside *v*. abgedrayt.
turned aside *v*. auskfoahra.
turned off *v*. abgedrayt.
turned out *v*. ausgedrayt.
turned over *v*. ivvah-gedrayt.
turned (usually in a negative
   sense) *v*. fadrayt.
turns *(f)*. drayya.
turtle dove *(f)*. daddel-daub.
turtle doves *(f)*. daddel-dauva.
twelfth - zvelft.
twelve - zvelf.
twenty - zvansich.
twig *(f)*. fitz.
twig *(f)*. hekk.
twigs *(f)*. fitza.
twigs *(f)*. hekka.
twins *(m)*. zvilling.
twist the truth *v*. fadrayya.
twisted *v*. farenkt.
twisted the truth *v*. fadrayt.
two - zvay.
two-faced - zvay-ksichtich.
type of - satt.
types - sadda.

U - u

udder *(neu)*. eidah.
udders *(f)*. aedra.
udders *(f)*. eidahra.
ugly - hatt-gukkich
    (lit. - hard looking).
umbrella *(f)*. amberell.
umbrellas *(f)*. ambrella.
unbelief *(m)*. unglawva.
unbelieving - unglawvich.
unborn - ungeboahra.
unbridle *v*. abzohma.
unbridled *v*. abgezohmd.
uncircumcised - unbeshnidda.
uncircumcision *(f)*.
    unbeshneiding.
unclean - unsauvah.
unclean by sinning *v*. fasudla
    (present, future).
unclean by sinning *v*.
    fasuddeld. *(past)*
unclothed - ungeglayt.
uncoil *v*. abvikla.
uncoil *v*. ausvikla.
uncoiled *v*. abgvikkeld.
uncoiled *v*. ausgvikkeld.
unconcerned - unbekimmaht.
unconscious (as a result of
    fainting) ummechtich.
uncover *v*. abdekka.
uncover *v*. ufdekka.
uncovered *v*. abgedekt.
uncovered *v*. ufgedekt.
undecided - eevel-ab.
under (located down below,
    at the bottom). unna

under - unnah *(prefix)*.
under - unnich.
under obligation - shuldich.
underneath - drunnah.
understand *v*. fashtay.
understanding *(m)*. fashtand.
understanding *(f)*. fashtendnis.
understood *v*. fashtanna.
undertake *v*. foahnemma.
undertake *v*. unnah-nemma.
undertaken *v*. unnah-gnumma.
undertook *v*. foahgnumma.
undesirable *v*. aykla.
undesireable *v*. gaykeld.
undoubtedly - gevislich.
unexpected - unfahoft.
unfair - fazatt.
unfamiliar - fremd.
unfortunate - ungliklich.
unfruitful - unfruchtboah.
ungodliness *(f)*. ungetlichkeit.
ungodly - gottlohs.
ungodly - ungetlich.
unhappy - bloosich.
unharness *v*. abkshadda.
unharnessed *v*. abgekshatt.
unhitch *v*. ausshpanna.
unhitched *v*. auskshpand.
unholy - ungeishtlich.
unhook *v*. abhenka.
unhooked *v*. abkanka.
unity *(f)*. aynichkeit.
unkept - zodlich.
unknown - unbekand.
unleavened - unksavvaht.

unless - unni.
unload *v.* abdu.
unload *v.* ablawda.
unload (with a fork) *v.* abgavla.
unloaded *v.* abgedu.
unloaded *v.* abglawda.
unloaded (with a fork) *v.*
        abgegavveld.
unmarried - leddich.
unnecessary - unaydich.
unnecessary fuss *(neu)*.
        vaysa.
unrest *(f)*. unroo.
unrighteous - ungerecht.
unrighteous - ungerechtich.
unrighteousness *(f)*.
        ungerechtichkeit.
unruly - ausgedrivva.
unsaddle *v.* absadla.
unsaddled *v.* abksaddeld.
unscrew *v.* abdrayya.
unscrewed *v.* abgedrayt.
unspiritual - ungeishtlich.
unstable - unshtandhaftich.
untaught - ungland.
unthankful - undankboah.
unthread *v.* ausfaydla.
unthreaded *v.* auskfaydelt.
until - biss.
untruth *(m)*. leek.
untruth *(f)*. unvoahret.
untruths *(f)*. leeya.
unusual - fremd.
unusual - kshpassich.
unwilling - unvillich.

unworthy - unveahdich.
unwrap *v.* abvikla.
unwrap *v.* ausvikla.
unwraped *v.* abgvikkeld.
unwraped *v.* ausgvikkeld.
up (toward a higher location)
        nuff
up (from below)   ruff
up - uf.
up ahead - fanna-draus.
up there - drovva.
upon - druff.
upon - uf.
upper (located above) ovva
uppermost - evvahsht.
upright - ufrichtich.
uprightness *(f)*. ufrichtichkeit.
upset *v.* abdu.
upset *v.* abgedu.
upset - ausfix.
upset *v.* umshmeisa.
upside down - unnahs-evvahsht.
upstairs *(m)*. shpeichah.
upstairs *(f)*. shpeichahra
upwards - nuftzus.
us - uns.
use *v.* yoosa.
used *v.* gyoost.

V - v

value *(f)*. veaht.
vault *(f)*. sayf.
vaults *(f)*. sayfa.
ventilate *v*. auslufta.
ventilated *v*. ausgluft.
verbaly grumpy *(adj.)*
    gneiksich.
verse *(m)*. feahsht.
verses *(f)*. feahshta.
very - oahrich.
very small - fei.
very warm (ambient
    temperature) brohdich.
vessel (for liquid) *(f)*. kann.
viewpoint - denkes.
vile - greislich.
village (little) *(neu)*. shtetli.
villages (little) *(f)*. shtetlen.
vinegar *(neu)*. essich.
vineyard *(neu)*. drauva-feld
    (lit. - grape field).

vineyard *(m)*. drauva-goahra
    (lit . - grape garden)
vineyard *(m)*. vei-goahra.
vinyards *(f)*. drauva-feldah
    (lit. - grape fields).
visit *v*. psucha.
visited *v*. gepsucht.
visitor *(f)*. psuch.
visitors *(f)*. psuch-leit.
voice *(f)*. shtimm.
voices *(f)*. shtimma.
vomit *(m)*. kotz.
vomit *v*. kotza.
vomited *v*. gekotzt.
voracious *v*. fafressa.
vote *v*. rohda.
voted *v*. grohda.
vow *v*. shveahra.
vowed *v*. kshvoahra.

W - w

wade *v*. bawda.
waded *v*. gebawda.
wages *(m)*. lohn.
wagon *(m)*. vauwa.
wagon (little) *(neu)*. vaykli.
wagon tongue *(f)*. deiksel.
wagon tongues *(f)*. deiksla.
wagons (little) *(f)*. vayklen.
waist *(m)*. bauch.

waists *(f)*. beich.
wait *v*. voahra.
wait out *v*. ausvoahra.
waited *v*. gvoaht.
waited out *v*. ausgvoaht.
wake up *v*. vekka.
walk *v*. lawfa.
walk away from *v*. ablawfa.
walk of life *(m)*. layves-lawf.

(m) = da   (f) = di   (neu) = es

walked *v.* gloffa.
walking stick *(m).* shtokk.
walking sticks *(f).* shtekk.
wall *(f).* vand.
wall in *v.* eivanda.
walled in *v.* eigvand.
walls *(f).* vanda.
wander *v.* vandla.
wandered *v.* gvandeld.
want *(m).* falanga.
want *v.* vella *(verb conj.*
　　　used with "miah", "si").
want *v.* vellet *(used with "diah").*
want *v.* vill *(used with*
　　　"Ich", "eah", "see", "es").
want *v.* vitt *(used with "du").*
war *(m).* greek.
war club *(m).* greeks-shtekka.
war horse *(m).* greeks-gaul.
war horses *(f).* greeks-geil.
warm *v.* veahma.
warm *(adj.)* voahm.
warmed *v.* gveahmd.
warmer - veahmah.
warmest - veahmsht.
warn *v.* vanna.
warn from *v.* abveahra.
warned *v.* gvand.
warned about *v.* abgveaht.
warning *(f).* vanning.
warnings *(f).* vanninga.
wars *(f).* greeka.
wart *(f).* voahtz.
warts *(f).* voahtza.
was *v.* voah.
wash *v.* vesha.
wash off *v.* abvesha.
wash out *v.* ausvesha.
washbowl *(f).* vesh-shissel.

washbowls *(f).* vesh-shisla.
washcloth *(m).* vesh-lumba.
washed *v.* gvesha.
washed off *v.* abgvesha.
washed out *v.* ausgvesha.
wasp *(f).* veshp.
wasps *(f).* veshpa.
waste time *v.* fasauma.
waste time *v.* faseima.
wasted time *v.* fasaumd.
watch *(f).* vatsh.
watch *v.* vatsha.
watched *v.* gvatsht.
watches *(f).* vatsha.
water *(neu).* vassah.
water (such as: to water plants).
　　　v. vessahra.
water glass *(neu).* glaws.
water glasses *(f).* glessah.
water livestock *v.* drenka.
water spring *(f).* vassah-shpring
water springs *(f).*
　　　vassah-shpringa.
watered (such as: to water
　　　plants). *v.* gvessaht
watering can *(f).* geeskann.
watering cans *(f).* geeskanna.
watering hole *(neu)* vassah-loch
watering holes *(f).*
　　　vassah-lechah.
waters *(f).* vassahra.
wave of water *(f).* vell.
wave off *v.* abshlenkahra.
waves of water *(f).* vella.
way *(m).* vayk.
ways *(f).* vayya.
we - miah.
weak - eahmlich.
weak (to feel) - matt

weak - shvach.
weaken *v.* fashvecha.
weakened *v.* fashvecht.
weaker - shvechah.
weakest - shvechsht.
weakness *(f).* shvachheit.
weaknesses *(f).* shvachheida.
wean *v.* abgvayna.
weaned *v.* abgegvaynd.
wear *v.* veahra.
wear off *v.* abveahra.
wear out *v.* ausveahra.
weasel *(neu).* visli.
weasels *(f).* vislen.
weather *(neu).* veddah.
weave *v.* flechta.
wedding *(f).* hochtzich.
weddings *(f).* hochtzicha.
wedge *(m).* keidel.
wedges *(f).* keidla.
Wednesday *(m).* mitvoch
      (lit. - mid-week).
Wednesdays *(f).* mitvocha.
weeds *(neu).* veetz.
week *(f).* voch.
weeks *(f).* vocha.
weep *v.* heila.
weep *v.* veina.
weigh *v.* veeya.
weighed *v.* gvohwa.
weight *(f).* gvicht.
weights *(f).* gvichta.
weighty - vichtich.
well (preface to a remark) vell
well behaved - brawf.
well meaning - goot-maynich.
well (water) *(m).* brunna.
went *v.* ganga.
went in *v.* eiganga.

went off (alarm) *v.* abganga.
went there *v.* anna-ganga.
wept *v.* gveind.
wept *v.* keild.
were *v.* voahra.
west - vest.
wet - nass.
whale *(m).* valfish.
what - vass.
whatever - vass-evvah.
wheat *(m).* vaytza.
wheel *(neu).* rawt.
wheelbarrow *(m).* shubkaych.
wheelbarrows *(f).* shubkaycha.
wheels *(f).* reddah.
when - vann.
when - vo *(conjunction).*
whenever - vann-evvah.
where - vo.
wherefore - doch.
wherefore - vo-heah.
wherever - vo-evvah.
whether - eb.
which - vass *(relative pronoun).*
which - vo *(relative pronoun).*
which one - vels.
which - es / 's *(relative pronoun)*
while - veil.
whimper *v.* vimsla.
whimpered *v.* gvimseld.
whip *v.* fagayshla.
whip *(f).* fitz.
whip *(f).* gayshel.
whip *v.* gayshla.
whipped *v.* fagaysheld.
whipped *v.* gegaysheld.
whipping *(f).* gayshtling.
whippings *(f).* gayshtlinga.
whips *(f).* fitza.

(m) = da   (f) = di   (neu) = es

whips *(f)*. gayshla.
whisper *v*. pishpahra.
whispered *v*. gepishpaht.
whistle *(f)*. peif.
whistle *v*. peifa.
whistled *v*. gepiffa.
whistler *(m)*. peifah.
white - veis.
whitewash *v*. veisla.
whitewashed *v*. gveiseld.
whittle *v*. shnefla.
whittled *v*. kshneffeld.
who - vass *(relative pronoun)*.
who - veah.
who vo *(relative pronoun)*.
who knows how - favaysvi.
who knows what all -
      favaysvass.
who es / 's *(relative pronoun)*.
whoever - veah-evvah.
whole - gans.
wholesome - heilsam.
whom - vemm.
whooping cough *(m)*.
      bloh-hooshta.
whose - vemm sei.
why - favach.
why - favass.
why (preface to a mark) vei
why - vo-heah.
wick on a lamp *(m)*. veecha.
wickedest (most evil)
      alli-veeshta.
wickedly - veeshtahlich.
wide - brayt.
widow *(f)*. vitt-fraw.
widow *(neu)*. vitt-veib.
widower *(m)*. vitt-mann.
widowers *(f)*. vitt-mennah.

widows *(f)*. vitt-veivah.
width *(f)*. brayding.
wife *(f)*. fraw.
wife - veib *(**not** common)*.
wiggle *v*. vakla.
wiggled *v*. gvakkeld.
wiggly - vaklich.
wild - vild.
wilderness *(f)*. vildahnis.
wildernesses *(f)*. vildahnissa.
will (document of direction after
      death). *(m)*. villa
will *v*. zayl.
willing - villich.
willing to share - mitt-daylich.
willingly - frei-villich.
willingly - villichlich.
willow tree *(m)*. veida-bohm.
wilt *v*. favelka.
wilted *v*. favelkt.
wilted - velk.
win over *v*. ivvah-vinna.
wind *(m)*. vind.
window *(neu)*. fenshtah.
window curtain *(neu)*.
      fenshtah-duch.
window curtains *(f)*.
      fenshtah-dichah.
windows *(f)*. fenshtahra.
winds *(f)*. vinda.
windstorm *(m)*. vind-shtoahm.
windstorms *(f)*. vind-shteahm.
windy - vindich.
wine *(m)*. vei.
wine drinker *(m)*. vei-saufah.
wine vat *(m)*. vei-drohk.
wine vats *(f)*. vei-drayk.
winepress *(f)*. vei-press.
winepresses *(f)*. vei-presses.

wineskin *(m)*. vei-sakk.
wineskins *(f)*. vei-sekk.
wing *(m)*. flikkel.
wings *(f)*. flikla.
winnowing fork *(f)*.
    dresha-shaufel.
winnowing forks *(f)*.
    dresha-shaufla.
winter *(m)*. vindah.
winters *(f)*. vindra.
wipe dry *v*. abbutza.
wiped dry *v*. abgebutzt.
wire *(m)*. droht.
wires *(f)*. drohda.
wisdom *(f)*. veisheit.
wise - foahsichtich.
wish *v*. vinsha
(example: "We wish you the best.")
wish *v*. vodda
   (example: "I wish it was warm.")
wished *v*. gvinsht.
wished *v*. gvott.
with - mitt.
wither *v*. dadda.
wither completely *v*.
    fadadda.
withered *v*. gedatt.
withered completely -
    v. fadatt.
without - unni.
without understanding -
    unfashtendlich.
without understanding *(f)*.
unfashtendlichkeit *(state of being)*
witness *(neu)*. zeiknis.
witness *v*. zeiya.
witness *(m)*. zeiyah
    (one who witnesses).
witnessed *v*. gezeigt.

wives *(f)*. frawwa.
wives - veivah *(not common)*.
wobble *v*. vakla.
wobbled *v*. gvakkeld.
wobbly - vaklich.
woe *(f)*. vay.
woes *(f)*. vayya.
woke *v*. gvekt.
wolf *(m)*. volf.
wolfs *(f)*. velf.
woman *(f)*. fraw.
woman *(neu)* veib *(not common)*
woman *(neu)*. veibsmensh.
womb *(f)*. muddahs-leib.
wombs *(f)*. muddahs-leivah.
women *(f)*. frawwa.
women *(f)*. veibsleit.
women *(f)*. veivah *(not common)*
won *v*. gebodda.
won *v*. gvunna.
won over *v*. ivvah-gvunna.
wonder *(m)*. vunnah.
wonder *v*. vunnahra.
wondered *v*. gvunnaht.
wonders *(f)*. vunnahs.
wood *(neu)*. hols.
wood strip *(f)*. latt.
wood strips *(f)*. ladda.
woodchuck *(f)*. grundsau.
woodchucks *(f)*. grundsei.
wooden - holsich.
wooden beam *(m)*. balka.
woods *(m)*. bush.
wool *(f)*. vull.
wooly - vullich.
word *(neu)*. vatt.
word of blasphemy *(neu)*.
    leshtah-vatt.
words *(f)*. vadda.

words of blasphemy *(f)*.
  leshtah-vadda.
words of prophecy
  broffetzeiya-vadda.
work *(f)*. eahvet.
work *(neu)*. ksheft.
work *v*. shaffa.
work *(neu)*. verk.
work off (debt) *v*. abshaffa.
work out *v*. ausshaffa.
work out a conflict *v*.
  ausrichta.
worked *v*. kshaft.
worked as a carpenter *v*.
  gezimmaht.
worked off (debt) *v*. abkshaft.
worked out *v*. auskshaft.
worked out a conflict *v*.
  ausgricht.
worker of evil *(m)*eevil-shaffah
worker of evil *(m)* evil-shaffah
works *(f)*. kshefta.
works *(f)*. verka.
world *(f)*. veld.
worldly - veldlich.
worlds *(f)*. velda.
worm *(m)*. voahm.
worms *(f)*. veahm.
worn *v*. gvoahra.
worn off *v*. abgveaht.
worn out *v*. ausgvoahra.
worried - bang.
worse - shlechtah.
worship *v*. deena.
worship *v*. ohbayda.
worship service *(f)*. gmay.
worship service *(m)*.
  Gottes-deensht.
worshipped *v*. gedeend.

worshipped *v*. ohgebayda.
worst - shlechsht.
worth *(f)*. veaht.
worthwhile - veahtfollich.
worthwile - diveaht.
worthy - veahtfol.
would - dayt.
would be *v*. veahra.
would be able to *v*. kend.
would be allowed *v*. deift.
would have *v*. hedda.
would have needed *v*.
  gebreicht.
would know *v*. vista.
would need *v*. breichta.
would perhaps *v*. mechta.
would want *v*. vedda.
woven *v*. kflochta.
wrap *v*. vikla.
wrap in *v*. eivikla.
wrap up *v*. favikla.
wrapped *v*. gvikkeld.
wrapped in *v*. eigvikkeld.
wrapped up *v*. favikkeld.
wrinkle *v*. farunsla.
wrinkle *(m)*. runsel.
wrinkled *v*. farunseld.
wrinkles *(f)*. runsla.
write *v*. shreiva.
write down *v*. anna-shreiva.
write off *v*. abshreiva.
writer *(m)*. shreivah.
written *v*. kshrivva.
written covenant *(neu)*.
  bund-shreives.
written document *(neu)*.
  shreives.
written down *v*. anna-kshrivva.
written off *v*. abkshrivva.

wrong *v.* faletza.
wrong letz.

wronged *v.* faletzt.
wrote *v.* kshrivva.

Y - y

yard *(m).* hohf.
yard (36 inches) *(m).* yoaht
yards *(f).* hohfa.
yardstick *(m).* yoaht-shtekka.
year *(neu).* yoah.
years *(f).* yoahra.
yell *v.* greisha.
yell at *v.* fagreisha.
yelled *v.* gegrisha.
yelled at *v.* fagrisha.
yellow - gayl.
yes - yau.
yes - yo *(only used when contradicting a negative statement).*
yesterday - geshtah.
yet - alsnoch.
yet - noch.
yield to *v.* blatz-gevva.
yoke *(neu).* yoch.

yokes *(f).* yocha.
you - dich *(accusative singular).*
you all - eich *(accusative plural)*
you - diah *(nominative plural) (dative singular).*
you - du *(nominative singular).*
young - yung.
younger - yingah.
youngest - yingsht.
your - dei.
your - deina.
your - deinra.
your - deim. *(dative case)*
your - eiyah. *(plural)*
your - eiyahm. *(plural) (dative case)*
yours - dein.
yourself - dich-selvaht.
yourselves - eich-selvaht.

Z - z

zeal *(m).* eahnsht.

Made in the USA
Middletown, DE
09 September 2023

38251400R00129